POPE JOHN PAUL II

POCKET
GIANTS

POPE JOHN PAUL II

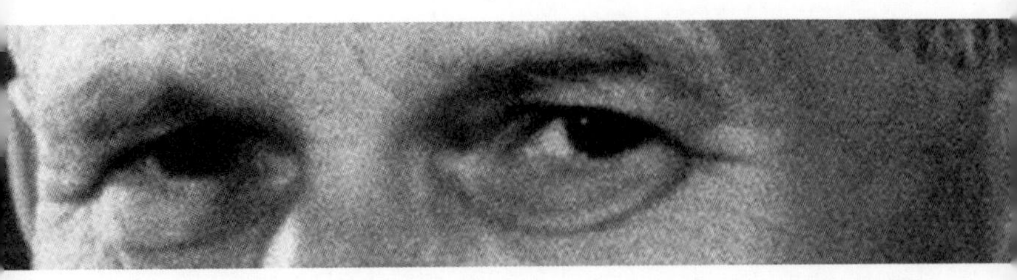

POCKET

GIANTS

HUGH COSTELLO

First published 2014

The History Press
The Mill, Brimscombe Port
Stroud, Gloucestershire, GL5 2QG
www.thehistorypress.co.uk

British Library Cataloguing in Publication Data.
A catalogue record for this book is available from the British Library.

ISBN 978 0 7524 9351 0

Typesetting and origination by The History Press
Printed in Europe

Contents

1	A Revolutionary Pope	7
2	'Upon This Rock': A Brief History of the Papacy	17
3	A Motherless Only Child	29
4	A Brother of the People	41
5	Called from a Faraway Land	51
6	The Portable Pope	61
7	Cold Warrior	75
8	Culture Wars	85
9	Millennial Pursuits	97
10	Legacy	107
	Notes	119
	Timeline	122
	Further Reading	125
	Web Links	126

1

A Revolutionary Pope

The Italians have a word for it: *papabile*. The literal English translation is 'popeable'. A more helpful interpretation is 'electable'. The man who is *papabile* is believed by his fellow cardinals to possess an elusive blend of personal qualities – authority, holiness, forbearance – that together equip him to take on the most demanding, and frequently most thankless, of jobs.

Over the centuries, many holders of this unique office have struggled to convert those pre-election *papabile* virtues into effective leadership of the worldwide Church. The majority have been sincere and capable figureheads; but others have proved spectacularly ill suited to the role. There have been vain popes, libidinous popes, ignorant popes and inept popes. Some have been downright corrupt, exploiting the office for their own distinctly unspiritual ends. Others have begotten chaos or presided helplessly over decline. Many, crushed by the weight of expectation, have simply subsided into inertia.

Every so often, however, a figure has ascended to St Peter's throne who has delivered on the promise he showed as a cardinal. These men have not pleased everyone (an impossible task for any pope), but they have demonstrated unquestionable qualities of leadership and vision. They have been true helmsmen, guiding the Church through hostile times and keeping it vital and relevant in the face of sometimes forbidding odds. Among these figures was the eleventh-century Pope Gregory VII, who stood up to state power and cemented the Church's primacy in medieval Europe. The controversial Pope Pius IX – or 'Pio Nono' as he was known in Italian – masterminded a resurgence in Catholicism in the nineteenth century. Another remarkable figure was the avuncular Pope John XXIII, who reigned for just five years (1958–63) yet began a series of reforms that radically overhauled the faith's relationship with secular society. These men could truly be said to have changed the world.

Another such figure, and one of the unlikeliest, was a little-known Polish prelate. In October 1978, when the College of Cardinals met to elect a pope for a second time in just two months, Karol Wojtyła, the Archbishop of Kraków, was not widely considered to be *papabile*. The college had recently elected one obscure figure: Albino Luciani, Pope John Paul I, who reigned for barely a month before his sudden (and some believe suspicious) demise. The College were hardly in the mood to choose another wild card. The expectation this time was that they would elect a senior figure from within the Curia, the administrative and political establishment of the Roman Church.

For reasons of factional infighting and ideological division (outlined in more detail in Chapter 5), the cardinals failed to give decisive backing to either of the main contenders. Since no conclave can break up without choosing a pope, a third way was required. Out of the pack emerged Wojtyła, the first non-Italian pope in 450 years. As a tribute to his late predecessor, he took the name John Paul II.

There were some who feared that Wojtyła's obscurity and his lack of a broad base of support prior to his election would undermine his authority as pope. How emphatically wrong they were. John Paul II revolutionised the office and dragged it into the modern age. In the process he became a global phenomenon. Where previous popes had barely featured in the mainstream media for years on end, John Paul II was rarely off the news pages. His relative youth – he was 58 when elected – meant he would have time to mould the Church in his own image and leave a legacy that might be sustained for generations. This he achieved with vigour and charisma, but at a cost.

His reign – one of the longest in papal history – was marked by controversy and division. John Paul II became a *bête noire* in the eyes of liberals for his staunch refusal to allow contraception or to reconsider the Church's position on priestly celibacy and the ordination of women. But for others he was a Churchillian figure who took on the forces of godlessness and moral relativism. He gained a stature that left secular statesmen in his shadow. It is these qualities that make John Paul II a worthy subject for this book. He is an enduringly fascinating figure not despite but because of the strength of feeling he inspired – and continues to inspire – both among his legions of admirers and his armies of critics.

Karol Wojtyła was unquestionably a man of intelligence, a gifted theologian and philosopher who also had the ability to communicate complex ideas in plain language – a rare combination even among democratically elected public figures. He took over an institution reeling from the loss of influence it had suffered in post-war Europe and the United States. His immediate predecessors had remained immured in Vatican City, showing little apparent interest in an increasingly diverse world outside. John Paul changed all that. He had a message and he was determined to deliver it personally. If the world had stopped listening to the Vatican, he believed, maybe it was time for the Vatican to increase the volume.

He was uniquely suited to the task. Handsome, charismatic, energetic, he bore no resemblance to the often remote and desiccated figures who had traditionally held the office. Where they had kept the world at arm's length, he embraced it; where they had located the epicentre of faith in the confines of the Holy See, he set out to discover it in the hearts and minds of every individual believer, whatever benighted corner of God's earth they lived in. This difference of approach was encapsulated in his trademark gesture: where earlier popes would extend an imperious ringed hand to be kissed by the supplicant, John Paul got down on his knees and kissed the ground in each new country he visited. As a signifier of humility and openness it was hugely effective; as a visual motif, a photogenic 'moment' for an image-hungry mass media to capture and disseminate, it was beyond compare.

There were, of course, other reasons for Wojtyła's rapid rise to global prominence. Here was a man who had lived most of his life under totalitarian regimes. The Cold War was not, for him, some theoretical construct but a harsh fact of daily life. At the time of his election in 1978, the Soviet Bloc was still a powerful and implacable reality, but the cracks were beginning to show. In the West, a generation of leaders was emerging who would share Wojtyła's conviction that the twentieth century's Marxist experiments had run their course. Margaret Thatcher would become the British prime minister less than a year after Wojtyła's election. In 1980, the hawkish Ronald Reagan won the White House. They would become John Paul's ideological soulmates, and together they were in the vanguard of events that led to the collapse of what Reagan called 'the Evil Empire'. The timing of Wojtyła's election, then, could hardly have been more serendipitous – but it was the man himself, through his steely single-mindedness, who capitalised on this opportunity.

Many Catholics look back on John Paul II's pontificate as a golden age. For others it marked a descent into autocracy and fundamentalism. His detractors, while acknowledging that he advanced the cause of freedom and made the Church relevant again, point out his failure to provide effective leadership when sexual abuse scandals rocked the institution. This failure, they argue, was consistent with John Paul's earlier refusal to show any flexibility on issues that have come to define the Church's relationship with the modern, secular world. John Paul insisted on excluding from the sacraments all Catholics who had divorced, those living together out of wedlock and those in homosexual relationships. These doctrinaire positions, while applauded by traditionalists in the Church, alienated millions of otherwise devout Catholics.

His obstinacy when it came to artificial birth control was even more draconian. He rejected arguments that Catholics in AIDS-ravaged parts of the world, particularly Africa, should be allowed to wear condoms – an absolutist position that condemned many thousands to death. In his war on what he described as a 'culture of death' in the modern world, symbolised by abortion and contraception, he himself added to the toll of casualties.

Absolutism is generally near the top of the charge sheet against John Paul. While his many overseas trips carried a message to the world, it was, say critics, his own distinctly narrow message. Far from opening up the papacy to a conversation with the wider world, he shut down debate, stifled dissent and demanded unquestioning loyalty and obedience. For that reason, he left the Church weakened, divided and deeply unpopular with many of its own members.

As time goes by, the debate about his legacy shows no sign of mellowing. Where one stands on John Paul's pontificate has become a litmus test of Catholic opinion. Those who seek an accommodation with the secular sphere tend to see his tenure of office as a missed opportunity. Advocates of traditional values view him as an arch defender of truth and godliness. The former group aim to roll back many of John Paul's measures; the latter have been a driving force behind an unusually rapid process of canonisation.

This ongoing schism of opinions reflects the fact that he was a man of compelling contradictions: doctrinaire and conservative on some issues, bracingly libertarian on others. In the words of respected Vaticanologist John L. Allen: 'Outside the church a democrat, inside the church an autocrat.'[1]

This short book does not aspire to be an exhaustive account of John Paul's life and times. Rather, it aims to explore what it was that made him such an important and iconic figure in late twentieth-century history. What were the forces that shaped his ideas and his attitudes? What clues can we find in his early life to help us understand this most contradictory of men? What gave him the strength to survive an assassination attempt and to keep going during his long, very public battle with Parkinson's disease with his authority and – among many – his popularity undiminished? Even in his final days in April 2005, as thousands waited in St Peter's Square for news of his passing, he continued to exert a dominant hold on the Church and many of its faithful.

John Paul II remains a man to be reckoned with. A giant. This book explains why.

2

‘Upon This Rock’: A Brief History of the Papacy

A favourite story among professional Vatican watchers concerns a young priest who arrives in Rome to start a new job in the Church's civil service. He tries to open the window beside his desk but it will not budge. When he asks his superior why the window has been painted shut, he is told: 'That's how it was when I got here.' Our enterprising young priest decides to take action. The Vatican might be stuck in its ways, but he isn't, and nor is his window. He prises it open, breathes in the fresh air, and goes for lunch. When he gets back he finds half a dozen pigeons sitting on his desk and a very unpleasant mess all over that day's copy of the *Osservatore Romano*.

Like other 'be careful what you wish for' parables, this one may well be apocryphal, but it illustrates an essential truth: resistance to change, whether due to hard-earned wisdom or mule-like stubbornness, is at the very heart of the Catholic Church's culture and philosophy. This is not, as many of the Church's critics argue, a knee-jerk conservatism. Continuity at all costs is the core principle on which the Church and its institutions are built. Those who expect the Church to change with the times as if it were a political party simply do not understand how it works. Witness the worldwide astonishment that greeted Pope Benedict's decision to retire in early 2013. Such dramatic change happens only once or twice in a millennium in the Church.

When Karol Wojtyła was chosen by his fellow cardinals in October 1978, he became the 263rd custodian of that precious continuity. Popes have many roles but by far the most important is to be a strong link in the chain that goes all the way back to St Peter, the man Jesus chose to propagate the faith with the words (according to Matthew's Gospel): 'You are Peter and upon this rock I will build my Church and I will give to you the keys to the kingdom of heaven.'

What made Peter worthy of such special treatment?

Throughout the New Testament, Peter is described as leader of the apostles. He stands out from the crowd right from his first appearance when, as a fisherman called Simon, he is told by Jesus that he will soon become a 'fisher of men'. Jesus then renames him Petrus, or 'rock' – a foreshadowing of Peter's later status as the foundation stone of Christianity. Peter is present at a number of miracles and when Jesus is arrested at Gethsemane. Perhaps the key event in this relationship is when – under interrogation – Peter thrice denies that he knows his master. This betrayal is forgiven by Jesus after his resurrection, and Peter's standing as his most trusted lieutenant is confirmed when Jesus instructs Peter to 'feed my lambs, feed my sheep'.

The clear message is that possession of the keys to the kingdom of heaven comes with a heavy weight of responsibility – nothing less than the spiritual nourishment of Christ's flock. In return for bearing this responsibility, Peter's successors are granted an authority unrivalled by that of any secular leader. The Code of Canon Law leaves one in no doubt as to the extent of a modern pope's powers: '… by virtue of his office, he has supreme, full, immediate and universal ordinary power in the Church and he can always freely exercise this power.' To some outside the Church, such absolute power might seem autocratic, even dictatorial. Yet in the eyes of most of the faithful the pope's authority is not only tolerable, but essential. While a constitutional monarch is a symbolic figurehead providing an important but largely honorific link to the past, the pope is much more than that: he is the *living presence* of Peter among Christ's followers. Among his many official titles are Successor to St Peter and Prince of the Apostles. In effect, all popes are St Peter incarnate, anointed by Christ, chosen with the guidance of the Holy Spirit. The pope is God's man on earth.

The idea of a seamless through-line linking Peter the Apostle with globetrotting John Paul II (or, indeed, John Paul's Twitter-friendly successors) is, of course, fanciful. In reality, the emergence of what we now call the papacy was a gradual and messy process, driven not by divine will or human masterplan, but by resourceful pragmatism. In this regard, papal history is as prone to contingency, confusion and misinterpretation as any other branch of history.

The papacy was originally conceived as a solution to a dangerous problem. Early Christians in first-century Rome were notoriously factional, their loyalties divided along lines of ethnicity and language. This diverse membership led, in turn, to conflicting interpretations of the scriptures and disagreements about rites. To adjudicate in such disputes and keep heresy at bay, a single authoritative voice was required. This figure – it is believed that the first was called Linus – became known as Bishop of Rome. We know little about Linus or his immediate successors, Cletus and Clement, but it appears that their attempts to keep a lid on dissent and unite Christ's followers were largely successful. Critics of the papacy have observed that, from the very outset, the imposition of a central controlling force lay behind the office of Bishop of Rome. The roots of papal autocracy run deep.

It was not enough simply to claim authority for the bishop. Over the first two centuries of the Christian era, a link had to be forged between the rapidly growing Church and certain key biblical figures who founded it. A cult grew up around the tombs of St Peter and St Paul, both of whom were believed to have been martyred and buried in or near the Eternal City. It seemed expedient in this context to trace the lineage of the bishops of Rome back to Peter and the other apostles, men who had served Jesus, passed on his words, witnessed his miracles. Thus, while the connection between Peter and his later successors was contrived retroactively, it had the desired effect of creating a powerful mythology which added gravitas to the office.

If the origins of the papacy were local, its influence gradually became widespread. Pope Gregory the Great (590–604), for example, revolutionised the liturgy and dispatched missionaries to England. By the early Middle Ages, popes had become adjudicators of last resort, pronouncing judgement in theological disputes from Canterbury to Constantinople. Popes came to be seen as operating above the fray: repositories of a divine wisdom that superseded the temporal interests of mere mortals. Kings and emperors craved the authority a papal stamp of approval might give them, to the extent that it became common for the pope to preside at secular coronations.

One source of this ever-growing papal power came from the office's role as custodian of the values and virtues of ancient Rome. As the Roman Empire disintegrated, its political and military power exhausted, the Church came to embody all that had been best about Rome. In the fractious early Middle Ages, law and order were at a premium. Christendom at this time had a dizzying range of secular leaders, most aspiring to stability but delivering chaos. Against this backdrop, the appeal of a single unquestioned moral and legal arbiter was obvious.

The high point of papal authority came between the ninth and fourteenth centuries. It was Pope Urban II who unleashed the Crusades and, with them, an age of inter-religious strife, the repercussions of which are still felt today. It was also during this period that popes regularly faced down kings and emperors. The most celebrated example of this came in the eleventh century, when Pope Gregory VII threatened to excommunicate the Holy Roman Emperor, Henry IV, over the latter's insistence on appointing his own bishops. The story goes that Henry, his bluff called, walked to Canossa in northern Italy, where Gregory was staying, and stood barefoot in the snow awaiting the pope's forgiveness. This incident provided symbolic evidence of papal supremacy for centuries thereafter.

In 1378, political infighting led to a schism. For more than thirty years, Christendom had two popes: one in Rome, the other in Avignon. Although the split was resolved, the papacy entered a period of disrepute, particularly under the Borgias. The corruption of the office in this period is rightly notorious. Nepotism was the norm, any pretence of leading a holy life disappeared and Rome's fixation with raising money to fund its lavish architectural and artistic projects fuelled the righteous ire of men like Martin Luther. With the Reformation came the repudiation of Rome and the pope in large areas of northern Europe, and the erosion of Rome's authority elsewhere. When, in 1606, Pope Paul V threatened to excommunicate the entire Republic of Venice, he no longer wielded the power that had enabled his predecessor, Gregory VII, to triumph at Canossa 500 years earlier. The Venetians carried on regardless and Paul was forced to back down.

The Counter-Reformation saw a cleansing of the institution. Popes became serious and holy again, as they sought to claw back some of the authority squandered by their reckless predecessors. But the Church's hold over secular rulers had been broken. No longer would the monarchs of Catholic Europe bow down before the Holy See. They ran their kingdoms in their own ways, appointed bishops, imposed taxes and kept a wary eye on papal attempts to interfere. Roles had been reversed by 1789, when the French Revolution set in train events that would bring an end to what remained of the Holy Roman Empire and diminish still further Rome's influence on the political affairs of Europe. As if to confirm this, a French Revolutionary army kidnapped Pope Pius VI and took him back to France, where he died in prison.

The nineteenth century was a time of unremitting woe for the Vatican. The forces of industrialisation and nationalism changed Europe's socio-political landscape almost beyond recognition, and the Church struggled to keep up. This culminated in the incorporation of Rome into a newly independent Italy in 1870 and the Vatican's loss of a sovereignty it had held for a millennium. Pope Pius IX responded in startling fashion. Refusing to recognise the Italian state, he declared himself a prisoner in the Vatican (though he was at liberty to come and go had he chosen to do so). For Pius, the Vatican's loss of liberty was an inevitable consequence of a period of declining moral values. What was required, he decided, was a strengthening of the papacy. Henceforth, he – and all future popes – would be infallible on matters of doctrine. Those who opposed this lurch into authoritarianism, and there were many, were marginalised and denounced. In Prussia, the Protestant Otto von Bismarck, already concerned about growing Catholic influence, reacted by launching his *Kulturkampf*, closing monasteries and imprisoning clergymen. Liberal Catholic opinion across the world reacted with dismay, but the die had been cast.

Pius IX's reframing of the relationship between his Church and modern society set up a confrontation that continues to this day. Indeed, John Paul II spent much of his pontificate fighting on the front line of that confrontation, further alienating moderate Catholics.

The papacy and the Vatican continue to exert a powerful fascination in the eyes of the world. As well as an aura of rarefied holiness, the Vatican gives off a whiff of secrecy and scandal, exploited so profitably by works of pulp fiction such as Dan Brown's *The Da Vinci Code* (2003). Much of this has its origins in the post-1870 'infallibility' era. Defensive of its own status and intellectually aggressive in its treatment of those who would undermine it, the Vatican has acquired an unfortunate reputation for intrigue. Frequently this leads outsiders to see conspiracies where none exist. The failure of wartime Pope Pius XII to condemn Nazi atrocities against Jews was thus interpreted by many as an example of virulent papal anti-Semitism, whereas indecision and diplomatic fence-sitting on Pius' part provide a more persuasive explanation. Likewise, when in 1978 Pope John Paul I was found dead in bed barely a month into his pontificate, conspiracy theorists leapt on the fact that the late pope was embalmed before an autopsy could be conducted: proof that he was murdered, claimed many. Equally plausibly, it was proof that those running the Vatican handled the situation with a not untypical combination of ineptitude and insensitivity. As more recent events have demonstrated, each new pontificate seems to generate its own scandals – whether financial, sexual or diplomatic – reinforcing the sense that the institution is irredeemably dysfunctional.

In the wake of John Paul I's death, it fell to his immediate successor, Karol Wojtyła, to redefine the powers and limits of his office, and the global perception of how that office was relevant in the modern world. Like his predecessors, he inherited an unfeasibly wide range of roles: Vicar of Christ; Primate of Italy; Bishop of Rome; Patriarch of the West; Servant of the Servants of God; Archbishop and Metropolitan of the Province of Rome; Sovereign of the Vatican City State. Like so many other aspects of Vatican reality, this list seems almost wilfully daunting and hard to understand, further reinforcing the sense that the job of a pope is to preside over an arcane cult with its own impenetrable rules and rituals.

Wojtyła set about redefining the papal image with a gusto that few could have predicted. In part this was due to the particular historical circumstances prevailing at the time of his election. But there are other reasons, to do with Wojtyła's status as an outsider and as a man whose character and world view had been formed in conditions utterly unlike those experienced by any previous pontiff.

3

A Motherless Only Child

Death was a major theme of John Paul II's pontificate. He believed the secular modern world to be obsessed with – and morally crippled by – a 'culture of death'. By this he meant abortion, contraception and euthanasia, practices that removed God's will from the equation of when a human life should begin or end. John Paul wrote and spoke about the culture of death at length (see Chapter 8). So much so, indeed, that it came to symbolise his refusal to compromise with progressive forces within the Church, especially on the issue of artificial birth control.

It is not hard to trace the roots of Karol Wojtyła's preoccupation with mortality. His mother, Emilia, died, probably of kidney failure, when he was only 9. Karol was reported to have coped stoically with her loss: 'It is God's will,' he told a teacher. Premature death also claimed his older brother Edmund, a newly qualified doctor and very much the star of the family. Edmund caught scarlet fever from a patient and died within four days. On his deathbed, the 26-year-old was reported to have said, 'Why now, why me?' That was in 1932, when the future pope was just 12 years old. Add to this the elder sister who had died as a baby and one can understand Wojtyła's adult observation that he had become, early in life, 'a motherless only child'.[2]

Wojtyła addressed this subject half a century later, a few years after he had become pope. 'These are events that became deeply engraved in my memory,' he said, 'my brother's death perhaps even deeper than my mother's death.'[3]

Karol Wojtyła was born on 18 May 1920 in Wadowice, 50km from Kraków in southern Poland. His home town was a provincial backwater (even by the 1930s the motor car had scarcely reached there), but it was close enough to Kraków to have at least some pretension to metropolitan sophistication. His father, also called Karol, was a career officer in the army of the Austro-Hungarian Empire, and subsequently in that of newly independent Poland. He was a disciplinarian, though apparently not in any sadistic way: the future pope had only appreciative things to say about his father.

Young Karol was born into dramatic times. A Second Polish Republic had been created following the Great War – the first time Poles had lived free of foreign rule since 1795. But already this once mighty nation was under threat. Lenin's vastly larger Red Army invaded from the east just months after Karol was born. Only an unexpected victory – known to this day in Poland as 'the miracle of the Vistula' – preserved Polish independence.

Following the deaths of Emilia and Edmund, Karol's father became increasingly devout. 'Sometimes I would wake up during the night and find my father on his knees,' Wojtyła recalled many years later.[4] A friend described the sadly reduced household as 'a community of two people'.

Father and son shared a devotion to the Virgin Mary, a figure who has been treated with profound reverence in Poland for more than 600 years – one icon of the Virgin is even credited with repulsing an invading Swedish army in 1655. Together they made pilgrimages to shrines and devoutly observed her feast days. Young Karol prayed to her statue in the local church every day on his way to school. His attachment to the Virgin remained intense throughout his life. He had special affection for the great Marian pilgrimage sites, including the celebrated 'Black Madonna' icon at Jasna Gora, in the Polish city of Czestochowa, which he first visited with his father at the age of 10. For the young Wojtyła, the Mother of God, through her suffering and her consolation, was a source of strength. In particular, her intermittent 'visitations' at sites such as Lourdes, Fatima and Medjugorje were evidence of, in his words, 'a specific geography of faith'.

If Marian devotion was one important formative element of Wojtyła's early life, so too was the theatre. In the aftermath of his election as pope, the global media expressed fascination and amazement that this embodiment of piety should once have been a stage actor. (Equal astonishment greeted the revelation that the teenage Karol had been a skilled goalkeeper, as if athleticism and holiness were mutually exclusive.) The effect of this coverage was to trivialise the significance of drama in Wojtyła's teens and early adulthood. In fact, contemporary accounts suggest that the young Karol was never more at ease than when on stage.

The attraction began early. By the age of 8 Karol was carrying messages for Wadowice's local theatre company, which was run by a family he knew well, the Kotlarczyks. To suggest that the motherless boy was looking for an alternative to the rather austere home he shared with his father might seem rather simplistic – though Wojtyła himself later explained his relationship with the Kotlarczyks in terms of 'trying to find friends and close family'.

Many of the amateur dramas Karol acted in – and, on occasion, directed – told stories from Poland's chequered past. Patriotic and imbued with the nation's intense brand of Catholicism, these plays had a strong element of ritual. National traumas were recalled, triumphs celebrated. Karol's father did nothing to encourage his son's passion for theatre, and there is no evidence of his having attended any of the productions. He studiously avoided befriending the Kotlarczyks, leaving the way clear for young Karol to build a parallel life with his 'stage' family. Nor was the acting bug simply a passing phase: Wojtyła would carry on performing throughout his time at university and up to the point where he embraced an alternative type of performance art, the priesthood.

Although Wadowice was provincial and unremarkable, it was far from homogenous in its make-up. Approximately one-fifth of the town's population in the 1920s was Jewish. The Wojtyłas rented their apartment from a Jewish small businessman who ran a shop downstairs. The future pope's best friend was a Jewish boy, Jerzy Kluger: the pair were known around the town as Jurek and Lolek, the affectionate Polish abbreviations of their names. Lolek even learned some Yiddish. In their biography of Wojtyła, Carl Bernstein and Marco Politi observe that 'since the time of the Apostle Peter, no Roman pontiff has ever spent his childhood in such close contact with Jewish life'.[5]

To read accounts of the young Wojtyła's childhood philo-Semitism is to get a misleading picture of relations between Jews and Catholics in Poland at that time. Although the country was traditionally less violently anti-Semitic than some of its neighbours, there remained a profound and superstitious mistrust of Jews, particularly among rural Poles. Wojtyła bucked this trend. His friendship with Kluger lasted for decades, with Jurek later visiting Pope John Paul in Rome. But a clearer sense of Catholic–Jewish relations is revealed in a speech written by the Primate of Poland, Cardinal Hlond, in 1936, and read from every church pulpit in the land: 'There will be a Jewish problem as long as the Jews remain … It is a fact that the Jews are fighting against the Catholic Church, persisting in free-thinking and are the vanguard of godlessness, Bolshevism and subversion …'

Hardly surprising, then, that many of the Jews Wojtyła knew growing up in Wadowice would end up in the gas chambers at Auschwitz-Birkenau, less than 20 miles away.

If Lolek's passion for football and acting are established beyond doubt, his relationships with girls remain shrouded in sanctified mystery. He was known to be fond of a neighbour, Ginka Beer, described by Jerzy Kluger as having 'stupendous eyes and jet-black hair'. She was sent by her Jewish family to Palestine in 1937 and later recalled that the Wojtyłas, father and son, had been the most tolerant family in Wadowice. Another alleged romantic interest was the daughter of the headmaster at Wojtyła's school. In later years she steadfastly maintained that they had been just good friends, though she complicated matters somewhat by claiming, after John Paul's death in 2005, that he was 'the love of my life'. The pope himself had previously reacted with irritation to speculation about his youthful love life. 'Can't you believe,' he wrote to one biographer, 'that a young man can live without committing mortal sin?'

Wojtyła left school in 1938 with impressive grades and an assessment that he was 'mature and adequately prepared to pursue higher studies'. Like his brother before him, he chose to attend the Jagiellonian University in Kraków. He and his father moved to the city and took up residence in the basement of a house owned by relatives of his late mother. In his first year at university he immersed himself in those subjects to which he was already temperamentally drawn: Polish language, culture and history. By all accounts, Karol was a sensitive and cerebral young man, and his faith, far from becoming diluted by exposure to city life and its many temptations, appears to have deepened. But that faith was to be tested when Kraków found itself in the eye of an unprecedented historical storm.

On 1 September 1939, Germany invaded Poland. Britain declared war, offering some fleeting hope to the

Poles, but Hitler's blitzkrieg ensured that the country was rapidly subdued. Kraków became the base for Hans Frank, Germany's governor general in what it called the 'New Reich'. Frank spelled out with chilling clarity his plans for occupied Poland:

> Every vestige of Polish culture is to be eliminated. Those Poles who seem to have Nordic appearance will be taken to Germany to work in our factories ... The rest? They will work. They will eat little. And in the end they will die out. There will never again be a Poland.

Like tens of thousands of their compatriots, Wojtyła and his father fled the city, heading for the Romanian border. Their column of refugees was strafed by German fighter planes, and Karol's father, who was in poor health, struggled to make progress. News then reached the column in mid-September that the Soviets had invaded from the east, fulfilling the terms of the nefarious Molotov-Ribbentrop pact, according to which Germany and the Soviet Union would divide and annihilate Poland. Trapped between invading armies, the Wojtyłas had little choice but to return to Kraków.

Hans Frank's war on Polish culture led to mass arrests of priests and academics; the university's faculties were decimated as professors were arrested and deported or killed. Nonetheless, in November 1939 Wojtyła enrolled for a second year of study. It was now that his dedication to the theatre paid dividends. Throughout that brutal winter,

Wojtyła wrote and staged several plays, most performed in semi-darkness in basement apartments. This was a risky business, theatre productions having been expressly outlawed. But for Wojtyła, these stories celebrating Polish history and culture were a form of resistance. 'I am not a cavalier of the sword,' he wrote to a friend, 'but an artist.'

He also risked arrest by taking part in prayer meetings led by a self-styled mystic called Jan Tyranowski. From contemporary accounts, there appears to have been something of the cult leader about Tyranowski. He encouraged younger members of the group to call him 'Master' – one later recalled that 'he knew how to convince people and bind them to himself'. Tyranowski's influence on the future pope was strong. As the Church's public role diminished under Nazi and Soviet tyranny, Wojtyła increasingly internalised his faith and developed a fascination for mysticism that would persist for the rest of his life.

By the autumn of 1940, Germany had made good its bleak promise to turn Poland into a nation of slave labourers. In September, Wojtyła was forced to take a job at a quarry run by the Solvay chemicals company. Accounts vary as to how arduous this work was, but it is certain that for a few months at least Wojtyła broke rocks with a pickaxe, gaining an insight into hard physical toil that makes him unique among Roman pontiffs. While the work meant his studies had to be put on hold, there was a positive side: because the quarried minerals went towards Germany's war effort, Wojtyła was safe from any immediate threat of deportation. Later he obtained a transfer on to a night shift at the company's water purification plant, which enabled him to keep up with his reading.

In February 1941, Wojtyła returned home to his basement apartment to find his father dead. This time, the stoicism he had shown following the deaths of his mother and brother was absent. Wojtyła wept openly and berated himself for not having been present when his father had died. According to one old friend, Wojtyła walked several miles to the city cemetery every day for weeks to pray at his father's graveside.

Wojtyła sought consolation in his clandestine stage productions and in fervent prayer meetings with Tyranowski. Life on the streets of Kraków became ever more dangerous, with mass arrests and deportations becoming increasingly common. The growing horror of war had a galvanising effect on Wojtyła's hitherto latent ambition to enter the priesthood. Writing half a century later, Wojtyła acknowledged the significance of this dark period: 'It helped me to understand in a new way the value and importance of a vocation. In the face of the spread of evil and the atrocities of war, the meaning of the priesthood and its mission in the world became much clearer to me.'[6]

So it was that in October 1942, Wojtyła presented himself at the palace of the Archbishop of Kraków, Adam Sapieha, and asked to be given a place at the secret seminary operating within its walls. Sapieha was on a mission to preserve the Catholic soul of Poland, and that meant training young men to replace the thousands of priests who were being rounded up and killed. For the remainder of the war, Wojtyła would prepare himself to embrace the vocation that had given his life fresh purpose (a vocation that was further strengthened when he survived a serious road accident in February 1944). He had embarked on a path that would lead him back to the palace twenty-two years later, as Archbishop of Kraków.

The young Karol Wojtyła's world view was inevitably shaped by the atrocities and deprivation he witnessed during these war years. In a world where morality appeared to have disappeared, he found strength in faith and patriotism and in exploring the inner mysteries of the soul. These became the bedrocks of his later life. The sanctity of life and the unique importance of the priesthood would be major – and controversial – themes of his pontificate.

Wojtyła was ordained on 1 November 1946. Many of the survival skills he had learned in wartime would now be needed again, as he fought to preserve the Church's freedom in the face of a new type of totalitarianism.

4

A Brother of the People

> **I could ... see** the church in Niegowić in the distance. It was harvest time. I walked through the fields of grain with crops in part already reaped and in part still waving in the wind. When I reached the territory of the Niegowić parish I knelt down and kissed the ground ...[7]

Karol Wojtyła's trademark gesture was established long before he became pope. The passage of memoir above recounts his journey to his first parish in a remote corner of southern Poland. The 28-year-old Fr Wojtyła already had a powerful sense of destiny and an abiding taste for the dramatic flourish. Indeed, there is something immodest about his description of kneeling and kissing the earth. One can't help feeling that, while the gesture may have been one of humility, the decision to set it down for all posterity suggests a certain egocentricity.

The young parish priest was far from callow. Immediately after his ordination he had been sent by Archbishop (now Cardinal) Sapieha to study in Rome. This was a rare honour; Poland had lost many of her priests, as we have seen, and most of the newly ordained were put straight to pastoral work. At the

Angelicum University in Rome, Wojtyła was tutored by the theologian Reginald Garrigou-Lagrange, noted for his strict devotion to St Thomas Aquinas, the thirteenth-century monk whose teachings continued to dominate Catholic theology. 'Reginald the Rigid', as he was known to anglophone students, was a fierce defender of orthodox Catholic teaching and a strong believer in the special, even mystical, nature of the priesthood. This chimed with Fr Wojtyła's own sense that he had been marked out by God – not just ordained but preordained. 'My priesthood, even at its beginning, was in some way marked by the great sacrifice of countless men and women of my generation,' he later wrote:

> Providence spared me the most difficult experiences and so my sense of indebtedness is all the greater, both to people whom I knew and to many more whom I did not know; all of them … by their sacrifice on the great altar of history, helped make my priestly vocation a reality.[8]

After eighteen months in Rome, incorporating occasional intellectually stimulating forays to France and Belgium, Wojtyła was brought back to Poland to run the rural parish of Niegowić. But not for long. Talent-spotted again by Sapieha, he was sent to the parish of St Florian near the Old Town quarter of Kraków. Many of his parishioners were students, and he took a special interest in guiding them through the moral pitfalls of early adult life, speaking frankly with them about love and marriage and, as many later recalled, sexuality. In a 2005 obituary of John Paul, the distinguished American Vaticanologist John L. Allen observed:

> That period in his life later flowered during his pontificate in a remarkable set of teachings delivered in general audiences about human sexuality. He spoke openly and warmly about sexuality as a gift that unites men and women in the depths of their being. Critics said that John Paul, in refusing to budge on issues such as birth control or homosexuality, refused to draw the conclusions of his own reasoning on human dignity as the ultimate basis of sexual morality.[9]

Wojtyła was, by all accounts, a vigorous pastor, organising retreats, theology evenings and stage productions, and indulging his own passion for the outdoors by taking groups of young people on hiking trips. Such excursions were not without risk, as Poland's communist regime increasingly clamped down on Church activities. The impression one gets of Wojtyła at this time is of a man preoccupied with philosophy and theatre, with hiking and skiing, and not at all engaged with politics. He combined parish work with a position teaching philosophy at Lublin, which was the only Catholic university in the communist world allowed to remain operational – remarkably, given that many seminaries and monasteries were closed down, religious schools and hospitals taken over by the state, and priests harassed and jailed or forced to become informants for the party.[10] At this early stage of Wojtyła's ecclesiastical career, confrontations with state authority were not on the agenda.

In July 1958 Wojtyła was chosen, to some surprise, to be the auxiliary Bishop of Kraków. At 38, he was comfortably the youngest bishop in Poland. Wojtyła chose as his motto the Latin phrase *Totus Tuus* (All Yours), an acknowledgement of his deep commitment to the cult of the Virgin Mary. Now Wojtyła was a public figure, expected by the faithful to show leadership in the ongoing struggle with godless state ideology. He threw his weight behind a campaign to build a chapel for workers at the giant Nowa Huta steelworks on the outskirts of Kraków. On Christmas Eve 1959, he celebrated Midnight Mass in a field near the steelworks, in defiance of the authorities. The Masses became an annual tradition until a church at the site was finally consecrated (by Wojtyła himself, then a cardinal) in 1977.

The timing of Wojtyła's elevation to bishop was opportune. One month after his consecration at Wawel Cathedral in Kraków, the reigning pope, Pius XII, died. Under this controversial pontiff, who had steered the barque of St Peter through the fire of the Second World War and the ice of the early Cold War, the Church had remained steadfastly introspective. Pius' successor, John XXIII, would change its direction in dramatic fashion – and Wojtyła would play a significant part in making that happen.

The Second Vatican Council, or Vatican II, saw the biggest overhaul of Catholic procedures and rituals in centuries. The first session convened by John XXIII opened in Rome in October 1962. Among its delegates was Karol Wojtyła: one of the younger men invited, and one of the most proficient Latin speakers – a fact which was noted with approval by his peers. The appreciation was not mutual. Coming from a society where state oppression demanded discipline and unity among Catholics, Wojtyła was unimpressed by the conduct of his Western colleagues. Infighting and regular leaks to the press dogged council meetings. Later, as pope, Wojtyła would show little tolerance for such off-message behaviour. As Edward Stourton points out in his biography of John Paul: 'Many of the critics of John Paul's pontificate complained that, while he insisted on human rights when he was fighting a totalitarian State, he seemed unwilling to grant them to members of the Church.'[11]

Wojtyła had a hands-on role in helping to frame the modernising measures that emerged from Vatican II – such as celebration of the Mass in the vernacular and an increased role for the laity. Yet an enduring mystery concerns the part he played (or did not play) in drafting one of the most controversial papal documents of modern times.

During Vatican II, Pope John XXIII gave his blessing to a Birth Control Commission, formed to re-examine the Church's position on contraception and over-population. Given the hard-line stance the Church would go on to take under John Paul II, it is easy to forget that in the mid-1960s some senior prelates believed the Church should drop its historic intolerance of contraception and avoid what one called 'another Galileo moment'. Indeed, the commission concluded that the Church should change its teaching. Liberal Catholics hoped that John XXIII's successor, Pope Paul VI, would endorse the commission's findings. Instead, he issued an encyclical called *Humanae Vitae* (*On Human Life*), which included an unequivocal defence of established thinking: '… to have recourse to contraceptives is a serious sin that offends God, destroys the life of grace, prevents access to the sacraments and … wounds the life of the couple.'

Many detected the hand of Wojtyła in the conclusions and wording of *Humanae Vitae*. His status enhanced by his appointment as Archbishop of Kraków in 1964, Wojtyła had been asked by Paul VI to join the commission, though travel restrictions imposed by the communist regime prevented him from attending all but a handful of meetings. Yet he had sent the pontiff many letters and articles supporting traditional teaching. While no irrefutable evidence exists that Wojtyła contributed directly, there is little doubt that *Humanae Vitae* was a victory for him and like-minded clergy.

The late 1960s and early 1970s saw Wojtyła augment his standing at home and abroad. As Poland celebrated a thousand years as a Christian country in 1966, he was at the forefront of ceremonies attended by millions. By 1970, he had gained sufficient authority to speak out in support of workers' rights in the shipyards of Gdansk and elsewhere, demanding 'the right to food, the right to freedom … an atmosphere of genuine freedom … not questioned or threatened in any practical sense'.

Cardinal Wojtyła – he had been elevated again in 1967 – became an increasingly prominent figure within Vatican circles. He sat on various synods of bishops, earning praise for clear thinking. His position as a leading Churchman in an officially atheistic society lent him a certain celebrity status. He travelled widely, to the United States, the Philippines and Australia as well as within Europe, and cultivated a discreet but influential network of contacts.

There is a tradition in Rome that, at the start of Lent, the pope and a group of senior curial officials attend a five-day retreat in a chapel within the Vatican's walls. Each year, a cardinal, bishop or theologian is invited to deliver a series of talks, or homilies, on themes pertinent to the Church's place in the world. Outside the Vatican little attention is paid to the identity of this guest speaker. Within that cloistered world, however, the invitation is seen to be a sign that the speaker is admired or considered ripe for advancement. At the very least, it is a sign that he has friends in high places.

In 1976, the aged and ailing Pope Paul VI asked Cardinal Wojtyła to deliver the Lenten homilies. This was no junket: over the course of five days, the Polish cardinal gave more than twenty talks. In one particularly noteworthy homily, he brought together two of the themes that would later come to define his pontificate – freedom and the right to life: 'Dignity must not be made to consist in unbridled exercise of one's own freedom … The freedom sought after by the campaigners in favour of abortion is a freedom in the service of pleasure unrestrained by norms of any kind.'

This reaffirmation of traditional teaching went down well with the assembled Vatican heavy-hitters.

Over the course of the next two years, Wojtyła became increasingly well known. A short theology book he had written, entitled *Sign of Contradiction*, was deemed essential reading in the seminaries and colleges of Rome. Meanwhile, back in Poland, Wojtyła and his Church were growing in confidence as the Communist Party's iron grip was loosening. In a memoir of forty years working alongside Wojtyła, his aide and secretary Stanisław Dziwisz (who would himself later become Archbishop of Kraków) recalled the mood in 1978: 'The [Polish] regime was too much a prisoner in its own ideological mechanisms and its own absolute rigidity to notice the threat hanging over its head,' he wrote.[12] In this atmosphere, Wojtyła delivered a stirring speech on a visit to the shrine at Kalwaria Zebrzydowska. 'Something completely new is being born,' he declared. 'I would call it a spontaneous, passionate search for the "faithful witness". Jesus is this witness.'

With his usual flair for the theatrical, some might even say the melodramatic, Cardinal Wojtyła was summoning into being an era of renewal for Catholicism. That job was well in hand in Poland, where the Church had become a de facto opposition to totalitarian control. The challenge now was to export Catholic renewal to those parts of the world where the Church had become increasingly outdated and irrelevant. Few would have predicted at the time that this challenge would be spearheaded by the man from Wadowice.

5

Called from a Faraway Land

On Wednesday 4 October 1978, hundreds of thousands of mourners gathered in St Peter's Square for the funeral of Albino Luciani, the former Patriarch of Venice, who had become Pope John Paul I just weeks earlier, on 26 August. A mild, self-deprecating man, dubbed 'the Smiling Pope', he won instant popularity both with the faithful and with the global media. It was typical of his humility that he chose as his regnal name a compound of his two immediate predecessors: John XXIII, who had made Luciani a bishop, and Paul VI, who had elevated him to the College of Cardinals.

John Paul I had been found dead in bed just thirty-three days after his election, throwing the Church into a state of shock worldwide. The circumstances of his death were unclear, prompting suspicions (never substantiated) that he had been eliminated by enemies within the Vatican. A *Time* magazine reporter captured the scene at the funeral: 'As the plain cypress coffin was borne through the portals of the great basilica, the huge, tearful crowd standing in the rainswept square burst into applause.'[13]

At the Requiem Mass that preceded the burial, it rained intermittently. As if to counteract the rain clouds, in his funeral address, reported in *Time*, 85-year-old Cardinal

Carlo Confalonieri compared Pope John Paul I to 'a meteor that unexpectedly lights up the heavens and then disappears, leaving us amazed and astonished'.

Luciani had been chosen by his fellow cardinals because he was reassuringly pastoral, a nurturing man of the people, unlike the aloof intellectual Paul VI, who directly preceded him. He had a reputation as a good communicator, was doctrinally a moderate conservative, and had not (again unlike Paul VI) spent his career in the rarefied confines of the Roman Curia.

Karol Wojtyła's aide and secretary, Stanisław Dziwisz, recalled his superior's reaction on hearing the news of John Paul I's death: 'He wanted to be alone at that sad moment … we only heard him whispering, "this is unbelievable … unbelievable." From the other end of the hall we saw him going in to the chapel. And he stayed there for a long time, praying.'[14]

The question preoccupying the faithful now was: with John Paul I gone, would the cardinals dare to choose another charismatic outsider or would they revert to type and elect a known quantity from within the Church establishment? Because Catholic doctrine maintains that the Holy Spirit guides the choice of pope, open campaigning is strictly taboo. A candidate who knows he has support among cardinals must strive not to show that he knows. Likewise, any would-be kingmaker must be discreet in the way he advances the claims of his preferred candidate. There is a saying in Rome that 'the man who goes into the conclave a pope comes out a cardinal'.

Some biographers have speculated that Wojtyła had a strong inkling that this time, when he went to Rome for the conclave, he would not be returning. Such claims owe more to Wojtyła's later reputation as a man of destiny than to any firm evidence.

The period before a conclave is known as the *Sede Vacante*, or Vacant See. It is the ultimate power vacuum. The heads of the various Vatican departments relinquish their posts and bureaucracy grinds to a halt. Only the *camerlengo*, or chamberlain, grows in authority. (In October 1978 it was the chain-smoking French cardinal Jean Villot.) He oversees the mourning process, controls access to the Lateran Palace and presides over the conclave. Because power in the Vatican resides in the person of the pope, the rest of the clergy present have been compared to orphans. One effect of Pope Benedict XVI's surprise resignation in February 2013 was to change this dynamic. Because there was no solemn funeral and no mourning period, cardinals had more time and freedom to meet and discuss their preferred candidates.

Before the October 1978 conclave began, there were two clear favourites. Giuseppe Siri, the Archbishop of Genoa, was the most prominent conservative cardinal. He was an unabashed reactionary, dismissive of the reforms of Vatican II and determined to turn the clock back to an era of Latin Masses, all-powerful clergy and icy disapproval of the secular world. His chief rival was Giovanni Benelli, the recently appointed Archbishop of Florence. Benelli, a clever and well-connected moderniser, had been influential in the previous conclave, advancing the case for Luciani despite the latter's profound reluctance to be considered *papabile*. While both Siri and Benelli were backed by significant numbers of their fellow cardinals, each lacked broader appeal. Siri could rely on the votes of his fellow traditionalists but was mistrusted by many on the reformist wing. Benelli, while championed by many, was a similarly divisive figure. With a deadlocked conclave looming, something had to give.

The moment was propitious for a compromise candidate: conservative enough to appeal to Siri's constituency yet sufficiently progressive to draw support from cardinals in the Benelli camp. A number of elderly Italians were cast in the role, while some cardinals began to consider a possibility that would have seemed ludicrous even a decade earlier: what about a non-Italian pope? There were strong contenders: Lorscheider from Brazil, Willebrands from Holland, Westminster's own Basil Hume. Also on this list was the name of the energetic Archbishop of Kraków.

Back in Rome, Wojtyła wisely refused to entertain the possibility that he might become pope. Even privately, with Dziwisz and other Polish friends, he dismissed such talk as idle speculation. But he must have been aware that a coalition of interests was lining up behind him. He had, after all, received nine votes at the August conclave – enough to suggest that his name was in the frame even then.

The key figure behind Wojtyła's transformation from dark horse to serious contender was Cardinal Franz König, the much-admired Archbishop of Vienna. Under

Pope Paul VI, König had been a roving Vatican ambassador in communist Eastern Europe. He knew Wojtyła well and was impressed by the Pole's calm defiance in the face of state oppression. As the start of the conclave drew closer, König took steps to make sure Wojtyła's name was prominent in the minds of his fellow cardinals.

While König's assessment that the Polish cardinal had both personality and gravitas was growing in popularity, Wojtyła chose to escape Rome in the days immediately preceding the conclave. His devotion to the Virgin Mary was never more apparent than at key moments such as this, and now he took himself off to the Marian shrine at Mentorella, 25 miles from the capital. Three Polish priests who accompanied him later described how the exceptionally hale and hearty 58-year-old cardinal strode up the mountainside to the shrine, leaving his much younger companions trailing behind. In the aftermath of John Paul I's sudden death, such youthful vigour would be a significant factor as cardinals weighed up the Archbishop of Kraków's suitability for the top job.

A papal conclave is a ritual so arcane and secretive that it seems to belong to another world, another time. Those members of the College of Cardinals under the age of 80 and eligible to vote – at that time numbering 111 – together with those required to meet the cardinals' daily needs, are locked into the Sistine Chapel (the word conclave derives from the Latin *cum clave*, or 'with a key'). There, with Michelangelo's *The Creation of Man* on the ceiling above and his *Last Judgement* over the altar, they gather to choose a successor to St Peter. The ballots are held in complete silence. If no cardinal gains the required number of votes, the ballot papers, tally sheets and any notes made by cardinals are collected by the Master of the Sacred Palace. It is he who places them in the stove, adding moistened straw and a black flare to indicate to the waiting crowds in St Peter's Square that no pope has yet been chosen. The cardinals then vote again.

Between ballots, they pray, seeking guidance from the Holy Spirit, and they take soundings, weighing the merits of each contender. Food and drink are provided by silent nuns, flitting about with bowls of pasta and salad, and carafes of wine. In the twenty-first century, the cardinals are housed in relative comfort at a hotel-like residence within the Vatican, but back in 1978 they slept on camp beds and used chamber pots – a strong incentive to reach a swift decision.

Despite the secrecy surrounding conclaves, details of the ballots routinely make their way into the public domain, suggesting that at least one cardinal believes the historical record to be of more importance than the tradition of confidentiality. Thus we know that in the first ballot Cardinal Siri received twenty-three votes, while his arch-rival Benelli got twenty-two. The rest were distributed among various compromise candidates, including Wojtyła, who garnered five votes.

This spelled the end for Siri. Aware that he had no chance of outflanking Benelli, the cardinals abandoned him in droves. The second ballot saw Benelli's support rise to sixty-five votes. Wojtyła was now in second place with twenty-four. This was the moment at which König and others went into full campaign mode. Their calculation was that Benelli had peaked. Disgruntled conservatives, deprived of their champion, simply would not countenance a Benelli papacy. Benelli's erstwhile supporters were lobbied about the attractions of the cardinal from Kraków. Over the course of several more ballots, support shifted inexorably towards Wojtyła, until he passed the two-thirds majority required to be elected. At 6.19 p.m. on 16 October white smoke appeared above St Peter's Square, and the waiting crowd, along with millions watching worldwide, were given the startling news that the new pope came not from Italy, as most had expected, but was, in John Paul II's own words, 'called from a faraway land'.

In an interview with the *National Catholic Reporter* more than twenty years later, Franz König argued that the idea of a non-Italian pope had proven irresistible: the fact that Wojtyła came from the wrong side of the Iron Curtain made it even more so.[15] König also disclosed that he was approached by one cardinal shortly after the conclave ended and asked, 'What have we done?' König himself would go on to wonder the same thing. (See Chapter 8.)

Beyond the College of Cardinals, the reaction to Wojtyła's election was one of bewilderment, even shock. John Cornwell quotes an unnamed Vatican source describing the effect on Italian clergy from lower down the Vatican hierarchy:

> When [Wojtyła's] name was announced, I had the presence of mind to take a sidelong look around me to see how they had taken it. Their faces were frozen in sheer horror – a foreigner! Then the old *bella figura* complex took over, and they grinned and clapped![16]

If those Italian priests were unpleasantly surprised, that was as nothing compared to the reaction at Communist Party headquarters in Warsaw. Poland's leader, Edward Gierek, is reported to have greeted the news with the inadvertently apt exclamation: 'Holy Mother of God!'[17] While the Polish people celebrated with candlelit parades, the party leadership met in emergency session to consider the implications. Pope Paul VI had implemented a policy of *Ostpolitik*, hoping to forge working relationships with Eastern Europe's godless regimes. Gierek had an uneasy sense that the erstwhile Archbishop of Kraków would prove to be less emollient in his relations with the Soviet Bloc. Some in the leadership even concluded that Wojtyła's election was an American-led conspiracy.

Gierek was faced with an intractable political problem. The overwhelming majority of Poles now looked for moral and spiritual leadership to Rome, and their exiled king. In the game of thrones that was about to take place, Wojtyła unquestionably had the support of the people. The first set-piece battle in this struggle for Poland's soul would take place just nine months later, when Wojtyła returned to his homeland for a visit that announced the arrival of a major new player on the world stage.

6

The Portable Pope

No one could be sure exactly how many were present. Officially, 230,000 tickets had been issued, but most estimates put the crowd in Warsaw's Victory Square at 300,000. Up to 1 million more thronged the surrounding, flower-strewn streets. Many wept or laughed. Others sang hymns. Whatever the precise figures, all had come to witness what they saw as a miracle. As Pope John Paul II, their newly minted national hero, addressed them in their own tongue, his audience left the Polish government in no doubt as to their priorities. 'We want God', was the chant that reverberated around the square.

Papal biographer George Weigel has deftly summed up the immediate impact of Karol Wojtyła's return to Poland on 2 June 1979: 'Seven hours after he had arrived, a crucial truth had been clarified by a million Poles' response to John Paul's evangelism,' he wrote. 'Poland was not a Communist country. Poland was a Catholic nation saddled with a Communist state.'[18]

This impression was shared by Zbigniew Brzezinski, the Polish-born national security adviser to US President Jimmy Carter: 'The dominant mood [in Poland] until then was the inevitability of the existing system. After [John Paul II] left, the dominant mood was the non-inevitability of the existing system. I think that was a fundamental transformation.'[19]

Edward Gierek was left to reflect on this inconvenient reality as he watched John Paul II sweep the nation (the pope made no fewer than forty public appearances in nine days, including a Mass in his home town of Wadowice). The party boss had endured a difficult few months. On the telephone from Moscow, Leonid Brezhnev had urged Gierek to downplay the visit: 'Don't give him any reception, it will only cause trouble' was the Soviet leader's impractical advice.[20] In the event, Poland's defiant Catholics provided a reception of their own.

John Paul surprised both Gierek and Brezhnev by avoiding a full-scale denunciation of the regime. Instead, he accentuated the positive, as Norman Davies, the distinguished historian of Poland, has observed:

> He did not waste words condemning the Communist system or the iniquities of Soviet domination. He spoke of truth, mercy, justice, compassion and, above all, love … As a result, the Soviet Bloc was irreparably holed beneath the waterline. The Communist leaders were helpless. They would probably have survived a nuclear attack. But they could not resist a barrage of good will and simple truths.[21]

Just over a year later, shipyard workers in the Baltic port of Gdansk would form a new trade union, *Solidarnosc*, or Solidarity. Led by Lech Wałęsa – a devout Catholic –

and vigorously supported by John Paul, Solidarity rapidly became the focal point for opposition in Poland. It would be simplistic to attribute the rise of Solidarity to John Paul's intervention alone. Conditions in Poland were ripe for an upsurge of dissent. In 1979, the year of John Paul's first visit (in all, he would return to his homeland nine times), Poland's economy shrank for the first time since the Second World War, though standards of living had been declining throughout the 1970s. There can, however, be no doubt that the pope's active support emboldened his compatriots. John Paul helped spark a slow-burning revolution that would culminate in the collapse of communism across the entire face of Europe.

John Paul's triumphant Polish visit established one theme of his pontificate: a personal crusade against the kind of state tyranny he had endured at first hand throughout his adult life. Equally significant, in his first two years in office, was the manner in which he marked out a second battlefront. This would be an altogether less heroic struggle, fought behind closed doors. To describe it as civil war may be to overstate the case, but John Paul's assault on freedom of expression *within* the Church led to internal divisions and mistrust that persist into the twenty-first century. He started early, in Mexico, on his first overseas trip as pope in January 1979. Most headlines focused on his visit to the shrine of Our Lady of Guadalupe. But what came next was of greater long-term significance. His Marian devotions concluded, John Paul went on to the city of Puebla, where the Latin-American

Bishops' Conference was in session. As many observers recalled, the smiling public man who had greeted the crowds transformed, away from the cameras, into a stern, occasionally hectoring martinet.

John Paul's ire was directed at those who had embraced liberation theology, a peculiarly Latin-American idea which mixed elements of Marxism-Leninism with Christianity. For adherents of liberation theology, Christianity's primary duty was to help the poor, the oppressed and the downtrodden. While John Paul certainly sympathised with that ambition, he disagreed fundamentally with the approach adopted by some of the local clergy. To this implacable enemy of Eastern European communism, any Marxist contamination of the Christian message was anathema. John Paul spelled this out unambiguously to the bishops assembled in Puebla. Just a few months into his pontificate, he had made two things clear: that unorthodox thinking would be discouraged and that he personally would be the judge of what 'unorthodox' meant.

Back in Europe, French theologian Jacques Pohier was first to feel the backlash. He had dared to reinterpret Christian teaching using psychoanalytic theory and was stripped of his licence to teach, celebrate Mass or participate in liturgical gatherings. Edward Schillebeeckx, a Belgian Dominican, was threatened with a similar fate when one of his books explored the human side of Jesus' nature at the expense of the divine – an interpretation that was not encouraged in Rome.

Perhaps the most high-profile theologian to be singled out for censure was Professor Hans Küng. An influential figure during the Second Vatican Council more than a decade earlier, Küng was a critic of the Church's hierarchical structure. In particular, he questioned the doctrine of papal infallibility, which had been introduced in 1870 at a time when the pope, Pius IX, had felt that his office was being besieged and threatened. Küng was now warned 'not to persist in the teaching of erroneous or dangerous doctrines' and summoned to the Vatican. When he refused to go, he too was deprived of his teaching licence and declared *persona non grata.*

The list goes on: Father Anthony Kosnik from Detroit, forced to resign from a teaching job because of an essay on human sexuality; Father Matthew Fox of Chicago, silenced and forced out of the Dominican Order; Leonardo Boff, a liberation theologist from Brazil, censured and silenced; Mary Agnes Mansour, a nun forced to choose between her job in Michigan's Department of Social Services and the religious life – like many others during John Paul's pontificate, she chose to leave her order.

Further confirmation that John Paul would be a doctrinally conservative pontiff came with the publication of his first encyclical, *Redemptor Hominis.* Encyclicals (circular letters addressed to bishops clarifying Church teaching) issued early in a pontificate often act as signposts indicating the direction the Church is likely to take under the latest successor to St Peter.

In *Redemptor Hominis*, or *Redeemer of Man* (1979), John Paul identified human rights as the most important issue of his time. Specifically, he called for a renewed recognition of the dignity of the individual, so often forgotten in the course of history's bloodiest century. John Paul made it clear, however, that there was only one path to human freedom. In a phrase that could only alienate those who did not share his beliefs, John Paul wrote that 'the name for that deep amazement at man's worth and dignity is the Gospel … It is also called Christianity'.

Reactions to the encyclical confirmed that John Paul was a divisive figure from the very outset of his pontificate. For George Weigel, an unabashed admirer, '*Redemptor Hominis* offered the world a Church in love with humanity, and for the most weighty of reasons – because God had so loved the world that he had sent his only son as the redeemer of man'.[22] Michael Walsh, another papal biographer, took a different view: 'As the guardian of the Gospel message … the Church can claim a privileged status when the dignity of the person is to be debated … There was no longer any common ground when talking of moral issues with those who did not share the Christian faith.'[23]

Critics of John Paul also saw in *Redemptor Hominis* the blueprint for an increasingly authoritarian approach to Church governance. 'There were ominous signs of what was in store for dissidents who exercised their right to freedom of conscience within the Catholic Church,' wrote John Cornwell. '[John Paul] warned Catholic theologians that they should engage in "close collaboration with the magisterium", the body of doctrine approved by the papacy.' For Cornwell, this suppression of unorthodox voices had a lasting effect on the intellectual life of the church: '[John Paul's] determination to exert discipline unfortunately imposed heavy restrictions and penalties on creative theologians who were non-conformist and different rather than erroneous or heretical.'[24]

Throughout 1979 and 1980, travelling extensively in Africa, Latin America and Europe, John Paul preached to millions, inspiring them with his message of freedom and dignity. He continued to intervene personally in the affairs of his homeland; in a frank letter to Soviet leader Leonid Brezhnev, John Paul warned that 'what is at stake here is, and always will be, a strictly internal matter for the people of Poland'. Meanwhile, the new pope continued to tighten his grip on the internal affairs of the Church. When bishops from around the world went to Rome in 1980 for the first Synod of his reign, they quickly learned that John Paul would rarely be receptive to fresh thinking. Several groups of bishops, including those from England and Wales, sought to reopen a debate on the Church's outright ban on artificial birth control and on the withholding of the sacraments from divorced Catholics. John Paul's response was to issue an apostolic exhortation (another form of communiqué from a pontiff to the faithful) overruling the views of many bishops and reaffirming existing Church teaching. It was a pattern that would be repeated on many occasions over the following decades.

Two and a half years into his pontificate, John Paul had become arguably the most newsworthy pope in history. His already high profile would be raised to spectacular new levels by events in St Peter's Square on the afternoon of 13 May 1981. Around 20,000 people (modest by John Paul's standards) had gathered in the square to receive a blessing. As John Paul's 'popemobile' Jeep moved slowly through the crowd, two shots rang out. One bullet entered the pope's abdomen, the other nicked his arm and subsequently hit two American tourists, neither of whom was seriously injured.

As the pope fell back into the arms of his ever-present secretary, Stanisław Dziwisz, his vehicle sped from the square. John Paul was transferred to an ambulance, which got him to the Gemelli Hospital in eight minutes, during which time, recalled Dziwisz, the pope was fading but still conscious:

> He was groaning quietly and his voice kept getting weaker. He was praying, too. I heard him saying: 'Jesus, Mother Mary.' As soon as we got to the Gemelli [hospital] he lost consciousness. And at exactly that moment it dawned on me that his life was in danger. Even the doctors who performed the surgery confessed to me later … that they didn't believe the patient would survive.[25]

John Paul had lost 6 pints of blood, but the bullet had missed arteries and vital organs by millimetres. After undergoing an emergency colostomy, he spent four days in intensive care, while the world came to terms with news of this latest horrifying attack on a public figure (the shooting came a few months after the murder of John Lennon and just weeks after the attempted assassination of Ronald Reagan).

The man who shot John Paul with a semi-automatic pistol was Mehmet Ali Agca. He was apprehended as he tried to escape. Agca refused to reveal his motives: within days, theories abounded as to his motives. The two most popular were that Agca, already wanted by police in his native Turkey, was either working for Bulgarian intelligence or that he was a lone Islamic fundamentalist acting out of hatred of the Catholic Church. Rumours circulated that the Italian secret services knew more than they were saying. Inevitably, given John Paul's forceful support of Solidarity in Poland, the KGB was also under suspicion.

In their biography of John Paul, Carl Bernstein and Marco Politi claim to have seen documents demonstrating 'the increasing Soviet preoccupation with the Pope and the Church – and the Soviet leaders' frustration with the Polish authorities for not cracking down on the Church – in the weeks and months preceding the assassination attempt'. The authors stop short of laying blame at Moscow's door, however, arguing that the diplomatic fall-out from a Soviet-backed conspiracy would have been counter-productive.[26]

More than thirty years on, no proven explanation exists for the assassination attempt. Certainly Agca had links to

Bulgaria's secret services and most commentators now believe he was not acting alone. One school of thought, perhaps the most plausible, is the 'Becket Theory', named in honour of the Archbishop of Canterbury murdered in the twelfth century; it argues that diverse shadowy forces within communist Eastern Europe let it be known that they wanted the pope dead and issued a 'who will rid me of this turbulent priest?' appeal for willing assassins. Agca fitted the bill. He was a professional hitman with a track record, having previously taken part in the killing of a newspaper editor in Istanbul. What's more, he had threatened in print to kill the pope prior to John Paul's visit to Turkey in November 1979. Yet Agca, even after his eventual release more than twenty years later, has never provided a motive – perhaps, some believe, because he never knew who his ultimate paymasters were.

Once his condition had stabilised and his recovery was under way, John Paul again displayed his trademark talent for the dramatic, weaving a narrative around the shooting in which he managed to cast himself and his beloved Virgin Mary in starring roles. By coincidence, Agca had carried out his attack on the feast day of Our Lady of Fatima, marking the occasion more than sixty years earlier when the Virgin supposedly appeared to a group of children in rural Portugal. One of those children, who later became a nun, claimed to have been told three secrets by the apparition. The first two concerned global carnage, while the third had never been disclosed. Struck by the coincidence of the date, John Paul called for the envelope containing this secret and learned that it predicted the violent death of a 'bishop in white'. The pope became convinced that the Blessed Virgin had intervened to save his life: a glorious confirmation of his lifelong conviction that she was a vital source of security and comfort in the world. 'Again I have become indebted to the Blessed Virgin,' he told an audience of the faithful in St Peter's Square on 7 October 1981. 'I felt the extraordinary motherly protection, which turned out to be stronger than the deadly bullet.'

One year to the day after he was shot, John Paul would visit Fatima with the bullet that had been removed from his body. In an act of almost medieval supplication, he placed the bullet on the crown worn by a statue of the Virgin. The gesture was, as George Weigel observes:

> John Paul's answer to the question of how his papacy, and indeed his life, should be understood … Arriving in Fatima, the Pope succinctly summarised his view of life, history and his own mission in one pregnant phrase: 'In the designs of Providence there are no mere coincidences.'[27]

7

Cold Warrior

On 22 May 1982, in the middle of the Falklands Conflict, John Paul sent a telegram to the British Prime Minister, Margaret Thatcher. 'In deep anguish at the news from the South Atlantic,' he wrote, 'where the armed conflict with Argentina is causing grievous loss of human life … I urgently appeal to you to act decisively in order to secure an immediate ceasefire that will open the way to a peaceful solution of the dispute.'[28]

If John Paul's tone was typically peremptory, Thatcher's reply was equally characteristic. She readily shared John Paul's 'anguish … at the loss of life', before adding a sharp proviso: 'That our cause is just and that the principles which we uphold are shared and understood by democratic nations, I have not the slightest doubt.'[29]

What made the situation difficult for Thatcher was a threat from within the Vatican to cancel John Paul's first visit to Britain. Previously classified documents, released in 2012, show that John Paul was unhappy when his pleas for a negotiated ceasefire were ignored. Just a fortnight before the papal visit was due to begin, Sir Mark Heath, Britain's ambassador to the Holy See, reported on a meeting between John Paul and Cardinal Basil Hume: 'The kernel of this,' Sir Mark wrote, was that 'if the Pope's prayers and hopes for a peaceful settlement were not answered and if armed conflict were to continue then the visit would be "reconsidered"'.

Some in London suspected that the pope was trying to blackmail the Thatcher government into suing for peace (he had reportedly also threatened to call the disputed islands the Malvinas, which would have amounted to a clear declaration of partisanship). In the event, Sir Mark Heath's warning to the Vatican that cancelling the trip would have a damaging effect on public opinion in Britain were heeded. The status of the visit, however, was radically downgraded. The foreign secretary, Francis Pym, wrote that: 'If it would help the Pope to stand by his visit, Her Majesty's Government would be ready to treat the visit … as a purely pastoral event and therefore remove from the present programme most or all aspects of government involvement.'[30] In effect, this meant there would be no official greeting at the airport and no meeting between the pope and Thatcher. The visit went ahead and was deemed a success. The spectacle of John Paul and the Archbishop of Canterbury, Robert Runcie, walking together in the cloisters of Canterbury Cathedral was seen as evidence of a growing rapprochement between Catholics and Anglicans. That optimism would be dashed within a few years, however, as John Paul's continued resistance to women priests drove a wedge between the two churches.

British anxiety over John Paul's visit illustrates the extent to which he had become a man whose views counted on the world stage. Just days after his tour of Canterbury, the pope had his first meeting with the US President, Ronald

Reagan. Unsurprisingly, the two Cold Warriors found much common ground. Reagan is known to have shared US intelligence with John Paul on developments behind the Iron Curtain, prompting a long-standing theory that the two men actively conspired to destroy communism in Eastern Europe. George Weigel dismisses this analysis as 'journalistic fantasy', but others cite evidence of a trade-off: John Paul kept quiet about his objections to the deployment of cruise missiles in Europe, the theory goes, while Reagan cut federal spending on abortion and family planning programmes in the US and elsewhere. Carl Bernstein and Marco Politi note this 'synergy' of interests, though they conclude that US-Vatican co-operation fell short of a formal series of 'clandestine activities together'.[31]

Whatever the extent of their collaboration, there can be no doubt that John Paul found an ideological soulmate in Reagan, and to a certain extent in Thatcher, as he pursued his campaign for freedom in Poland. His second papal visit to his homeland, in June 1983, took place against a very different backdrop from the first. The martial law declared by Poland's leader, General Wojciech Jaruzelski, two years earlier had been suspended but Solidarity remained outlawed. Many of its leaders, including Lech Wałęsa, had spent periods of time in prison.

Some in the Vatican, notably John Paul's secretary of state, Cardinal Casaroli, were uneasy about the pope's eagerness to confront Jaruzelski, fearing that such an intervention might provoke violent civil unrest in Poland. In the event, John Paul demanded a private meeting with

Wałęsa, word of which soon spread among opposition supporters. Wałęsa, whose ability to influence events had been severely curtailed, gained huge prestige from the meeting. Far from inflaming the situation, however, John Paul showed his diplomatic nous by promising Jaruzelski that he would urge Western governments to ease their economic sanctions against Poland.

By the time the pope made his next visit home, in June 1987, it was Jaruzelski's position that had weakened. The murder in 1984 by Poland's secret police of Father Jerzy Popiełuszko, a prominent Solidarity supporter and popular preacher, had been greeted with outrage. The opposition was galvanised. Strikes were called, weakening Poland's already ailing economy. John Paul visited Gdansk – previously kept off limits by the regime – where a congregation of more than 1 million heard him preach in praise of 'solidarity and the common good'. Within three years Jaruzelski would be gone, Wałęsa would be Poland's president and John Paul would be hosting a meeting in the Vatican with another principal player in the drama of communism's downfall, Russian leader Mikhail Gorbachev. By then the hard work had been done, yet their meeting still stood as an extraordinary testament to the changes that had swept Europe since John Paul's election.

For the pope personally, the 1980s saw the resolution of a lifelong struggle. As Edward Stourton has observed:

> Europe suffered three great traumas during the twentieth century, but if you look at them from the

> perspective of a Pole born in 1920, the Great World War, the Second World War and the Cold War can appear to be one long conflict interrupted by anxious and uncertain periods of peace.[32]

The meeting with Gorbachev symbolised the end of that conflict.

As the 1980s saw the systematic fall of totalitarianism in Europe, John Paul's global image matured. The youthful whirlwind of those first two years gave way to a graver and more reflective figure. This impression was enhanced by John Paul's decision to visit his would-be killer in an Italian prison – an event that attracted front-page coverage around the world. Far from casting light on his motives, Agca was preoccupied with the Fatima legend. Having read that John Paul believed the Blessed Virgin had interceded to save his life, Agca now feared she would take revenge. John Paul reassured Agca that Mary represented love of all humanity and would leave earthly powers to see to his punishment.

Stanisław Dziwisz, who accompanied the pope, was not impressed with Agca's attitude. 'The Pope had already publicly pardoned him in his very first address after the attack,' recalled Dziwisz. 'I did not hear the prisoner utter a single word to ask forgiveness. He was only interested in the mystery of Fatima – troubled by the force that had got the better of him.'[33] John Paul, however, continued to show compassion, successfully petitioning Italy's president in 2000 to release Agca and repatriate him to Turkey.

(Agca would serve another decade in jail there before his eventual release in 2010.)

Less understanding would be shown to those within the Church who continued, in John Paul's view, to undermine his doctrinal authority. A key figure in the pope's continued clampdown on dissent was Cardinal Joseph Ratzinger. A one-time progressive teacher and theologian, Ratzinger had grown to share John Paul's belief that the reforms of Vatican II had gone too far. He was appointed by John Paul in 1981 to head the Congregation for the Doctrine of the Faith (once known as the Holy Inquisition and still seen by many as the Vatican's thought police). Ratzinger first set his sights on Nicaragua, where several priests served in the revolutionary left-wing Sandanista government. When John Paul visited the country in 1983 he took the opportunity to reiterate his disdain for liberation theology, notably going so far as to upbraid one priest/minister with a wagging finger and the firm instruction: 'Regularise your position with the Church.'[34]

John Paul's ongoing conflict with liberation theology came as a surprise to many in the Church. As the historian Tony Judt observed, many supporters of liberation theology were initially optimistic that the new pope would give them a sympathetic hearing. 'Here was a man who would understand their fight because he understood oppression,' said Judt. 'Intellectuals thought here was a man they could talk to because he read the same books that they read.' In Judt's view, they had misjudged John Paul's true agenda: 'This was a Pope for whom modernity was not the enemy or something to be avoided, but simply a passing mistake to be exposed, to be argued against ... You don't engage [with] mistakes. You reveal them and you move on.'[35]

Despite his avowal, in a speech to a thousand journalists, that he wanted to make the Church transparent, 'a house of glass', John Paul (aided by Ratzinger, who would in due course become his successor as pope) continued through the 1980s to stamp his authority on matters of doctrine and ritual. He summoned the world's bishops to Rome for an Extraordinary Synod in 1985, yet refused to allow any 'progressive' topics on to the agenda (this gathering marked the effective end of any Anglican hopes that women clergy might make it into this pope's reckoning). John Paul further tightened the reins by choosing to appoint all bishops personally, thereby ensuring that the vast majority of local Church leaders around the world were doctrinally in sympathy with his position.

This period in John Paul's pontificate was remarkable for its continued engagement with issues of global human rights and ecumenism – despite his impasse with the Anglicans, he continued to build relationships with other religions, convening an unprecedented gathering of multi-faith leaders in Assisi in 1986 to pray for world peace. Yet this was also a period in which signs of neglect became apparent in the conduct and management of Church affairs. When the chairman of Banco Ambrosiano, Roberto Calvi, was found hanging from Blackfriars Bridge in London, a damaging scandal erupted which revealed the extent of Church dealings with organised criminals, including the mafia. Matters were not helped when it emerged that Calvi had written in desperation to the pope just a fortnight before his death, warning of the rotten state of the Vatican's financial ethics. There has been no suggestion that John Paul knew of the Vatican's murky dealings at the time, but therein lies a deeper problem: while John Paul was an undisputed maestro on the world stage, he was frequently tone deaf when it came to his own organisation's internal machinations.

He was deaf on other important topics too. As the decade ended, John Paul gathered experts on AIDS to a conference in Rome, only to ignore their insights and reaffirm the Church's total and implacable opposition to the use of condoms under any circumstances. As we shall see, his continued insistence that the Church knew best, on this and other issues, would alienate millions of devout Catholics, and would turn out to have grave and lasting consequences.

8

Culture Wars

John Paul turned 70 in 1990. By papal standards he was still relatively youthful – his two successors, Popes Benedict and Francis, were 78 and 76 when they were elected. A dozen years on the throne of St Peter had taken a toll, however. In the course of the next few years, John Paul would suffer a number of illnesses and accidents. In 1992 he had a benign tumour removed from his intestine. The following year he fell and broke his shoulder. He had barely recuperated from that injury when he slipped and fell in the bath; a hip replacement operation was required to rectify the damage. Another operation followed in 1996, to remove his appendix. Most ominously, the first signs appeared around this time of the Parkinson's disease that would later devastate him. Although he continued to travel widely, John Paul's days of kissing the ground were over (though, with typical theatricality, he asked that a tray of native soil be raised to meet the papal lips).

Despite the difficulties caused by age and infirmity, John Paul remained a vivid figure on the world stage. Far from retreating into a weary dotage, he continued to think and act on a grand scale. In the wake of Saddam Hussein's invasion of Kuwait, John Paul made clear his belief that a war would be 'unworthy of humanity'. His efforts intensified after the US, Britain and their allies launched a counter-offensive, Desert Storm, in 1991: 'Have the courage to end this war,' he urged, in letters to George W.H. Bush and Saddam Hussein. 'Abandon this bellicose road. Negotiate, collaborate.' This contrasted with the stand taken by many bishops, including Basil Hume, who had identified the liberation of Kuwait as a 'just war'.

While John Paul's anti-war stance went down badly in Washington and London, he also succeeded in antagonising many in the Middle East when his encyclical *Redemptoris Missio* (*Mission of the Redeemer*) appeared to call on Catholics to proselytise the faith among all peoples, including Muslims and Jews. 'Since [Christ's] salvation is offered to all, it must be made concretely available to all,' he wrote. If this seems to hint at an obligation on Christians to spread the Gospel (the 'Good News'), he later becomes more explicit: 'While respecting the beliefs and sensitivities of all, we must clearly assert our faith in Christ, the one Saviour of mankind …' As American bombs fell on Baghdad and Iraqi Scud missiles flew towards Tel Aviv, the moment was clearly not propitious for a call to global religious unity under Christ.

Not content with seeking to influence the course of world events, John Paul had set his sights on a new bogeyman: what he saw as the spiritually destructive side effects of consumer capitalism. Nowhere was this more apparent than in his native Poland. Far from replacing communism with a system built on Christian values of community and self-restraint, Poles had rapidly succumbed to Western materialism. Where once they had chanted 'We Want God' at his first Mass as pope in Warsaw, it appeared to John Paul that the refrain of the average Pole now was 'We Want Goods'. On his fourth visit to Poland, in 1991, the pope was dismayed by this state of affairs. It provided further evidence, he argued, that capitalist societies, while claiming to honour individuals' rights and freedoms, failed to provide their citizens with a moral compass. This was, in the eyes of Rome, a deepening of the crisis of moral relativism that had plagued developed societies since the Enlightenment.

In a series of papal encyclicals – perhaps the most important intellectual mission statements of his pontificate – John Paul crafted a blueprint for a kind of ethical capitalism. Anticipating the philosophy behind the secular movements which would emerge a decade later, he warned of the dangers of untrammelled market forces. Just as communism had recast individuals as units of economic activity, so free-market capitalism was dehumanising those who succumbed to its relentlessly consumerist world view. The idealist from Wadowice was not afraid to use traditionally left-wing language to enforce his arguments. In both his 1991 encyclical *Centesimus Annus* (*Hundredth Year*) and in *Veritatis Splendor* (*The Splendour of Truth*, 1993) he defended workers' rights and the value of trades unions, and identified a just distribution of wealth and opportunity as an essential precursor of universal moral norms. Academics Jonathan Luxmoore and Jolanta Babiuch have suggested that the pope was significantly influenced by the very ideology he helped to overthrow. Citing obscure essays by the young Fr Wojtyła, written in the early 1950s, they observe: 'Evidence exists that [he] nursed radical sympathies, and a passionate critique of capitalist injustices, that made him interested in Marxist ideals.'[36]

By the mid-1990s, John Paul's disillusion with the post-Cold War slide into godless consumerism had found a familiar focus: what he saw as an increasing disregard for the sanctity of life. Symbolic of this was the defeat of a 1993 campaign in Poland to ban abortion and the vigorously pro-choice policies of US President Bill Clinton both at home and in the developing world. These concerns would be encapsulated by John Paul in one of his most memorable phrases. There existed, he said, 'a culture of death', against which he would target whatever remaining intellectual energies he could muster. From now on, historian Eamon Duffy has observed, 'John Paul's moral teaching was directed above all against the "culture of death" which he believed pervaded the modern world. We had created a culture in which birth control or abortion, rather than a just redistribution of the world's resources, were proposed as remedies for world hunger.'[37]

Evangelium Vitae (*The Gospel of Life*), John Paul's fourth encyclical in five years (an exceptional rate of papal productivity), is a powerful denunciation of the culture of death. Having documented the 'alarmingly vast scale' of threats to life, he goes on to bemoan the 'broad sectors of public opinion [which] justify certain crimes against life in the name of the rights of individual freedom'. Legislators are held to account for allowing abortion and birth control to become socially acceptable. The medical profession is singled out for being 'willing to carry out these acts against the person', thereby allowing its very nature to become 'distorted and contradicted'. He concludes, in apocalyptic terms, that 'conscience itself, darkened as it were by such widespread conditioning, is finding it increasingly difficult to distinguish between good and evil in what concerns the basic value of human life'.

While John Paul's encyclicals were powerful counterblasts, many in the Church felt the time had come for action rather than words. In this new moral – or amoral – landscape, the Church might make itself more relevant, or at least less marginal, by showing a willingness to engage with some aspects of modernity. Under John Paul and his doctrinal commissar, Cardinal Ratzinger, the promised reforms of Vatican II had been slowed or, in many cases, shelved. As a result, John Paul was increasingly viewed in the wider world as a reactionary figure. Given his views on war, poverty and the rights of workers, this perception was sometimes inaccurate and even unfair. Yet he did little to alter it. In his unwillingness to compromise, his insistence that all power in the Church lay at the centre and his belief that his Church represented the only path to salvation, John Paul was complicit in his own demonisation as a fundamentalist. John Cornwell has argued that the pope's failure to come to terms with pluralism 'may well prove the greatest failing of his papacy'.[38] Cornwell cites an example of the consequences of John Paul's intransigence: the invidious position of Catholic aid workers in the third world, who must either remain loyal to the pope on the issue of condoms and watch many die of AIDS or disobey and save lives.[39] Yet resistance to pluralism was not invented by John Paul. The magisterium of the Catholic Church has been fundamentally opposed to pluralism throughout its history, characterising itself as the one true and universal path to salvation.

For many progressive Catholics, there was one area in particular where the Church might have gained enormously from a change of direction. In 1994, the Anglican Church had ordained its first group of women priests. While no one expected Rome to follow suit immediately (to do so would have been hugely divisive), an open discussion began to take place about the long-term merits, or otherwise, of allowing women to take Holy Orders. John Paul's response was to issue an apostolic letter called *Ordinatio Sacerdotalis* (*On Priestly Ordination*). In it, he acknowledged that existing Church teaching which excludes women from ordination 'has merely disciplinary force' and was therefore 'still considered open to debate'. In his next paragraph, certainly one of the most important and most shocking to be found in all of John Paul's writings, he asserted: 'In order that all doubt may be removed regarding a matter of great importance … I declare that the Church has no authority whatsoever to confer priestly ordination on women and that this judgement is to be definitively held by all the Church's faithful.'

Far from refining the debate or introducing new theological justifications, *Ordinatio Sacerdotalis* amounted to a stern command: put up or shut up. In this it failed. The document provoked a vigorous response from Cardinal Carlo Maria Martini of Milan, a noted theologian, who questioned its validity, and from lay groups and women's organisations. In response to this dissent, Cardinal Ratzinger delivered a ruling in which he conferred upon John Paul's instruction the status of infallibility. The subject had been declared closed and for any future pope to reopen it would be tantamount to declaring that John Paul was not, after all, infallible. The otherwise reform-minded Pope Francis acknowledged as much when, in July 2013, he said, 'With regard to the ordination of women the Church has spoken and says "no". Pope John Paul said so with a formula that was definitive. That door is closed.'[40]

Some refused to be silenced. Hans Küng, the veteran dissident, was moved to write:

> I cannot help asking what people may have thought in Geneva or Canterbury (let alone among Old Catholics) when the Pope now infallibly condemns a practice that has long since been tried and tested in the Churches of the Reformation. It is hardly possible to kick our ecumenical brothers and sisters in the teeth more roughly than this Pope has done.[41]

Similarly angry was the Benedictine nun Sister Joan Chittister. 'The suppression of honest and credible questions,' she wrote, '... damages the Church, dispirits the people of God, depresses churchgoing fathers who know their girl children to be as fully human as themselves, and drains the Church of more and more women every day ...'[42]

Again, the pope responded to criticism by hardening his line. A new apostolic letter (with a postscript by Cardinal Ratzinger) spelled out the fate that would await theologians and other Catholics who continued to question papal teaching on subjects such as artificial birth control and the ordination of women – nothing less than excommunication.

As John Paul celebrated the twentieth anniversary of his election as pope in 1998, he remained an inspiring figure to many. His World Youth Days were wildly popular among young Catholics, particularly in the developing world, and the attendances at his open-air Masses regularly broke world records. His opinion was still sought by secular leaders. Books of papal theology and memoir sold by the millions. His achievements in the area of ecumenism were concrete and important: John Paul's efforts had seen diplomatic relations established between the Holy See and Israel in 1993, and he was to become the first pope to set foot in a mosque, in Damascus in 2001.

Yet a sense was growing within the Church that the enormous promise of John Paul's early years had been squandered. Franz König, the respected Austrian cardinal who had pushed for Cardinal Wojtyła's election in 1978, was among those for whom the pope's actions had come as a disagreeable surprise. The journalist Hella Pick, who knew König well, wrote that 'though he never regretted his backing for Wojtyła, he did not hide his dismay over the Pope's conservatism on issues of theology'.[43] Edward Stourton also found König 'deeply disillusioned'.[44] As a rather pointed corrective, König questioned the theological basis of the ban on women priests. He also predicted an end to the celibate priesthood (an implausible suggestion when he made it in 1995, but one that is starting to look less so in the wake of clerical sex abuse scandals).[45] König escaped excommunication, but was sidelined by the Vatican.

Writing about Lyndon Johnson, the historian Robert Caro makes a telling observation. While the old adage that 'power corrupts' is certainly true, writes Caro, 'what is seldom said, but what is equally true, is that power always reveals'.[46] In other words, far from becoming obscured behind the mask of power, men such as Johnson revealed their true nature through their decisions at key moments. John Paul's heavy-handed approach to differences of opinion within the Church suggests that he was a man who, for all his undoubted talents and virtues, was revealed to have had a tragic flaw: an inability to see the merit in beliefs he did not share or to escape his own controlling nature.

9

Millennial Pursuits

The Great Schism of 1054 remains, a thousand years later, a source of trauma for the Christian Churches. The fall-out between Rome and Constantinople is often characterised as having been a semantic dispute about the wording of the Nicene Creed. In fact, the Schism came about because Rome, which was supposed to be *primus inter pares* among the great centres of Christianity, had begun to assert its authority in an increasingly non-egalitarian fashion. Despite numerous attempts to heal the rift, and occasional polite ecumenical gatherings of popes and patriarchs, the Roman Catholic and Eastern Orthodox Churches have never since managed to resolve their differences.

As the Millennium approached, it was one of Pope John Paul's most cherished ambitions to engineer a reconciliation between the two branches. To that end, the globetrotting pontiff planned to add Moscow to his list of destinations. The fall of communism in Europe appeared to have created a spiritual vacuum, which John Paul's brand of crowd-pleasing evangelism might aspire to fill. In fact, the Christian Churches of the East, many of them freed from decades of state control, were determined to effect their own renewal, without interference from Rome. The Moscow visit never materialised, and the pope met with a frosty reception from the Orthodox hierarchy when he visited Greece in 2001. As with Poland's lurch into consumerism, John Paul found that shifting geopolitical forces had stymied his best efforts to impose his will on events. His cause was not helped by inept, sometimes obstructive, diplomatic bungling on the part of senior curial officials, which succeeded only in further alienating the Eastern Orthodox Churches. While John Paul's agenda was clearly for détente, others, notably Cardinal Ratzinger, were wary of the implications. Priests in the Eastern Orthodox Churches were allowed to marry: would a healing of the Schism not put pressure on Rome to follow suit?

With reconciliation no longer a viable option, some of the gloss was taken off John Paul's grandest theatrical project. Throughout the year 2000, dubbed 'the Jubilee Year' in Rome, he hosted a series of extravagant set pieces; millions of Catholics travelled to the Italian capital to take place in these mass gatherings. For two decades he had been promoting the idea that the coming of a third Christian millennium would see a resurgence and renewal of the faith, 'a new springtime of Christian life'. In John Paul's estimation, the job of a pope was, first and foremost, to spread the Good News. He had devoted his entire pontificate to that task (often at the expense of more mundane but nonetheless important responsibilities). Despite the debilitating effects of Parkinson's disease, he kept up with a demanding schedule both in Rome and overseas as he campaigned to make the Millennium year a great showcase for the Christian message.

The gravity of John Paul's condition had encouraged rumours in Rome that he would be unable to see out his pontificate. One careless bishop even let slip the word 'resignation'. At the time, the suggestion was widely derided as preposterous (though subsequent events have shown that a pontiff can indeed step down without occasioning the collapse of civilisation). Certainly, it is unlikely that this most mystical of popes, a great believer in Providence and divine will, would even have considered such a course. Just as he avowed that Mary had saved him from the assassin's bullet in 1981, so he would leave the decision as to when his pontificate ended in God's hands.

As part of the process of millennial renewal, John Paul decreed a Day of Pardon, to salve the conscience of the Church. In a remarkable ceremony at St Peter's Basilica, a succession of eminent cardinals confessed the sins of their predecessors. The Crusades, the Inquisition and various human rights abuses were among those historical offences for which the Church now apologised, though there was something equivocal about the title given to this ritual: 'The Confession of Sins Committed in the Service of Truth.' While certain deeds were wrong, this title suggested, the intention behind them was not. This linguistic qualification was a victory for those in the hierarchy who believed John Paul was going too far down the road of compromise.

Those same traditionalists were generally wary of the many ecumenical initiatives launched by John Paul in the course of his reign. It was their most powerful representative, Cardinal Ratzinger, who set the record straight by publishing an extraordinarily provocative document in September 2000. *Dominus Iesus* (*The Lord Jesus*) rejects any possibility that the Vatican might view other faiths, including other branches of Christianity, as equals. 'The Church's constant missionary proclamation is endangered today by relativistic theories which seek to justify religious pluralism,' it asserts, in Ratzinger's characteristically prolix style. These theories, it goes on, lead to 'certain theological proposals … in which Christian revelation and the mystery of Jesus Christ and the Church lose their character of absolute truth and salvific universality …' In effect, Ratzinger was declaring that all other Churches and belief systems were built on falsehoods. George Weigel, among others, defends the document, seeing in it a 'humble confession of Catholic faith' and observing that 'those who expected the Catholic Church to present itself as one consumer option in a supermarket of religious possibilities were thus mistaken'.[47] Weigel makes a fair point, yet the question remains: was it necessary, in the middle of Jubilee Year, when the pontiff was voicing contrition and compromise, to undermine that agenda in so pointed a fashion? The fact that John Paul himself wholeheartedly endorsed *Dominus Iesus* leads one to conclude that either the rapidly deteriorating 80-year-old pope was being manipulated by those around him or much of what he had previously said about inter-faith relations had been misunderstood. John Paul's vociferous support for political change led the wider world to expect flexibility in internal Church affairs too, an expectation he was never likely to fulfil.

The one ecumenical enterprise in which John Paul scored an undoubted success was his initiative to ease historic tensions between the Catholic Church and the Jewish people. The Jews were among those to receive an apology on the Day of Pardon, and this prepared the ground for what would turn out to be one of the most important of John Paul's foreign trips. In a memorable ceremony at Yad Vashem, the Holocaust memorial near Jerusalem, John Paul met a group of Holocaust survivors, including a woman he had personally helped in Poland during the Second World War. Observers were struck by the intense emotions clearly visible on the face of the frail and infirm Pope. Stanisław Dziwisz, John Paul's increasingly influential secretary, later offered a telling explanation: 'Maybe – I say maybe because I am just speculating – the Holy Father, feeling the end of his life approaching, was worrying that he hadn't done enough to condemn the people and the ideologies responsible for the … Holocaust.'[48] Later in the visit, John Paul prayed at the Western Wall, Judaism's holiest site. The prayer he placed, as befits tradition, between the stones in the wall, was a further plea for forgiveness of Christian sins against Jews. For many in Israel, the visit represented a significant break with past mistrust. Elie Wiesel, the Romanian-born writer and Nobel Peace Prize winner, summed up the feelings of many Jews: 'When I was a child I was always afraid of walking by a church. Now all of that has changed.'[49]

John Paul earned further international respect for his measured response to the 9/11 attacks on America in September 2001. In contrast to the fervent brutality of al-Qaida and the Old Testament wrathfulness of George W. Bush and Tony Blair, he came across as a voice of reason (and, with hindsight, something of a prophet) when he warned against a military response the consequences of which could not be predicted. The episode demonstrated that a role as calming elder statesman would have provided a perfect grace note to his long and sometimes fractious pontificate. It was not to be.

In 2002, the *Boston Globe* newspaper ran a series of articles detailing the shocking extent of clerical abuse against children in and around its city. Previously, reports of such abuse were commonplace but relatively diffuse: as would soon become apparent, efforts by the Church to downplay or even cover up individual cases had been disturbingly successful. Now, however, the floodgates opened, and the paedophile priests scandal threatened to wash away much of Rome's remaining credibility.

John Paul's first public reaction came in a letter to priests, delivered during Easter week. While repentant in tone, it contained an emphasis that would taint the Vatican's response to the issue for years to come. The pope described himself as 'personally and profoundly afflicted' by the behaviour of some priests, which, he noted, 'cast a dark shadow of suspicion' over the virtuous majority. When it came to the victims, however, the best he could muster was that 'the Church shows her concern' over what he then described, with astonishing understatement, as 'painful situations'.

Since his days as a student in Rome, John Paul had had a view of the priesthood that bordered on the mystical. Priests were not mere teachers or pastors or glorified social workers; they were repositories of grace and wisdom. They were, in short, special (the young Karol Wojtyła, as we have seen, had felt personally called by God). The fault for this mass outbreak of paedophile abuse, therefore, must lie elsewhere. Over the following years, as new scandals erupted in Europe and in the developing world, Cardinal Ratzinger and his propaganda machine went into overdrive. Culpability resided not in any inherent problem of priestly celibacy or inadequate training and preparation. Instead, blame lay with the sexual permissiveness of society and with that old bogeyman, moral relativism. Edward Stourton has observed that 'when the Boston story broke, those at the heart of John Paul's circle instinctively looked for their villains where they had always done – in the secular culture they saw flourishing beyond the walls of the Vatican …'[50]

Evasiveness and sophistry became hallmarks of the Church's response to the abuse scandals. While it would be inaccurate to lay primary responsibility for this at John Paul's door, he had allowed a climate to develop in which senior churchmen failed in their duty to victims and, frequently, to the law. As John Paul's health declined and the end of his life drew closer, it became apparent that this legacy of failure was threatening to cast a permanent shadow over those achievements of which he was most proud.

10

Legacy

Ever since Pope Pius IX asserted papal infallibility in 1870, there has been a paradox at the heart of the Roman Catholic Church. As an institution it craves a strong and charismatic leader whose authority is absolute – how else could the 'infallibility' claim be made to work? Yet a strong pope comes at a price. The longer he reigns and the more authority he possesses, the more likely a pope is to accumulate an unhealthy amount of power. As a consequence, other sections of the Church, notably bishops and priests, tend to become enfeebled, unable or unwilling to make decisions at a local level for fear of displeasing the magisterium in Rome. John Henry Newman, the nineteenth-century English Anglican who defected to Rome and became a cardinal, put it bluntly: 'It is not good for a pope to live twenty years. He becomes a god and has no one to contradict him.'[51]

Even many of John Paul's most ardent admirers would have had sympathy with Newman's analysis. At a time when the Church desperately needed fresh leadership to deal with fall-out from the sexual abuse scandals, a kind of paralysis gripped the Vatican. The pope became so debilitated by illness that he appeared at times to be a ghost of his former self. Yet absolute power continued to reside with the Holy Father and a small number of his closest advisers. The result was a failure to respond satisfactorily to the sexual abuse scandals that erupted in the early years of the century. The fact that John Paul II's successor Benedict XVI would, after just eight years, choose to step down rather than suffer a similar crisis of leadership, demonstrates just how traumatic John Paul's very public decline had been for the Vatican hierarchy.

There were occasional flashes, during these final years, of the old John Paul. He presided over a huge gathering in October 2003 marking the beatification (the first step on the road to sainthood) of Mother Teresa. Although his speech was barely comprehensible, he was clearly aware of what was going on (which was not always the case around that time). The following year he showed great physical resilience in travelling to Lourdes and addressing a crowd of 200,000. The magic was gone, however, and in its place was the pitiful, sometimes painful spectacle of a very ill old man struggling to cope with his demanding workload.

The end came on 2 April 2005, one month short of his eighty-fifth birthday. His last words, whispered into the ear of a Polish nun who had been among those taking care of him, were: 'Let me go to my father's house.' Stanisław Dziwisz was present as the pope was pronounced dead. Among the first to pay his respects at the papal deathbed was Joseph Ratzinger, the man who would, weeks later, step into John Paul's shoes.

Even in death, Karol Wojtyła retained his box-office appeal. Tens of thousands of pilgrims were in St Peter's Square on that night, along with an army of journalists.

And Rome was not the only focal point of mourning. Throughout the Catholic world, from Rio de Janeiro to Manila, candlelit vigils attracted huge crowds. Nowhere was the loss felt more deeply than in the pope's homeland. Irish television journalist Tony Connelly was reporting from outside Kraków's St Mary's Basilica when news came of John Paul's death. 'Some [people] fell to their knees, others turned and went straight back into the basilica …' he recalled. 'The man they simply knew as Papa, their spiritual guide, was gone. As I watched the agony on the faces of the young people who had gathered – not just tears but great shuddering cries – I felt I was looking at a nation that had just been orphaned.'[52]

The reaction to John Paul's death among secular leaders and media commentators demonstrated both the scale of his international stature and the sharply conflicting opinions his pontificate had provoked. For British Prime Minister Tony Blair, John Paul had been 'an inspiration, a man of extraordinary faith, dignity and courage. Throughout a hard and often difficult life, he stood for social justice and on the side of the oppressed …' US President George W. Bush couched his praise in terms that would appeal to his supporters on the Christian right:

> Pope John Paul II left the throne of St Peter in the same way he ascended to it – as a witness to the dignity of human life … Throughout the West, John Paul's witness reminded us of our obligation to build a culture of life in which the strong protect the weak.

Much liberal opinion was less enamoured of John Paul's reputation as a seeker of freedom and justice. 'How dare Tony Blair genuflect on our behalf before the corpse of a man whose edicts killed millions,' thundered Polly Toynbee, for whom the pope's record on AIDS, contraception and 'turning a blind eye' to priestly paedophilia far outweighed his achievements.[53] The *New York Times* noted that: 'For all his worldwide evangelism, John Paul left behind a Church with a dwindling number of priests and nuns and a shrinking percentage of the world's population; Islam has overtaken Catholicism as the globe's most popular religion.'[54]

The funeral was, in diplomatic terms, an A-list event. President Bush found himself next to his French counterpart, Jacques Chirac, who had been downright unco-operative in the build up to the US-led invasion of Iraq a few years earlier. The leaders of Israel and Syria were in similarly uncomfortable proximity. Prince Charles postponed his wedding to Camilla Parker-Bowles in order to head the British delegation. Rome was overwhelmed with visitors. More than 800,000 people filled the square and surrounding areas during the funeral Mass, celebrated, fittingly, by Cardinal Ratzinger. Among the banners flying in the square was one bearing the single word 'Wadowice' – a reminder of the extraordinary journey Karol Wojtyła had made from provincial obscurity. As his plain cypress coffin was lifted from its bier and carried towards the doors of St Peter's Basilica, the pallbearers turned to face the crowd and inclined the coffin, as if in acknowledgement of the special bond between the pontiff and his faithful. When the funeral Mass ended, cries went up in the crowd: '*Santo Subito*! A saint immediately!' For John Paul's most passionate admirers, it was not enough that the pope be given a spectacular send-off. They wanted their man elevated to the ranks of the saints, a process that has been known to take centuries but which, in John Paul's case, gained irresistible momentum that day in Rome.

Was John Paul worthy of such acclaim? The bald statistics of his tenure are certainly impressive. He had been Pope for more than twenty-six years, the third-longest pontificate in history. He had made 104 foreign visits, taking in 129 countries and personally touching the lives of millions. He had created 482 saints, more than all his predecessors put together. These record-breaking statistics are part of his legacy, but they pale into insignificance beside his most enduring achievement. In his willingness to confront state oppression in Poland and elsewhere, and in the consistency of his message that the rights of the individual must never be sacrificed to those of the state, he became one of the most important global figures of the late twentieth century. The writer and historian Timothy Garton Ash described John Paul as 'the first world leader'. In contrast to 'national leaders who have a global impact', wrote Garton Ash, John Paul 'made the world his parish'.[55] This view is shared by Eamon Duffy, who wrote that 'no Pope since the Middle Ages has had so direct and measurable an impact on world history'.[56]

John Paul had a gift not just for inspiring those who heard him speak but for giving them courage.

In countries where intellectual and cultural life was rigorously controlled by the state, he reminded people that their nations had a rich past and the possibility of a bright future. As Anne Applebaum observed: 'John Paul's particular way of expressing his faith – publicly, openly, and with many cultural and historical references – was explosive in countries whose regimes tried to control both culture and history, along with everything else.'[57]

Within the Catholic Church, John Paul's legacy is less glowing. His lack of interest in Vatican governance left the Church rudderless at a time when close, hands-on management was required. This neglect continued through the reign of his successor, Benedict XVI, who had been chosen for reasons of continuity. Only with the election in 2013 of Pope Francis, who as a Jesuit is known to be an enthusiast for organisational clarity, has the Church acknowledged that its internal affairs were left in a mess by John Paul's preference for world travel over good housekeeping. John L. Allen has written: 'In pursuit of his great historical ambitions, John Paul left day-to-day management to his aides. Since nature abhors a vacuum, this laissez-faire approach encouraged a stranglehold over the internal life of the Church in the Curia …' This contrasted, Allen noted, with Vatican II's vision of a Church where decisions would be taken 'in parishes and missions'.[58]

John Paul's insistence on forbidding the use of artificial birth control under any circumstances had drastic consequences for which he will not quickly be forgiven by many – including Roman Catholics – especially in the developing world. Likewise, his decision not merely to resist calls for married clergy and women priests, but to declare discussion of such issues anathema, alienated considerable numbers of otherwise devout Catholics in the US and Europe. Although he always insisted he was a supporter of Vatican II reforms – the drafting of which he had contributed to – it seemed to many Catholics that John Paul was instinctively a pre-conciliar pontiff. He ignored – or even punished – those who called for greater collegiality, an enhanced role for bishops and an agenda in step with changes in the modern world. The long-term legacy of John Paul's autocratic stance on doctrinal matters may turn out to be a new schism in the Church. The historian Diarmaid MacCulloch has warned of 'a very great split over the Vatican's failure to listen to European Catholics'. MacCulloch believes that priestly celibacy could be the issue that provokes such a split. 'No other Church in history has ever made all its clergy celibate. It's a peculiarity of the Western Latin Church and it looks increasingly unrealistic.'[59]

At the root of John Paul's refusal to consider the possibility of married priests is his passionate devotion to the Blessed Virgin, one the consistent themes, as we have seen, of his religious life. Garry Wills has observed that 'modern popes tell priests to think of themselves as virgins consecrated to the Virgin'. Similarly, says Wills, the Virgin is deployed as an argument against the ordination of women: 'If Mary was not a priest, how can they be?' Under John Paul, the hierarchy of the Church became 'more Marianised than ever'. Wills argues that John Paul's insistence that Mary 'was the mediatrix of all graces' was not only counter-productive for the Church but theologically erroneous.[60]

John Paul also invited controversy over his promotion of unconventional religious organisations that operated without bishops. He consistently favoured Opus Dei, even giving it the privileged status of a 'personal prelature', reporting directly to Rome. Although Opus Dei does not merit the sinister reputation it acquired as a result of its depiction in Dan Brown's novel *The Da Vinci Code*, the organisation operates secretively and is viewed warily by many mainstream Catholics. Undeterred, John Paul fast-tracked the canonisation of Opus Dei's founder. Similarly favoured was the Mexican priest Marcial Maciel, who founded another freelance movement called the Legion of Christ. Even after Maciel was accused of abusing members of the movement, including children he himself had fathered (many of these accusations were later substantiated), John Paul continued to offer support to the Legion of Christ, which donated large sums of money to the Vatican and adhered to doctrinally austere practices of which the pope was known to approve. His enthusiasm for these allegedly 'cult-like' organisations has unquestionably deepened divisions within the Church.

John Paul was, throughout his life, a man of contradictions. While there is a case to be made that he was doctrinally a reactionary, favouring tradition over modernity at every turn, at other times he was sufficiently progressive to alarm his senior aides in the Curia. As we have seen, many traditionalists looked disapprovingly upon his vigorous ecumenical efforts. John L. Allen wrote that 'John Paul had a penchant for blending traditional Catholic theology with the philosophical insights of the twentieth century … another instance in which the stereotype of a "conservative" pope runs out of gas'.[61]

On other issues, John Paul had an agenda closer to the European tradition of social democracy than to knee-jerk conservatism. He used his office to argue against war and state-sponsored violence, to condemn capital punishment and to warn of the moral perils of unfettered market forces. Writing for a progressive think tank, Mark Engler commented that 'particularly in his teachings about the global economy, the Pope advanced a vision of social justice that challenges the current, narrow political debate about "moral values" … John Paul's vision of globalisation sharply countered the pro-corporate triumphalism spread by free-trade boosters'.[62]

John Paul is one of the most revered popes in history – and one of the most loathed. He revitalised the Church through his evangelism, yet weakened it through his doctrinal dogmatism. He became a touchstone of hope for oppressed peoples throughout the world, yet left an unholy mess within the institution, which his successors will spend many years trying to clean up.

Ultimately, what distinguished Pope John Paul II from the majority of his predecessors was his unshakable sense of destiny. Here was a man who believed from an early age that history was something not just to be experienced but to be shaped. He had a deep-seated mysticism that prompted him to view his own life and the future of the planet in cosmic terms. In the eyes of this one-time actor and director, a giant drama was being played out in which good and evil, light and dark were in perpetual conflict. He devoted his life to fighting on the side of good, to keeping the apocalypse at bay. And in the course of fighting that battle, he managed to achieve something that few among us can even dream of. He changed the world.

Notes

1 Allen, John L., obituary in *National Catholic Reporter* Online, April 2005.
2 From Frossard, Andre, *Be Not Afraid: Conversations with Pope John Paul II* (1984).
3 Speech at the Jagellonian University, Kraków, 1983.
4 John Paul II, *Gift and Mystery* (1997), p. 20.
5 Bernstein, Carl and Politi, Marco, *His Holiness* (1997), p. 42.
6 *Gift and Mystery*, op. cit., p. 34.
7 Ibid., p. 61.
8 Ibid., p. 39.
9 Obituary, op. cit.
10 Applebaum, Anne, *Iron Curtain: The Crushing of Eastern Europe 1944–56* (2012).
11 Stourton, Edward, *John Paul II* (2006), p. 124.
12 Dziwisz, Stanisław, *A Life with Karol* (2008), p. 54.
13 'A Light That Left Us Amazed', in *Time* magazine, 16 October 1978.
14 *A Life with Karol*, op. cit., p. 58.
15 *National Catholic Reporter*, 8 October 1999.
16 Cornwell, John, *The Pope in Winter* (2004), p. 61.
17 *His Holiness*, op. cit., p. 199.

18 Weigel, George, *Witness to Hope* (2005), p. 295.
19 Stourton, *John Paul II*, op. cit., p. 203.
20 Quoted in O'Sullivan, John, *The President, the Pope and the Prime Minister* (2006), p. 96.
21 'God and Mammon', in *The Spectator*, 9 April 2005.
22 *Witness to Hope*, op. cit., p. 290.
23 Walsh, Michael, *John Paul II* (1994), p. 53.
24 *The Pope in Winter*, op. cit., p. 68.
25 *A Life with Karol*, op. cit., p. 132.
26 *His Holiness*, op. cit., p. 333.
27 *Witness to Hope*, op. cit., p. 440.
28 The National Archives, PREM 19/630.
29 The National Archives, PREM 19/630.
30 The National Archives, PREM 19/627.
31 *His Holiness*, op. cit., p. 303.
32 Stourton, *John Paul II*, op. cit., p. 240.
33 Speech to the Catholic University of Lublin, 13 May 2001.
34 *Witness to Hope*, op. cit., p. 454.
35 Interview with PBS television, April 2005.
36 'John Paul's Debt to Marxism', in *The Tablet*, 14 January 2006.
37 Duffy, Eamon, *Ten Popes Who Shook the World* (2011), p. 131.
38 *The Pope in Winter*, op. cit., p. 124.
39 Ibid., p. 140.
40 Reported in the *Daily Telegraph*, 29 July 2013.
41 'Women's Ordination and Infallibility', in *The Tablet*, 16 December 1995.

42 'Ratzinger Raised Bigger Issues than Ordination', in *National Catholic Reporter*, 8 December 1995.
43 Obituary in *The Guardian*, 16 March 2004.
44 Stourton, *John Paul II*, op. cit., p. 271.
45 'Top Cardinal Predicts End to Celibacy Rule', in *Catholic Herald*, 11 August 1995.
46 Caro, Robert A., *The Years of Lyndon Johnson: Vol 4* (2012).
47 Weigel, George, *The End and the Beginning* (2010), pp. 249–50.
48 *A Life with Karol*, op. cit., p. 236.
49 Quoted in ibid., p. 237.
50 Stourton, *John Paul II*, p. 302.
51 Letter to Lady Simeon, 18 November 1870, from Dessain, Charles Stephen, *The Letters and Diaries of John Henry Newman*, Vol. 5 (1973).
52 Connelly, Tony, *Don't Mention the Wars*, p. 353.
53 *The Guardian*, 8 April 2005.
54 Editorial in the *New York Times*, 3 April 2005.
55 *The Guardian*, 4 April 2005.
56 *Ten Popes Who Shook the World*, op. cit., p. 135.
57 *Washington Post*, 6 April 2005.
58 Allen, obituary, op. cit.
59 *The Tablet*, 21 June 2012.
60 Wills, Garry, *Papal Sin* (2001), pp. 204–8.
61 Allen, obituary, op. cit.
62 Engler, Mark, 'John Paul II's Economic Ethics', in *Foreign Policy in Focus*, 30 September 2005.

Timeline

1920	18 May: Born Karol Wojtyła in Wadowice, Poland
1929	Death of his mother, Emilia
1932	Death of his brother, Edmund
1934	First theatrical performances at school
1938	Moves with his father to Kraków and starts philosophy studies at Jagellonian University
1939	Kraków occupied by Germans
1940	Meets Catholic 'mystic' Jan Tyranowski Acts and writes for experimental theatre company Avoids deportation by working as a stone cutter in a quarry
1941	Death of his father, Karol
1942	Begins clandestine studies for the priesthood
1945	Kraków 'liberated' by the Red Army
1946	Ordained as a priest; studies in Rome
1948	Becomes parish priest in rural Niegowić
1949	Returns to Kraków
1958	Appointed auxiliary Bishop of Kraków
1963	Participates in Second Vatican Council in Rome

1964	Becomes Archbishop of Kraków
1967	Consecrated a cardinal by Pope Paul VI
1976	Addresses the elite Lenten Retreat of Pope Paul VI
1978	Death of Paul VI; his successor, John Paul I, dies suddenly weeks later 16 October: Wojtyła is elected as Pope John Paul II
1979	First visit as pope to his native Poland; addresses huge crowds around the country
1981	Gives an audience at the Vatican to Lech Wałęsa and other leaders of Solidarity Injured in an assassination attempt in St Peter's Square
1982	Visit to Britain downgraded because of Falklands Conflict Meets Ronald Reagan and agrees to share intelligence Roberto Calvi found hanged in London; financial scandal embroils the Vatican Bank
1983	Visits his would-be assassin, Mehmet Ali Agca, in prison
1987	Meets Polish leader General Jaruzelski at the Vatican Visits Poland and praises Solidarity
1989	Meets with Mikhail Gorbachev at the Vatican
1990	Lech Wałęsa elected President of Poland
1991	Appeals for peace as Gulf War begins

1992	Has surgery to remove a tumour
1993	Diplomatic relations established with Israel
1994	Falls and breaks his hip
1996	Celebrates fiftieth anniversary of his ordination
2000	Launches 'Jubilee Year' of events in Rome Meets Holocaust survivors in Jerusalem; prays at the Western Wall
2001	Prays for peace following 9/11 Becomes the first pope to visit a mosque
2004	Makes pilgrimage to Lourdes
2005	2 April: Dies in the Vatican, aged 84

Further Reading

Allen, John L., *All the Pope's Men* (Doubleday, 2004)
Bernstein, Carl & Politi, Marco, *His Holiness* (Bantam, 1997)
Cornwell, John, *The Pope in Winter* (Viking, 2004)
Davies, Norman, *God's Playground: A History of Poland: Vol II* (Oxford University Press, 2005)
Duffy, Eamon, *Ten Popes Who Shook the World* (Yale, 2011)
Dziwisz, Stanisław, *A Life with Karol* (Doubleday, 2008)
Hebblethwaite, Peter, *The Year of Three Popes* (Fount, 1978)
John Paul II, *Gift and Mystery* (Doubleday, 1997)
John Paul II, *Memory & Identity: Personal Reflections* (Weidenfeld and Nicolson, 2005)
O'Malley, John W., *What Happened at Vatican II* (Belknap Harvard, 2010)
Stourton, Edward, *John Paul II: Man of History* (Hodder and Stoughton, 2006)
Tobin, Greg, *Selecting the Pope* (Robson Books, 2004)
Walsh, Michael, *John Paul II: A Biography* (HarperCollins, 1994)
Weigel, George, *Witness to Hope* (Harper Perennial, 2005)
Weigel, George, *The End and the Beginning* (Doubleday, 2010)
Wills, Garry, *Papal Sin* (Doubleday, 2001)

Web Links

www.vatican.va – Official website of the Holy See. Includes biographical information on every pope, plus the full texts of all modern papal encyclicals, letters and speeches

https://twitter.com/Pontifex – Twitter page of the reigning pontiff

www.vaticaninsider.lastampa.it/en – English-language version of *La Stampa*'s up-to-the-minute Vatican coverage

www.ncronline.org – Online service of the US-based *National Catholic Reporter*

www.thetablet.co.uk – UK-based Catholic news weekly, covering international developments in the Church. Subscription required for some articles

www.georgeweigel.blogspot.com – Website of the papal biographer and conservative commentator on Catholic issues

www.blogs.telegraph.co.uk/news/author/damianthompson – Home of 'Holy Smoke', the sometimes scurrilous but always entertaining blog of *Daily Telegraph* columnist Damian Thompson www.catholicherald.co.uk – Includes a useful free-to-view archive of articles related to John Paul's pontificate

www.chiesa.espresso.repubblica.it/?eng=y – English-language version of authoritative website run by veteran Vatican specialist Sandro Magister

www.whispersintheloggia.blogspot.co.uk – Rocco Palmo's witty blog gets the inside track on Church affairs

www.commonwealmagazine.org – Online version of the progressive religious affairs magazine

www.newadvent.org – Home of the exhaustive *Catholic Encyclopedia*

Giuseppe Verdi Henry V **Brunel** Pope John Paul II **Jane Austen** William the Conqueror **Abraham Lincoln** Robert the Bruce **Charles Darwin** Buddha **Elizabeth I** Horatio Nelson **Wellington** Hannibal & Scipio **Jesus** Joan of Arc **Anne Frank** Alfred the Great **King Arthur** Henry Ford **Nelson Mandela**

RAPHAEL'S ASTRONOMICAL

Ephemeris of the Planets' Places

for 2007

A Complete Aspectarian

Mean Obliquity of the Ecliptic, 2007, 23° 26′ 18″

INTRODUCTION

Greenwich Mean Time (G.M.T.) has been used as the basis for all tabulations and times (G.M.T. is essentially the same as U.T.). The tabular data are for Greenwich Mean Time 12h., except for the Moon tabulations headed 24h. All phenomena and aspect times are now in G.M.T. To obtain Local Mean Time of aspect, add the time equivalent of the longitude if East and subtract if West.

Both in the Aspectarian and the Phenomena the 24-hour clock replaces the old a.m./p.m. system.

The zodiacal sign entries are now incorporated in the Aspectarian as well as being given in a separate table.

BRITISH SUMMER TIME

British Summer Time begins on March 25 and ends on October 28. When *British Summer Time* (one hour in advance of G.M.T.) is used, subtract one hour from B.S.T. before entering this Ephemeris.

These dates are believed to be correct at the time of printing.

Printed in Great Britain

Strathearn Publishing Ltd. 2006

ISBN-13: 978-0-572-03182-4
ISBN-10: 0-572-03182-3

Published by

LONDON: W. FOULSHAM & CO. LTD.

BENNETTS CLOSE, SLOUGH, BERKS. ENGLAND

NEW YORK TORONTO CAPE TOWN SYDNEY

NEW MOON–Jan.19,04h.01m. (28°♑41′)

D M	D W	Sidereal Time	☉ Long.	☉ Dec.	☽ Long.	☽ Lat.	☽ Dec.	☽ Node	24h. ☽ Long.	24h. ☽ Dec.
		h m s	° ′ ″	° ′	° ′ ″	° ′	° ′	° ′	° ′ ″	° ′
1	M	18 43 03	10 ♑ 41 01	23 S 01	14 ♊ 22 51	5 N 01	27 N 31	19 ♓ 39	21 ♊ 17 50	28 N 11
2	T	18 46 59	11 42 09	22 56	28 09 47	4 58	28 24	19 35	4 ♋ 58 13	28 11
3	W	18 50 56	12 43 17	22 50	11 ♋ 42 44	4 38	27 32	19 32	18 22 58	26 30
4	Th	18 54 52	13 44 25	22 44	24 58 39	4 03	25 07	19 29	1 ♌ 29 36	23 25
5	F	18 58 49	14 45 34	22 37	7 ♌ 55 44	3 16	21 27	19 26	14 17 06	19 14
6	S	19 02 45	15 46 42	22 30	20 33 49	2 20	16 51	19 23	26 46 06	14 19
7	Su	19 06 42	16 47 50	22 23	2 ♍ 54 17	1 19	11 40	19 19	8 ♍ 58 46	8 56
8	M	19 10 39	17 48 58	22 15	15 00 00	0 N 15	6 09	19 16	20 58 32	3 N 19
9	T	19 14 35	18 50 06	22 07	26 54 58	0 S 48	0 N 29	19 13	2 ♎ 49 53	2 S 20
10	W	19 18 32	19 51 15	21 58	8 ♎ 43 58	1 50	5 S 08	19 10	14 37 52	7 54
11	Th	19 22 28	20 52 23	21 49	20 32 18	2 46	10 35	19 07	26 27 56	13 11
12	F	19 26 25	21 53 31	21 40	2 ♏ 25 27	3 36	15 41	19 04	8 ♏ 25 29	18 03
13	S	19 30 21	22 54 39	21 30	14 28 42	4 17	20 16	19 00	20 35 38	22 17
14	Su	19 34 18	23 55 47	21 19	26 46 50	4 46	24 05	18 57	3 ♐ 02 45	25 37
15	M	19 38 14	24 56 56	21 09	9 ♐ 23 44	5 03	26 51	18 54	15 50 03	27 46
16	T	19 42 11	25 58 03	20 57	22 21 52	5 05	28 18	18 51	28 59 14	28 27
17	W	19 46 08	26 59 11	20 46	5 ♑ 42 03	4 51	28 10	18 48	12 ♑ 30 07	27 28
18	Th	19 50 04	28 00 18	20 34	19 23 07	4 20	26 20	18 44	26 20 36	24 47
19	F	19 54 01	29 ♑ 01 25	20 21	3 ♒ 22 03	3 33	22 51	18 41	10 ♒ 26 52	20 34
20	S	19 57 57	0 ♒ 02 31	20 09	17 34 24	2 32	17 58	18 38	24 43 58	15 07
21	Su	20 01 54	1 03 36	19 55	1 ♓ 54 55	1 20	12 02	18 35	9 ♓ 06 37	8 48
22	M	20 05 50	2 04 40	19 42	16 18 28	0 S 03	5 S 27	18 32	23 29 56	2 S 02
23	T	20 09 47	3 05 43	19 28	0 ♈ 40 34	1 N 14	1 N 24	18 29	7 ♈ 49 58	4 N 48
24	W	20 13 43	4 06 46	19 14	14 57 51	2 26	8 09	18 25	22 03 56	11 22
25	Th	20 17 40	5 07 47	18 59	29 08 04	3 29	14 25	18 22	6 ♉ 10 04	17 17
26	F	20 21 37	6 08 47	18 44	13 ♉ 09 49	4 18	19 54	18 19	20 07 15	22 13
27	S	20 25 33	7 09 46	18 29	27 02 16	4 52	24 14	18 16	3 ♊ 54 46	25 53
28	Su	20 29 30	8 10 44	18 13	10 ♊ 44 40	5 09	27 09	18 13	17 31 51	28 00
29	M	20 33 26	9 11 41	17 57	24 16 13	5 08	28 26	18 10	0 ♋ 57 38	28 27
30	T	20 37 23	10 12 37	17 41	7 ♋ 35 59	4 50	28 03	18 06	14 11 09	27 15
31	W	20 41 19	11 ♒ 13 31	17 S 25	20 ♋ 42 59	4 N 17	26 N 05	18 ♓ 03	27 ♋ 11 25	24 N 35

D M	Mercury Lat.	Mercury Dec.		Venus Lat.	Venus Dec.		Mars Lat.	Mars Dec.		Jupiter Lat.	Jupiter Dec.
	° ′	° ′	° ′	° ′	° ′	° ′	° ′	° ′	° ′	° ′	° ′
1	1 S 30	24 S 44	24 S 43	1 S 21	22 S 08	21 S 55	0 S 18	23 S 16	23 S 21	0 N 42	21 S 00
3	1 39	24 40	24 36	1 23	21 41	21 26	0 20	23 25	23 28	0 42	21 04
5	1 47	24 30	24 23	1 26	21 10	20 54	0 21	23 32	23 35	0 42	21 08
7	1 53	24 14	24 04	1 28	20 38	20 20	0 22	23 38	23 41	0 42	21 11
9	1 59	23 52	23 39	1 29	20 02	19 44	0 24	23 43	23 46	0 42	21 15
11	2 03	23 25	23 08	1 31	19 25	19 05	0 25	23 48	23 50	0 42	21 18
13	2 05	22 50	22 31	1 32	18 45	18 25	0 26	23 51	23 53	0 42	21 22
15	2 06	22 10	21 48	1 33	18 03	17 42	0 28	23 54	23 55	0 42	21 25
17	2 06	21 24	20 58	1 34	17 19	16 57	0 29	23 55	23 56	0 42	21 28
19	2 03	20 31	20 02	1 35	16 34	16 10	0 30	23 56	23 56	0 42	21 31
21	1 58	19 32	19 01	1 35	15 46	15 21	0 32	23 55	23 55	0 42	21 34
23	1 51	18 28	17 53	1 35	14 57	14 31	0 33	23 54	23 53	0 42	21 37
25	1 42	17 17	16 40	1 34	14 06	13 40	0 34	23 51	23 50	0 42	21 39
27	1 29	16 02	15 23	1 34	13 13	12 46	0 36	23 48	23 46	0 42	21 42
29	1 14	14 43	14 S 02	1 33	12 19	11 S 52	0 37	23 44	23 S 41	0 42	21 44
31	0 S 56	13 S 21		1 S 32	11 S 24		0 S 38	23 S 38		0 N 42	21 S 47

FIRST QUARTER–Jan.25,23h.01m. (5°♉36′)

FULL MOON–Jan. 3,13h.57m. (12°♋48′)

D M	☿ Long.	♀ Long.	♂ Long.	♃ Long.	♄ Long.	♅ Long.	♆ Long.	♇ Long.	☉	☿	♀	♂	♃	♄	♅	♆	♇
	° ′	° ′	° ′	° ′	° ′	° ′	° ′	° ′									
1	7♑18	26♑41	18♐47	8♐18	24♌26	11♓33	18♒08	27♐03			⚼	☍	☍		□	△	
2	8 54	27 56	19 31	8 30	24R 23	11 35	18 10	27 05						⚹		⚼	☍
3	10 30	29♑11	20 14	8 42	24 20	11 38	18 12	27 07	☍	☍				∠	△		
4	12 06	0♒27	20 58	8 54	24 17	11 40	18 14	27 09			☍		⚼	⚺	⚼		
5	13 42	1 42	21 42	9 07	24 14	11 42	18 16	27 11				⚼	△				⚼
6	15 19	2 57	22 25	9 19	24 11	11 44	18 18	27 14				△		●		☍	
7	16 57	4 12	23 09	9 31	24 08	11 46	18 20	27 16	⚼	⚼							△
8	18 35	5 27	23 52	9 42	24 04	11 49	18 22	27 18	△	△			□		☍		
9	20 13	6 42	24 36	9 54	24 01	11 51	18 24	27 20			⚼	□		⚺			□
10	21 51	7 57	25 20	10 06	23 57	11 53	18 26	27 22			△		⚹	∠		⚼	
11	23 30	9 12	26 04	10 18	23 54	11 56	18 28	27 24	□	□		⚹	∠	⚹		△	
12	25 10	10 27	26 48	10 29	23 50	11 58	18 30	27 26							⚼		⚹
13	26 50	11 43	27 32	10 41	23 46	12 01	18 32	27 28			□	∠	⚺		△	□	∠
14	28♑30	12 58	28 16	10 52	23 43	12 03	18 34	27 30	⚹	⚹		⚺		□			⚺
15	0♒11	14 13	29 00	11 04	23 39	12 06	18 36	27 32	∠		⚹		☌		□		
16	1 52	15 28	29♐44	11 15	23 35	12 08	18 38	27 34	⚺	∠				△		⚹	☌
17	3 34	16 43	0♑28	11 26	23 31	12 11	18 40	27 36		⚺	∠	☌	⚺	⚼	⚹	∠	
18	5 15	17 58	1 12	11 38	23 26	12 14	18 43	27 38			⚺					⚺	
19	6 58	19 13	1 56	11 49	23 22	12 16	18 45	27 40	☌	●		⚺	∠		∠		⚺
20	8 40	20 28	2 40	12 00	23 18	12 19	18 47	27 42			●	∠	⚹	☍	⚺	☌	∠
21	10 23	21 42	3 24	12 11	23 14	12 22	18 49	27 44	⚺			⚹					⚹
22	12 05	22 57	4 09	12 22	23 09	12 25	18 51	27 46	∠	⚺			□		☌	⚺	
23	13 48	24 12	4 53	12 32	23 05	12 28	18 53	27 48	⚹	∠	⚺	□				∠	□
24	15 31	25 27	5 37	12 43	23 01	12 30	18 56	27 50		⚹	∠		△	⚼	⚺	⚹	
25	17 13	26 42	6 22	12 54	22 56	12 33	18 58	27 52	□		⚹		⚼	△	∠		△
26	18 55	27 57	7 06	13 04	22 52	12 36	19 00	27 54		□		△			⚹	□	⚼
27	20 36	29♒12	7 51	13 14	22 47	12 39	19 02	27 56			□	⚼		□			
28	22 16	0♓26	8 35	13 25	22 42	12 42	19 05	27 57	△				☍		□		
29	23 55	1 41	9 20	13 35	22 38	12 45	19 07	27 59	⚼	△				⚹		△	☍
30	25 32	2 56	10 04	13 45	22 33	12 48	19 09	28 01		⚼	△	☍		∠	△	⚼	
31	27♒07	4♓10	10♑49	13♐55	22♌28	12♓51	19♒11	28♐03			⚼			⚺			

D M	Saturn Lat.	Saturn Dec.	Uranus Lat.	Uranus Dec.	Neptune Lat.	Neptune Dec.	Pluto Lat.	Pluto Dec.
	° ′	° ′	° ′	° ′	° ′	° ′	° ′	° ′
1	1N12	14N31	0S45	7S56	0S13	15S37	6N53	16S32
3	1 13	14 33	0 45	7 54	0 13	15 35	6 52	16 32
5	1 13	14 36	0 45	7 52	0 13	15 34	6 52	16 32
7	1 13	14 38	0 45	7 51	0 13	15 33	6 52	16 32
9	1 14	14 41	0 45	7 49	0 13	15 32	6 52	16 33
11	1 14	14 43	0 45	7 47	0 13	15 30	6 52	16 33
13	1 15	14 46	0 45	7 45	0 13	15 29	6 52	16 33
15	1 15	14 49	0 45	7 43	0 13	15 28	6 52	16 33
17	1 15	14 52	0 45	7 41	0 13	15 27	6 52	16 33
19	1 16	14 55	0 45	7 39	0 13	15 25	6 52	16 33
21	1 16	14 58	0 45	7 37	0 14	15 24	6 52	16 33
23	1 16	15 01	0 45	7 34	0 14	15 23	6 52	16 33
25	1 16	15 05	0 45	7 32	0 14	15 21	6 52	16 33
27	1 17	15 08	0 45	7 30	0 14	15 20	6 53	16 33
29	1 17	15 11	0 45	7 28	0 14	15 18	6 53	16 33
31	1N17	15N14	0S44	7S25	0S14	15S17	6N53	16S33

Mutual Aspects

1 ♀∠♅. ♀⚺♇.
2 ☉⚹♅. ☉⊥♆. ☿⚺♃. ☿⚼♄.
4 ☿⚹♅. ☿⊥♆.
5 ☉⊥♃. ♀∥♃.
6 ☿⊥♃. ♀⊥♇.
7 ☉☌☿.
8 ☉±♄. ☿±♄. ☿⚺♆. ♀⊥♅. ♂△♄.
9 ☉⚺♆. 10 ☿∥♂.
11 ☿∇♄.
12 ☿∠♃. ♀⚹♃.
13 ☿∠♅. ☿⚺♇. ♀⚺♅. ♂☌♇.
14 ☉∇♄. ☿⚺♂. ♀∠♇. ☉∥♃.
15 ♀∠♂. 16 ☉∠♃.
17 ☉∠♅. ☿⊥♇. ♂Q♅. ☿∥♃.
18 ☉⚺♇.
19 ☿⊥♅. ♀☌♆. ♀∥♇.
20 ☿⊥♂. ☉∥☿.
22 ☿⚹♃. ☿⚺♅. ☿∠♇. ♀☍♄. ♂∠♆.
♃□♅. ♀∥♆.
23 ♀Q♃. ♀⋕♄.
24 ☉⊥♇.
26 ☉⊥♅. ☿☌♆. ♀⚹♇. ☿∥♇.
27 ♂⚼♄.
28 ☿☍♄. ☿⋕♄. ☿∥♆.
29 ☉⚺♂. ☿∠♂.
30 ☿Q♃.

LAST QUARTER–Jan.11,12h.45m. (20°♎54′)

NEW MOON – Feb.17,16h.14m. (28°♒37′)

D M	D W	Sidereal Time	☉ Long.	☉ Dec.	☽ Long.	☽ Lat.	☽ Dec.	☽ Node	24h. ☽ Long.	24h. ☽ Dec.
		h m s	° ′ ″	° ′	° ′ ″	° ′	° ′	° ′	° ′ ″	° ′
1	Th	20 45 16	12 ♒ 14 25	17 S 08	3 ♌ 36 22	3 N 32	22 N 47	18 ♓ 00	9 ♌ 57 47	20 N 44
2	F	20 49 12	13 15 17	16 50	16 15 41	2 37	18 27	17 57	22 30 07	16 00
3	S	20 53 09	14 16 08	16 33	28 41 10	1 35	13 25	17 54	4 ♍ 49 00	10 43
4	Su	20 57 06	15 16 58	16 15	10 ♍ 53 49	0 N 30	7 56	17 50	16 55 54	5 N 06
5	M	21 01 02	16 17 47	15 57	22 55 33	0 S 36	2 N 15	17 47	28 53 09	0 S 36
6	T	21 04 59	17 18 35	15 39	4 ♎ 49 07	1 40	3 S 27	17 44	10 ♎ 43 54	6 15
7	W	21 08 55	18 19 23	15 20	16 38 03	2 39	8 59	17 41	22 32 04	11 39
8	Th	21 12 52	19 20 09	15 01	28 26 34	3 31	14 13	17 38	4 ♏ 22 07	16 39
9	F	21 16 48	20 20 54	14 42	10 ♏ 19 21	4 15	18 57	17 35	16 18 53	21 04
10	S	21 20 45	21 21 38	14 23	22 21 21	4 48	23 00	17 31	28 27 22	24 41
11	Su	21 24 41	22 22 21	14 03	4 ♐ 37 31	5 08	26 07	17 28	10 ♐ 52 22	27 15
12	M	21 28 38	23 23 03	13 44	17 12 24	5 15	28 03	17 25	23 38 05	28 29
13	T	21 32 35	24 23 44	13 23	0 ♑ 09 44	5 06	28 32	17 22	6 ♑ 47 39	28 11
14	W	21 36 31	25 24 24	13 03	13 31 56	4 40	27 24	17 19	20 22 36	26 12
15	Th	21 40 28	26 25 02	12 43	27 19 30	3 58	24 35	17 16	4 ♒ 22 22	22 35
16	F	21 44 24	27 25 40	12 22	11 ♒ 30 44	3 00	20 13	17 12	18 44 03	17 31
17	S	21 48 21	28 26 15	12 01	26 01 34	1 49	14 33	17 09	3 ♓ 22 30	11 21
18	Su	21 52 17	29 ♒ 26 50	11 40	10 ♓ 45 56	0 S 30	7 59	17 06	18 10 56	4 S 30
19	M	21 56 14	0 ♓ 27 22	11 19	25 36 32	0 N 52	0 S 57	17 03	3 ♈ 01 47	2 N 37
20	T	22 00 10	1 27 53	10 57	10 ♈ 25 50	2 11	6 N 08	17 00	17 47 50	9 33
21	W	22 04 07	2 28 22	10 36	25 07 05	3 20	12 49	16 56	2 ♉ 22 59	15 53
22	Th	22 08 04	3 28 50	10 14	9 ♉ 35 04	4 15	18 42	16 53	16 42 57	21 14
23	F	22 12 00	4 29 15	9 52	23 46 23	4 53	23 27	16 50	0 ♊ 45 13	25 17
24	S	22 15 57	5 29 39	9 30	7 ♊ 39 22	5 14	26 44	16 47	14 28 53	27 47
25	Su	22 19 53	6 30 00	9 08	21 13 49	5 16	28 24	16 44	27 54 18	28 36
26	M	22 23 50	7 30 20	8 45	4 ♋ 30 29	5 01	28 23	16 41	11 ♋ 02 33	27 46
27	T	22 27 46	8 30 38	8 23	17 30 43	4 31	26 46	16 37	23 55 09	25 27
28	W	22 31 43	9 ♓ 30 53	8 S 00	0 ♌ 16 05	3 N 48	23 N 48	16 ♓ 34	6 ♌ 33 43	21 N 54

D M	Mercury Lat.	Mercury Dec.	Mercury Dec.	Venus Lat.	Venus Dec.	Venus Dec.	Mars Lat.	Mars Dec.	Mars Dec.	Jupiter Lat.	Jupiter Dec.
	° ′	° ′	° ′	° ′	° ′	° ′	° ′	° ′	° ′	° ′	° ′
1	0 S 45	12 S 39	11 S 57	1 S 31	10 S 56	10 S 28	0 S 39	23 S 35	23 S 32	0 N 42	21 S 48
3	0 S 22	11 15	10 34	1 29	9 59	9 30	0 40	23 28	23 24	0 42	21 50
5	0 N 04	9 53	9 14	1 27	9 01	8 32	0 41	23 20	23 16	0 42	21 52
7	0 33	8 36	8 00	1 25	8 02	7 32	0 43	23 11	23 06	0 42	21 54
9	1 04	7 27	6 56	1 23	7 03	6 32	0 44	23 01	22 56	0 42	21 56
11	1 37	6 28	6 05	1 20	6 02	5 32	0 45	22 50	22 45	0 42	21 58
13	2 09	5 45	5 30	1 17	5 01	4 30	0 47	22 39	22 32	0 42	22 00
15	2 40	5 19	5 13	1 13	3 59	3 28	0 48	22 26	22 19	0 42	22 02
17	3 07	5 12	5 16	1 10	2 57	2 26	0 49	22 12	22 05	0 42	22 03
19	3 27	5 25	5 38	1 06	1 55	1 24	0 51	21 57	21 50	0 42	22 05
21	3 40	5 54	6 14	1 02	0 S 52	0 S 21	0 52	21 42	21 33	0 42	22 06
23	3 44	6 37	7 02	0 58	0 N 10	0 N 42	0 53	21 25	21 17	0 42	22 07
25	3 38	7 29	7 56	0 53	1 13	1 44	0 54	21 08	20 59	0 42	22 09
27	3 25	8 24	8 51	0 48	2 16	2 47	0 56	20 49	20 40	0 43	22 10
29	3 05	9 17	9 S 43	0 43	3 18	3 N 49	0 57	20 30	20 S 20	0 43	22 11
31	2 N 41	10 S 06		0 S 38	4 N 20		0 S 58	20 S 10		0 N 43	22 S 12

FIRST QUARTER – Feb.24,07h.56m. (5°♊19′)

FULL MOON–Feb. 2,05h.45m. (12°♌59′)

D M	☿ Long.	♀ Long.	♂ Long.	♃ Long.	♄ Long.	♅ Long.	♆ Long.	♇ Long.	☉	☿	♀	♂	♃	♄	♅	♆	♇
	° ′	° ′	° ′	° ′	° ′	° ′	° ′	° ′									
1	28♒40	5♓25	11♑33	14♐05	22♌24	12♓54	19♒14	28♐04					⚼		⚼		
2	0♓10	6 40	12 18	14 15	22R 19	12 57	19 16	28 06	☍				△	●		☍	⚼
3	1 36	7 54	13 03	14 24	22 14	13 00	19 18	28 08		☍		⚼					△
4	2 58	9 09	13 47	14 34	22 09	13 04	19 20	28 10			☍	△	□		☍		
5	4 16	10 23	14 32	14 43	22 04	13 07	19 23	28 11						⚺			□
6	5 27	11 38	15 17	14 53	21 59	13 10	19 25	28 13	⚼					∠		⚼	
7	6 33	12 52	16 02	15 02	21 55	13 13	19 27	28 14	△	⚼		□	⚹	⚹		△	
8	7 31	14 07	16 47	15 11	21 50	13 16	19 30	28 16			⚼		∠		⚼		⚹
9	8 21	15 21	17 32	15 20	21 45	13 19	19 32	28 18		△	△		⚺		△		∠
10	9 03	16 36	18 17	15 29	21 40	13 23	19 34	28 19	□			⚹		□		□	⚺
11	9 36	17 50	19 02	15 38	21 35	13 26	19 36	28 21		□		∠					
12	9 59	19 04	19 47	15 46	21 30	13 29	19 39	28 22			□	⚺	☌	△	□	⚹	
13	10 11	20 18	20 32	15 55	21 25	13 32	19 41	28 23	⚹					⚼		∠	☌
14	10R 13	21 33	21 17	16 03	21 20	13 36	19 43	28 25	∠	⚹			⚺		⚹	⚺	
15	10 05	22 47	22 02	16 11	21 16	13 39	19 46	28 26	⚺	∠	⚹	☌	∠		∠		⚺
16	9 46	24 01	22 47	16 19	21 11	13 42	19 48	28 28		⚺	∠		⚹		⚺		∠
17	9 17	25 15	23 32	16 27	21 06	13 46	19 50	28 29	☌		⚺	⚺		☍		☌	⚹
18	8 39	26 29	24 17	16 35	21 01	13 49	19 52	28 30		☌		∠	□		☌		
19	7 52	27 43	25 02	16 43	20 56	13 53	19 55	28 32	⚺		☌	⚹				⚺	□
20	6 59	28♓57	25 48	16 51	20 51	13 56	19 57	28 33	∠	⚺			△	⚼	⚺	∠	
21	6 00	0♈11	26 33	16 58	20 47	13 59	19 59	28 34		∠	⚺	□	⚼	△	∠	⚹	△
22	4 57	1 25	27 18	17 05	20 42	14 03	20 01	28 35	⚹	⚹					⚹		⚼
23	3 51	2 39	28 04	17 13	20 37	14 06	20 04	28 36			∠	△		□		□	
24	2 45	3 53	28 49	17 20	20 33	14 09	20 06	28 38	□	□	⚹	⚼			□		
25	1 40	5 07	29♑34	17 26	20 28	14 13	20 08	28 39					☍	⚹		△	
26	0♓37	6 20	0♒20	17 33	20 24	14 16	20 10	28 40	△	△	□			∠		⚼	☍
27	29♒38	7 34	1 05	17 40	20 19	14 20	20 12	28 41		⚼				⚺	△		
28	28♒44	8♈47	1♒51	17♐46	20♌15	14♓23	20♒15	28♐42	⚼			☍	⚼		⚼		

D M	Saturn Lat.	Saturn Dec.	Uranus Lat.	Uranus Dec.	Neptune Lat.	Neptune Dec.	Pluto Lat.	Pluto Dec.
	° ′	° ′	° ′	° ′	° ′	° ′	° ′	° ′
1	1N17	15N16	0S44	7S24	0S14	15S16	6N53	16S33
3	1 18	15 19	0 44	7 22	0 14	15 15	6 53	16 33
5	1 18	15 23	0 44	7 19	0 14	15 14	6 53	16 33
7	1 18	15 26	0 44	7 17	0 14	15 12	6 53	16 33
9	1 18	15 29	0 44	7 14	0 14	15 11	6 53	16 32
11	1 18	15 33	0 44	7 12	0 14	15 09	6 53	16 32
13	1 19	15 36	0 44	7 09	0 14	15 08	6 54	16 32
15	1 19	15 39	0 44	7 07	0 14	15 07	6 54	16 32
17	1 19	15 43	0 44	7 04	0 14	15 05	6 54	16 32
19	1 19	15 46	0 44	7 01	0 14	15 04	6 54	16 32
21	1 19	15 49	0 44	6 59	0 14	15 02	6 54	16 32
23	1 19	15 52	0 44	6 56	0 14	15 01	6 55	16 31
25	1 19	15 55	0 44	6 54	0 14	15 00	6 55	16 31
27	1 19	15 58	0 44	6 51	0 14	14 58	6 55	16 31
29	1 20	16 01	0 44	6 48	0 14	14 57	6 55	16 31
31	1N20	16N04	0S44	6S46	0S14	14S56	6N56	16S31

Mutual Aspects

1 ☿⚹♇. ♄#♆.
2 ☉⚺♅. ☉∠♇.
3 ☉⚹♃. ♂⚹♅. ♂⊥♆. ☉∥♇.
5 ♀Q♇. ♂⚺♃.
7 ♀☌♅. ♂±♄. ☉#♄. ☉∥♆.
8 ☉☌♆.
9 ♀□♃. ☿∥♅. ♀∥♅.
10 ☉☍♄.
12 ♀⚺♆. ♂⚺♆.
13 ♀⚹♂.
14 ♀▽♄. ♂▽♄. ☿Stat.
15 ♂⊥♃.
17 ☉Q♃. ☉⚹♇. ♀⊥♆.
18 ☿∠♂. ♀±♄. ♂∥♃.
20 ♀□♇.　　21 ☉⊥♂.
23 ☉☌☿. ☿⊥♂.
24 ☿⚺♀. ♂∠♅. ♂⚺♇. ☿∥♅.
25 ♀⚼♄. ♀∠♆.
26 ☿⊥♀. ☿⚺♂.
27 ☿Q♃. ☉∥☿.
28 ☿⚹♇. ♄☍♆.

LAST QUARTER–Feb.10,09h.51m. (21°♏16′)

NEW MOON–Mar.19,02h.43m. (28°♓07′)

D M	D W	Sidereal Time	☉ Long.	☉ Dec.	☽ Long.	☽ Lat.	☽ Dec.	☽ Node	24h. ☽ Long.	24h. ☽ Dec.
		h m s	° ′ ″	° ′	° ′ ″	° ′	° ′	° ′	° ′ ″	° ′
1	Th	22 35 39	10 ♓ 31 07	7 S 37	12 ♌ 48 15	2 N55	19 N46	16 ♓ 31	18 ♌ 59 52	17 N26
2	F	22 39 36	11 31 19	7 15	25 08 47	1 54	14 56	16 28	1 ♍ 15 12	12 18
3	S	22 43 33	12 31 29	6 52	7 ♍ 19 17	0 N49	9 35	16 25	13 21 16	6 47
4	Su	22 47 29	13 31 37	6 29	19 21 21	0 S18	3 N56	16 22	25 19 47	1 N05
5	M	22 51 26	14 31 43	6 05	1 ♎ 16 48	1 23	1 S47	16 18	7 ♎ 12 40	4 S37
6	T	22 55 22	15 31 47	5 42	13 07 41	2 24	7 24	16 15	19 02 10	10 07
7	W	22 59 19	16 31 50	5 19	24 56 28	3 19	12 45	16 12	0 ♏ 50 58	15 16
8	Th	23 03 15	17 31 51	4 56	6 ♏ 46 05	4 06	17 38	16 09	12 42 15	19 52
9	F	23 07 12	18 31 50	4 32	18 39 56	4 42	21 54	16 06	24 39 39	23 43
10	S	23 11 08	19 31 48	4 09	0 ♐ 41 53	5 06	25 17	16 02	6 ♐ 47 11	26 35
11	Su	23 15 05	20 31 44	3 45	12 56 06	5 17	27 36	15 59	19 09 10	28 16
12	M	23 19 02	21 31 39	3 22	25 26 54	5 13	28 35	15 56	1 ♑ 49 49	28 31
13	T	23 22 58	22 31 32	2 58	8 ♑ 18 23	4 54	28 04	15 53	14 53 01	27 13
14	W	23 26 55	23 31 23	2 34	21 34 03	4 19	25 58	15 50	28 21 43	24 20
15	Th	23 30 51	24 31 13	2 11	5 ♒ 16 08	3 28	22 19	15 47	12 ♒ 17 19	19 57
16	F	23 34 48	25 31 00	1 47	19 25 04	2 23	17 16	15 43	26 39 04	14 18
17	S	23 38 44	26 30 46	1 23	3 ♓ 58 47	1 S07	11 06	15 40	11 ♓ 23 33	7 42
18	Su	23 42 41	27 30 30	0 59	18 52 31	0 N15	4 S10	15 37	26 24 41	0 S34
19	M	23 46 37	28 30 12	0 36	3 ♈ 58 56	1 37	3 N04	15 34	11 ♈ 34 06	6 N40
20	T	23 50 34	29 ♓ 29 52	0 S12	19 08 57	2 53	10 10	15 31	26 42 17	13 30
21	W	23 54 30	0 ♈ 29 30	0 N12	4 ♉ 12 59	3 56	16 37	15 28	11 ♉ 40 02	19 28
22	Th	23 58 27	1 29 06	0 35	19 02 31	4 42	22 00	15 24	26 19 44	24 09
23	F	0 02 24	2 28 40	0 59	3 ♊ 31 08	5 09	25 54	15 21	10 ♊ 36 21	27 14
24	S	0 06 20	3 28 11	1 23	17 35 10	5 16	28 06	15 18	24 27 33	28 32
25	Su	0 10 17	4 27 40	1 46	1 ♋ 13 34	5 05	28 31	15 15	7 ♋ 53 26	28 05
26	M	0 14 13	5 27 07	2 10	14 27 27	4 38	27 16	15 12	20 55 57	26 05
27	T	0 18 10	6 26 31	2 33	27 19 22	3 58	24 35	15 08	3 ♌ 38 08	22 48
28	W	0 22 06	7 25 53	2 57	9 ♌ 52 42	3 07	20 46	15 05	16 03 31	18 33
29	Th	0 26 03	8 25 13	3 20	22 11 03	2 08	16 08	15 02	28 15 44	13 36
30	F	0 29 59	9 24 30	3 44	4 ♍ 17 57	1 N05	10 56	14 59	10 ♍ 18 08	8 12
31	S	0 33 56	10 ♈ 23 45	4 N07	16 ♍ 16 36	0 S01	5 N24	14 ♓ 56	22 ♍ 13 43	2 N34

D M	Mercury Lat.	Mercury Dec.		Venus Lat.	Venus Dec.		Mars Lat.	Mars Dec.		Jupiter Lat.	Jupiter Dec.
	° ′	° ′	° ′	° ′	° ′	° ′	° ′	° ′	° ′	° ′	° ′
1	3 N05	9 S17	9 S 43	0 S 43	3 N18	3 N49	0 S 57	20 S 30	20 S 20	0 N 43	22 S 11
3	2 41	10 06	10 28	0 38	4 20	4 51	0 58	20 10	20 00	0 43	22 12
5	2 14	10 48	11 06	0 33	5 22	5 53	0 59	19 49	19 39	0 43	22 13
7	1 46	11 22	11 36	0 27	6 24	6 54	1 01	19 28	19 16	0 43	22 14
9	1 18	11 48	11 57	0 21	7 25	7 55	1 02	19 05	18 54	0 43	22 14
11	0 51	12 04	12 09	0 16	8 25	8 55	1 03	18 42	18 30	0 43	22 15
13	0 N25	12 12	12 13	0 10	9 24	9 54	1 04	18 18	18 06	0 43	22 16
15	0 00	12 12	12 09	0 S 03	10 23	10 52	1 05	17 53	17 40	0 43	22 16
17	0 S23	12 05	11 58	0 N 03	11 20	11 49	1 06	17 28	17 15	0 43	22 17
19	0 44	11 50	11 40	0 09	12 17	12 45	1 08	17 01	16 48	0 43	22 17
21	1 03	11 28	11 15	0 16	13 13	13 40	1 09	16 35	16 21	0 43	22 18
23	1 21	11 00	10 43	0 22	14 07	14 34	1 10	16 07	15 53	0 43	22 18
25	1 36	10 25	10 06	0 29	15 00	15 26	1 11	15 39	15 25	0 44	22 18
27	1 50	9 45	9 23	0 36	15 51	16 17	1 12	15 10	14 56	0 44	22 19
29	2 01	8 59	8 S 34	0 42	16 41	17 N06	1 13	14 41	14 S 26	0 44	22 19
31	2 S11	8 S07		0 N 49	17 N30		1 S 14	14 S 11		0 N 44	22 S 19

FIRST QUARTER–Mar.25,18h.16m. (4°♋43′)

FULL MOON–Mar. 3,23h.17m. (13°♍00′)

D M	☿ Long.	♀ Long.	♂ Long.	♃ Long.	♄ Long.	♅ Long.	♆ Long.	♇ Long.
	° ′	° ′	° ′	° ′	° ′	° ′	° ′	° ′
1	27♒56	10♈01	2♒36	17♐ 52	20♌10	14♓27	20♒17	28♐ 43
2	27R 14	11 15	3 22	17 59	20R 06	14 30	20 19	28 44
3	26 39	12 28	4 07	18 05	20 01	14 33	20 21	28 45
4	26 10	13 41	4 53	18 10	19 57	14 37	20 23	28 46
5	25 49	14 55	5 38	18 16	19 53	14 40	20 25	28 47
6	25 34	16 08	6 24	18 22	19 49	14 44	20 27	28 47
7	25 26	17 21	7 10	18 27	19 45	14 47	20 30	28 48
8	25D 25	18 34	7 55	18 32	19 41	14 51	20 32	28 49
9	25 30	19 47	8 41	18 37	19 37	14 54	20 34	28 50
10	25 41	21 00	9 27	18 42	19 33	14 58	20 36	28 50
11	25 57	22 13	10 12	18 47	19 29	15 01	20 38	28 51
12	26 19	23 26	10 58	18 51	19 25	15 04	20 40	28 52
13	26 46	24 39	11 44	18 56	19 21	15 08	20 42	28 52
14	27 18	25 52	12 30	19 00	19 18	15 11	20 44	28 53
15	27 54	27 05	13 15	19 04	19 14	15 15	20 46	28 54
16	28 34	28 17	14 01	19 08	19 11	15 18	20 48	28 54
17	29♒18	29♈30	14 47	19 11	19 07	15 21	20 50	28 55
18	0♓05	0♉42	15 33	19 15	19 04	15 25	20 52	28 55
19	0 56	1 55	16 19	19 18	19 01	15 28	20 54	28 55
20	1 50	3 07	17 05	19 21	18 58	15 32	20 55	28 56
21	2 47	4 19	17 51	19 24	18 55	15 35	20 57	28 56
22	3 46	5 32	18 36	19 27	18 52	15 38	20 59	28 57
23	4 49	6 44	19 22	19 30	18 49	15 42	21 01	28 57
24	5 54	7 56	20 08	19 32	18 46	15 45	21 03	28 57
25	7 01	9 08	20 54	19 34	18 44	15 48	21 05	28 57
26	8 10	10 20	21 40	19 36	18 41	15 52	21 06	28 58
27	9 22	11 32	22 26	19 38	18 38	15 55	21 08	28 58
28	10 36	12 43	23 12	19 40	18 36	15 58	21 10	28 58
29	11 51	13 55	23 58	19 41	18 34	16 01	21 12	28 58
30	13 09	15 07	24 44	19 43	18 32	16 05	21 13	28 58
31	14♓28	16♉18	25♒30	19♐ 44	18♌30	16♓08	21♒15	28♐ 58

Lunar Aspects

D M	⊙	☿	♀	♂	♃	♄	♅	♆	♇
1			△		△				⚼
2		☍	⚼			●		☍	△
3	●–●								
4				⚼	□	⚺	☍		
5				△		∠		⚼	□
6		⚼	☍		⚹				
7		△				⚹	⚼	△	⚹
8	⚼			□	∠				
9	△				⚺	□	△	□	∠
10		□	⚼						⚺
11				⚹	☌		□		
12	□	⚹	△	∠		△		⚹	☌
13		∠		⚺		⚼		∠	
14	⚹	⚺	□		⚺		⚹	⚺	
15	∠				∠		∠		⚺
16	⚺			☌	⚹	☍	⚺	☌	∠
17		●	⚹						⚹
18			∠	⚺	□		☌	⚺	
19	●	⚺	⚺	∠		⚼		∠	□
20		∠		⚹	△	△	⚺	⚹	
21	⚺	⚹	☌		⚼		∠		△
22	∠			□		□	⚹	□	⚼
23	⚹	□	⚺						
24			∠	△	☍	⚹	□	△	
25	□	△		⚼		∠		⚼	☍
26			⚹			⚺	△		
27		⚼					⚼		
28	△		□		⚼				⚼
29	⚼			☍	△	●		☍	
30									△
31		☍	△		□	⚺	☍		

D M	Saturn Lat.	Saturn Dec.	Uranus Lat.	Uranus Dec.	Neptune Lat.	Neptune Dec.	Pluto Lat.	Pluto Dec.
	° ′	° ′	° ′	° ′	° ′	° ′	° ′	° ′
1	1N20	16N01	0S44	6S48	0S14	14S57	6N55	16S31
3	1 20	16 04	0 44	6 46	0 14	14 56	6 56	16 31
5	1 20	16 07	0 44	6 43	0 14	14 54	6 56	16 30
7	1 20	16 09	0 44	6 40	0 14	14 53	6 56	16 30
9	1 20	16 12	0 44	6 38	0 14	14 52	6 56	16 30
11	1 20	16 14	0 44	6 35	0 14	14 50	6 57	16 30
13	1 20	16 17	0 44	6 32	0 14	14 49	6 57	16 29
15	1 20	16 19	0 44	6 30	0 14	14 48	6 57	16 29
17	1 20	16 21	0 44	6 27	0 14	14 47	6 57	16 29
19	1 20	16 23	0 44	6 24	0 14	14 45	6 58	16 29
21	1 20	16 25	0 44	6 22	0 14	14 44	6 58	16 28
23	1 20	16 27	0 44	6 19	0 14	14 43	6 58	16 28
25	1 20	16 29	0 44	6 17	0 14	14 42	6 58	16 28
27	1 20	16 30	0 44	6 14	0 14	14 41	6 59	16 28
29	1 20	16 32	0 44	6 12	0 14	14 40	6 59	16 27
31	1N20	16N33	0S44	6S09	0S14	14S39	6N59	16S27

Mutual Aspects

1 ⊙Q♇. ♂∠♃.
3 ⊙⚺♀. ☿∠♀. ⊙ ∥ ♅.
4 ♂⊥♇.
5 ⊙☌♅. ♀⚺♅.
6 ⊙#♀.
8 ♀△♃. ♀#♅. ☿Stat.
9 ⊙□♃. ♀△♄. ♂⊥♅.
10 ⊙∇♄. ♀⊥♅. ♀⚹♆.
11 ⊙⚺♆. ♀Q♂.
16 ⊙±♄. ☿⚹♇. ♂∠♇. ♃△♄.
17 ⊙⊥♆. ☿⚹♀. ♀△♇.
18 ♀∠♅. ♂⚺♅. ☿#♀.
19 ⊙□♇. ☿Q♃.
20 ♀Q♆.
21 ♀⚼♃. ♂ ∥ ♇.
22 ♂☍♄. ♂#♄.
23 ♂⚹♃.
24 ⊙⚼♄. ♀#♆. ♄#♇.
25 ♂☌♆. 26 ♀#♂.
27 ⊙∠♆.
28 ☿Q♇. ♀#♇.
29 ♀±♃. ♀⚼♇. ♀ ∥ ♄. ♂ ∥ ♆.
31 ⊙⊥♀. ⊙∠♂. ♀⚹♅. ♇Stat.

LAST QUARTER–Mar.12,03h.54m. (21°♐11′)

NEW MOON–Apr.17,11h.36m. (27°♈05′)

D M	D W	Sidereal Time	☉ Long.	☉ Dec.	☽ Long.	☽ Lat.	☽ Dec.	☽ Node	24h. ☽ Long.	24h. ☽ Dec.
		h m s	° ′ ″	° ′	° ′ ″	° ′	° ′	° ′	° ′ ″	° ′
1	Su	0 37 53	11 ♈ 22 58	4 N30	28 ♍ 09 48	1 S 06	0 S 17	14 ♓ 53	4 ♎ 05 07	3 S 07
2	M	0 41 49	12 22 09	4 53	9 ♎ 59 56	2 08	5 55	14 49	15 54 32	8 40
3	T	0 45 46	13 21 18	5 16	21 49 09	3 04	11 20	14 46	27 44 02	13 55
4	W	0 49 42	14 20 25	5 39	3 ♏ 39 25	3 52	16 22	14 43	9 ♏ 35 33	18 40
5	Th	0 53 39	15 19 30	6 02	15 32 42	4 30	20 48	14 40	21 31 09	22 43
6	F	0 57 35	16 18 33	6 25	27 31 10	4 57	24 25	14 37	3 ♐ 33 07	25 51
7	S	1 01 32	17 17 34	6 47	9 ♐ 37 18	5 10	27 01	14 33	15 44 07	27 51
8	Su	1 05 28	18 16 34	7 10	21 53 57	5 10	28 21	14 30	28 07 14	28 30
9	M	1 09 25	19 15 32	7 32	4 ♑ 24 23	4 56	28 17	14 27	10 ♑ 45 50	27 42
10	T	1 13 22	20 14 28	7 55	17 12 04	4 26	26 44	14 24	23 43 28	25 23
11	W	1 17 18	21 13 22	8 17	0 ♒ 20 29	3 42	23 41	14 21	7 ♒ 03 27	21 39
12	Th	1 21 15	22 12 15	8 39	13 52 39	2 44	19 17	14 18	20 48 19	16 38
13	F	1 25 11	23 11 05	9 01	27 50 31	1 35	13 43	14 14	4 ♓ 59 12	10 35
14	S	1 29 08	24 09 54	9 22	12 ♓ 14 10	0 S 18	7 15	14 11	19 35 01	3 S 48
15	Su	1 33 04	25 08 42	9 44	27 01 09	1 N 02	0 S 15	14 08	4 ♈ 31 49	3 N 21
16	M	1 37 01	26 07 27	10 05	12 ♈ 06 01	2 19	6 N 55	14 05	19 42 39	10 24
17	T	1 40 57	27 06 10	10 27	27 20 28	3 27	13 45	14 02	4 ♉ 58 07	16 53
18	W	1 44 54	28 04 52	10 48	12 ♉ 34 17	4 20	19 44	13 59	20 07 39	22 16
19	Th	1 48 51	29 ♈ 03 32	11 08	27 37 01	4 54	24 24	13 55	5 ♊ 01 20	26 07
20	F	1 52 47	0 ♉ 02 09	11 29	12 ♊ 19 42	5 09	27 22	13 52	19 31 29	28 09
21	S	1 56 44	1 00 45	11 50	26 36 13	5 03	28 26	13 49	3 ♋ 33 38	28 17
22	Su	2 00 40	1 59 18	12 10	10 ♋ 23 44	4 39	27 41	13 46	17 06 36	26 41
23	M	2 04 37	2 57 49	12 30	23 42 31	4 02	25 19	13 43	0 ♌ 11 52	23 40
24	T	2 08 33	3 56 18	12 50	6 ♌ 35 09	3 12	21 44	13 39	12 52 53	19 35
25	W	2 12 30	4 54 45	13 10	19 05 40	2 15	17 14	13 36	25 14 06	14 45
26	Th	2 16 26	5 53 10	13 29	1 ♍ 18 48	1 13	12 09	13 33	7 ♍ 20 22	9 27
27	F	2 20 23	6 51 32	13 48	13 19 24	0 N 09	6 42	13 30	19 16 27	3 N 54
28	S	2 24 20	7 49 52	14 07	25 12 02	0 S 54	1 N 04	13 27	1 ♎ 06 38	1 S 45
29	Su	2 28 16	8 48 11	14 26	7 ♎ 00 42	1 55	4 S 33	13 24	12 54 38	7 18
30	M	2 32 13	9 ♉ 46 27	14 N 45	18 ♎ 48 48	2 S 51	10 S 00	13 ♓ 20	24 ♎ 43 31	12 S 37

D M	Mercury Lat.	Mercury Dec.		Venus Lat.	Venus Dec.		Mars Lat.	Mars Dec.		Jupiter Lat.	Jupiter Dec.
	° ′	° ′	° ′	° ′	° ′	° ′	° ′	° ′	° ′	° ′	° ′
1	2 S 15	7 S 40	7 S 10	0 N 52	17 N 53	18 N 16	1 S 15	13 S 56	13 S 41	0 N 44	22 S 19
3	2 21	6 40	6 09	0 59	18 39	19 01	1 16	13 25	13 10	0 44	22 19
5	2 26	5 36	5 02	1 05	19 23	19 44	1 17	12 54	12 38	0 44	22 19
7	2 29	4 27	3 51	1 12	20 05	20 25	1 17	12 22	12 06	0 44	22 19
9	2 30	3 13	2 35	1 18	20 45	21 04	1 18	11 50	11 34	0 44	22 19
11	2 28	1 55	1 S 15	1 25	21 23	21 41	1 19	11 18	11 01	0 44	22 19
13	2 25	0 S 33	0 N 10	1 31	21 59	22 16	1 20	10 45	10 28	0 44	22 18
15	2 20	0 N 53	1 38	1 37	22 32	22 48	1 21	10 12	9 55	0 44	22 18
17	2 12	2 23	3 09	1 43	23 03	23 18	1 22	9 38	9 21	0 44	22 18
19	2 03	3 56	4 44	1 49	23 32	23 46	1 23	9 04	8 47	0 44	22 17
21	1 52	5 33	6 22	1 55	23 59	24 11	1 23	8 30	8 12	0 44	22 17
23	1 38	7 12	8 02	2 00	24 23	24 34	1 24	7 55	7 38	0 44	22 17
25	1 23	8 53	9 44	2 05	24 44	24 54	1 25	7 20	7 03	0 44	22 16
27	1 06	10 35	11 26	2 10	25 03	25 11	1 25	6 45	6 28	0 44	22 15
29	0 48	12 17	13 N 09	2 15	25 19	25 N 26	1 26	6 10	5 S 52	0 44	22 15
31	0 S 28	13 N 59		2 N 19	25 N 32		1 S 27	5 S 35		0 N 44	22 S 14

FIRST QUARTER–Apr.24,06h.35m. (3°♌43′)

FULL MOON–Apr. 2,17h.15m. (12°♎35′)

D	☿	♀	♂	♃	♄	♅	♆	♇	Lunar Aspects								
M	Long.	Long.	Long.	Long.	Long.	Long.	Long.	Long.	☉	☿	♀	♂	♃	♄	♅	♆	♇
	° ′	° ′	° ′	° ′	° ′	° ′	° ′	° ′									
1	15♓50	17♉30	26♒16	19♐45	18♌28	16♓11	21♒17	28♐58			⚼			∠			□
2	17 13	18 41	27 02	19 46	18R 26	16 14	21 18	28R 58	☍			⚼				⚼	
3	18 37	19 52	27 48	19 46	18 24	16 17	21 20	28 58					✱	✱		△	
4	20 04	21 03	28 34	19 47	18 22	16 20	21 21	28 58		⚼		△	∠		⚼		✱
5	21 31	22 14	29♒20	19 47	18 21	16 24	21 23	28 58					⊻	□	△	□	∠
6	23 01	23 25	0♓06	19R 47	18 19	16 27	21 24	28 58	⚼	△	☍	□					⊻
7	24 32	24 36	0 52	19 47	18 18	16 30	21 26	28 57									
8	26 05	25 47	1 38	19 46	18 16	16 33	21 27	28 57	△	□			☌	△	□	✱	
9	27 39	26 57	2 24	19 46	18 15	16 36	21 29	28 57				✱		⚼		∠	☌
10	29♓15	28 08	3 10	19 45	18 14	16 39	21 30	28 57	□		⚼	∠	⊻		✱	⊻	
11	0♈52	29♉18	3 56	19 44	18 13	16 42	21 31	28 56		✱	△	⊻	∠		∠		⊻
12	2 31	0♊29	4 42	19 43	18 12	16 45	21 33	28 56		∠			✱	☍	⊻		∠
13	4 12	1 39	5 28	19 42	18 12	16 48	21 34	28 56	✱		□					☌	✱
14	5 54	2 49	6 14	19 40	18 11	16 51	21 35	28 55	∠	⊻		●			☌		
15	7 38	3 59	7 01	19 38	18 10	16 54	21 37	28 55	⊻				□	⚼		⊻	□
16	9 23	5 09	7 47	19 36	18 10	16 56	21 38	28 54		☌	✱	⊻	△	△	⊻	∠	
17	11 09	6 19	8 33	19 34	18 10	16 59	21 39	28 54	☌		∠	∠	⚼		∠	✱	△
18	12 58	7 28	9 19	19 32	18 09	17 02	21 40	28 53		⊻	⊻	✱		□	✱		⚼
19	14 48	8 38	10 05	19 30	18 09	17 05	21 41	28 53	⊻	∠						□	
20	16 39	9 47	10 51	19 27	18D 09	17 08	21 43	28 52	∠	✱	☌	□	☍	✱	□		
21	18 32	10 57	11 37	19 24	18 09	17 10	21 44	28 51	✱					∠		△	☍
22	20 27	12 06	12 23	19 21	18 10	17 13	21 45	28 51			⊻	△				⚼	
23	22 23	13 15	13 09	19 18	18 10	17 16	21 46	28 50		□	∠	⚼		⊻	△		
24	24 21	14 24	13 55	19 15	18 11	17 18	21 47	28 49	□				⚼		⚼		
25	26 21	15 33	14 41	19 12	18 11	17 21	21 48	28 49			✱		△	●		☍	⚼
26	28♈22	16 41	15 26	19 08	18 12	17 23	21 49	28 48	△	△							△
27	0♉24	17 50	16 12	19 04	18 12	17 26	21 50	28 47		⚼	□	☍	□	⊻	☍		
28	2 28	18 58	16 58	19 00	18 13	17 28	21 50	28 46	⚼								□
29	4 33	20 06	17 44	18 56	18 14	17 31	21 51	28 45						∠		⚼	
30	6♉40	21♊14	18♓30	18♐52	18♌15	17♓33	21♒52	28♐45			△		✱	✱		△	

D	Saturn		Uranus		Neptune		Pluto	
M	Lat.	Dec.	Lat.	Dec.	Lat.	Dec.	Lat.	Dec.
	° ′	° ′	° ′	° ′	° ′	° ′	° ′	° ′
1	1N20	16N33	0S44	6S08	0S14	14S38	6N59	16S27
3	1 19	16 34	0 44	6 06	0 14	14 37	6 59	16 27
5	1 19	16 35	0 44	6 03	0 14	14 36	7 00	16 27
7	1 19	16 36	0 44	6 01	0 14	14 35	7 00	16 26
9	1 19	16 37	0 44	5 58	0 15	14 34	7 00	16 26
11	1 19	16 37	0 45	5 56	0 15	14 34	7 00	16 26
13	1 19	16 38	0 45	5 54	0 15	14 33	7 01	16 26
15	1 19	16 38	0 45	5 52	0 15	14 32	7 01	16 25
17	1 19	16 38	0 45	5 49	0 15	14 31	7 01	16 25
19	1 19	16 38	0 45	5 47	0 15	14 31	7 01	16 25
21	1 19	16 38	0 45	5 45	0 15	14 30	7 01	16 25
23	1 18	16 38	0 45	5 43	0 15	14 29	7 02	16 24
25	1 18	16 37	0 45	5 41	0 15	14 29	7 02	16 24
27	1 18	16 37	0 45	5 39	0 15	14 28	7 02	16 24
29	1 18	16 36	0 45	5 37	0 15	14 28	7 02	16 24
31	1N18	16N35	0S45	5S36	0S15	14S27	7N02	16S24

Mutual Aspects

1 ☿☌♅. 2 ♀□♄.
3 ☿▽♄. ♀▽♃.
4 ☿□♃. ♀□♆. ☿∥♅.
5 ☿⊻♆. ♂✱♇. ☉#☿. ☉#♅.
6 ☉⊻♅. ♀±♇. ♃Stat.
7 ☿✱♀. ☿±♄.
8 ☉△♄. ♂Q♃.
9 ☿⊥♆.
10 ☉△♃. ☿□♇. ♀Q♅.
11 ☉✱♆. ☿▽♇.
12 ☿⚼♄. 13 ☉⊥♅.
14 ☿⊻♂. ☿∠♆. ♀#♃.
16 ☉#♂. 17 ♀Q♄.
19 ☉△♇. ♄Stat.
20 ☿⊥♂. ☿⊻♅. ♂Q♇.
21 ☿△♃. ☿△♄. ☿#♅.
22 ☉∠♅.
23 ☿⊥♅. ☿✱♆. ♀□♂.
24 ☉⚼♃. ☉Q♆. ☿#♂.
26 ☿△♇.
27 ♀✱♄. ♀□♅.
28 ☿∠♂. ☿∠♅. ♀☍♃.
29 ☿⚼♃. ☿Q♆. ♂☌♅. ☉#♆.
30 ☿∠♀. ♂□♃. ♂▽♄.

LAST QUARTER–Apr.10,18h.04m. (20°♑29′)

NEW MOON–May 16,19h.27m. (25°♉33′)

D M	D W	Sidereal Time	☉ Long.	☉ Dec.	☽ Long.	☽ Lat.	☽ Dec.	☽ Node	24h. ☽ Long.	24h. ☽ Dec.
		h m s	° ′ ″	° ′	° ′ ″	° ′	° ′	° ′	° ′ ″	° ′
1	T	2 36 09	10 ♉ 44 42	15 N03	0 ♏ 39 02	3 S 39	15 S 07	13 ♓ 17	6 ♏ 35 38	17 S 30
2	W	2 40 06	11 42 55	15 21	12 33 30	4 18	19 42	13 14	18 32 50	21 44
3	Th	2 44 02	12 41 06	15 39	24 33 48	4 46	23 32	13 11	0 ♐ 36 33	25 05
4	F	2 47 59	13 39 15	15 56	6 ♐ 41 15	5 01	26 22	13 08	12 48 03	27 21
5	S	2 51 55	14 37 23	16 14	18 57 08	5 03	28 01	13 05	25 08 40	28 19
6	Su	2 55 52	15 35 30	16 31	1 ♑ 22 52	4 50	28 16	13 01	7 ♑ 39 58	27 51
7	M	2 59 49	16 33 34	16 47	14 00 13	4 23	27 04	12 58	20 23 56	25 55
8	T	3 03 45	17 31 38	17 04	26 51 23	3 43	24 26	12 55	3 ♒ 22 56	22 36
9	W	3 07 42	18 29 40	17 20	9 ♒ 58 53	2 50	20 28	12 52	16 39 34	18 03
10	Th	3 11 38	19 27 41	17 36	23 25 18	1 46	15 23	12 49	0 ♓ 16 20	12 29
11	F	3 15 35	20 25 40	17 51	7 ♓ 12 52	0 S 35	9 24	12 45	14 15 00	6 S 09
12	S	3 19 31	21 23 38	18 07	21 22 45	0 N 41	2 S 48	12 42	28 35 57	0 N 38
13	Su	3 23 28	22 21 35	18 22	5 ♈ 54 18	1 55	4 N 06	12 39	13 ♈ 17 19	7 33
14	M	3 27 24	23 19 30	18 36	20 44 18	3 03	10 55	12 36	28 14 25	14 10
15	T	3 31 21	24 17 25	18 51	5 ♉ 46 38	3 59	17 12	12 33	13 ♉ 19 48	20 00
16	W	3 35 18	25 15 18	19 05	20 52 40	4 39	22 27	12 30	28 23 59	24 33
17	Th	3 39 14	26 13 09	19 18	5 ♊ 52 29	4 59	26 12	12 26	13 ♊ 17 00	27 23
18	F	3 43 11	27 10 59	19 32	20 36 30	4 59	28 05	12 23	27 50 06	28 17
19	S	3 47 07	28 08 48	19 45	4 ♋ 57 10	4 40	28 01	12 20	11 ♋ 57 14	27 17
20	Su	3 51 04	29 ♉ 06 35	19 58	18 50 03	4 05	26 09	12 17	25 35 34	24 39
21	M	3 55 00	0 ♊ 04 20	20 10	2 ♌ 13 56	3 17	22 51	12 14	8 ♌ 45 24	20 47
22	T	3 58 57	1 02 04	20 22	15 10 25	2 20	18 31	12 11	21 29 27	16 04
23	W	4 02 53	1 59 46	20 34	27 43 07	1 18	13 29	12 07	3 ♍ 52 02	10 48
24	Th	4 06 50	2 57 26	20 45	9 ♍ 56 51	0 N 14	8 03	12 04	15 58 15	5 N 16
25	F	4 10 47	3 55 05	20 56	21 56 56	0 S 49	2 N 26	12 01	27 53 31	0 S 23
26	S	4 14 43	4 52 42	21 07	3 ♎ 48 40	1 50	3 S 12	11 58	9 ♎ 42 58	5 58
27	Su	4 18 40	5 50 18	21 17	15 37 00	2 45	8 41	11 55	21 31 16	11 20
28	M	4 22 36	6 47 53	21 27	27 26 14	3 33	13 53	11 51	3 ♏ 22 20	16 18
29	T	4 26 33	7 45 26	21 36	9 ♏ 19 55	4 13	18 35	11 48	15 19 18	20 42
30	W	4 30 29	8 42 58	21 45	21 20 43	4 41	22 37	11 45	27 24 24	24 17
31	Th	4 34 26	9 ♊ 40 29	21 N54	3 ♐ 30 29	4 S 57	25 S 42	11 ♓ 42	9 ♐ 39 04	26 S 50

D M	Mercury Lat.	Mercury Dec.		Venus Lat.	Venus Dec.		Mars Lat.	Mars Dec.		Jupiter Lat.	Jupiter Dec.
	° ′	° ′	° ′	° ′	° ′	° ′	° ′	° ′	° ′	° ′	° ′
1	0 S 28	13 N59	14 N 50	2 N 19	25 N32	25 N38	1 S 27	5 S 35	5 S 17	0 N 44	22 S 14
3	0 S 07	15 39	16 28	2 23	25 43	25 48	1 27	4 59	4 41	0 44	22 13
5	0 N 14	17 15	18 01	2 27	25 51	25 54	1 28	4 24	4 06	0 44	22 12
7	0 35	18 46	19 29	2 31	25 57	25 59	1 28	3 48	3 30	0 44	22 12
9	0 55	20 10	20 48	2 34	26 00	26 00	1 29	3 12	2 54	0 44	22 11
11	1 15	21 25	21 59	2 36	26 00	25 59	1 29	2 36	2 18	0 44	22 10
13	1 32	22 31	23 00	2 39	25 57	25 55	1 30	2 00	1 42	0 44	22 09
15	1 47	23 27	23 51	2 40	25 52	25 49	1 30	1 24	1 06	0 44	22 08
17	1 59	24 13	24 32	2 42	25 45	25 40	1 30	0 48	0 S 30	0 44	22 07
19	2 08	24 48	25 02	2 43	25 35	25 29	1 31	0 S 12	0 N 06	0 43	22 05
21	2 14	25 14	25 23	2 43	25 22	25 15	1 31	0 N23	0 41	0 43	22 04
23	2 17	25 30	25 35	2 43	25 08	24 59	1 31	0 59	1 17	0 43	22 03
25	2 17	25 38	25 39	2 43	24 51	24 41	1 31	1 35	1 52	0 43	22 02
27	2 13	25 38	25 36	2 42	24 31	24 21	1 31	2 10	2 28	0 43	22 00
29	2 06	25 32	25 N 27	2 40	24 10	23 N58	1 31	2 45	3 N 03	0 43	21 59
31	1 N55	25 N20		2 N 38	23 N46		1 S 31	3 N20		0 N 42	21 S 58

FIRST QUARTER–May 23,21h.02m. (2°♍21′)

FULL MOON–May 2,10h.09m. (11°♏38′)

EPHEMERIS]				MAY 2007													11
D	☿	♀	♂	♃	♄	♅	♆	♇	Lunar Aspects								
M	Long.	Long.	Long.	Long.	Long.	Long.	Long.	Long.	☉	☿	♀	♂	♃	♄	♅	♆	♇
	° ′	° ′	° ′	° ′	° ′	° ′	° ′	° ′									
1	8♉47	22♊22	19♓16	18♐47	18♌17	17♓36	21♒53	28♐44				⚼	∠		⚼		⚹
2	10 55	23 30	20 02	18R 43	18 18	17 38	21 54	28R 43	☍	☍	⚼			□	△		∠
3	13 05	24 37	20 48	18 38	18 19	17 40	21 54	28 42				△	⚺			□	⚺
4	15 14	25 45	21 33	18 33	18 21	17 43	21 55	28 41									
5	17 24	26 52	22 19	18 28	18 22	17 45	21 56	28 40				□	☌	△	□	⚹	
6	19 34	27 59	23 05	18 23	18 24	17 47	21 56	28 39	⚼	⚼	☍			⚼		∠	☌
7	21 44	29♊06	23 51	18 17	18 26	17 49	21 57	28 38	△				⚺		⚹		
8	23 53	0♋13	24 36	18 12	18 28	17 51	21 58	28 37		△		⚹	∠		∠	⚺	⚺
9	26 01	1 19	25 22	18 06	18 30	17 53	21 58	28 36				∠					∠
10	28♉08	2 25	26 08	18 00	18 32	17 55	21 59	28 35	□	□	⚼	⚺	⚹	☍	⚺	☌	⚹
11	0♊14	3 32	26 54	17 55	18 34	17 57	21 59	28 34			△						
12	2 18	4 38	27 39	17 49	18 37	17 59	21 59	28 32	⚹			☌	□		☌	⚺	□
13	4 21	5 43	28 25	17 42	18 39	18 01	22 00	28 31	∠	⚹	□			⚼		∠	
14	6 21	6 49	29 10	17 36	18 41	18 03	22 00	28 30	⚺	∠			△	△	⚺	⚹	
15	8 18	7 54	29♓56	17 30	18 44	18 05	22 01	28 29		⚺	⚹	⚺	⚼		∠		△
16	10 13	8 59	0♈42	17 23	18 47	18 07	22 01	28 28	☌		∠	∠		□	⚹	□	⚼
17	12 06	10 04	1 27	17 17	18 50	18 09	22 01	28 26		☌	⚺	⚹					
18	13 56	11 09	2 13	17 10	18 53	18 10	22 01	28 25	⚺				☍	⚹	□	△	
19	15 42	12 13	2 58	17 03	18 56	18 12	22 02	28 24				□		∠		⚼	☍
20	17 26	13 18	3 43	16 56	18 59	18 14	22 02	28 23	∠	⚺	☌			⚺	△		
21	19 07	14 21	4 29	16 49	19 02	18 15	22 02	28 21	⚹	∠		△	⚼		⚼		
22	20 44	15 25	5 14	16 42	19 05	18 17	22 02	28 20			⚺	⚼	△	●			⚼
23	22 18	16 29	5 59	16 35	19 08	18 18	22 02	28 19	□	⚹	∠					☍	△
24	23 49	17 32	6 45	16 28	19 12	18 20	22 02	28 17									
25	25 17	18 35	7 30	16 21	19 16	18 21	22R 02	28 16		□	⚹			□	⚺	☍	
26	26 41	19 37	8 15	16 14	19 19	18 22	22 02	28 14	△			☍		∠		⚼	□
27	28 02	20 40	9 00	16 06	19 23	18 24	22 02	28 13	⚼		□		⚹	⚹			
28	29♊20	21 42	9 45	15 59	19 27	18 25	22 02	28 12		△			∠			△	⚹
29	0♋34	22 43	10 30	15 51	19 31	18 26	22 02	28 10							⚼		∠
30	1 44	23 45	11 15	15 44	19 35	18 27	22 02	28 09		⚼	△	⚼	⚺	□	△	□	
31	2♋51	24♋46	12♈00	15♐36	19♌39	18♓29	22♒01	28♐07									⚺

D	Saturn		Uranus		Neptune		Pluto	
M	Lat.	Dec.	Lat.	Dec.	Lat.	Dec.	Lat.	Dec.
	° ′	° ′	° ′	° ′	° ′	° ′	° ′	° ′
1	1N18	16N35	0S45	5S36	0S15	14S27	7N02	16S24
3	1 18	16 34	0 45	5 34	0 15	14 27	7 02	16 24
5	1 18	16 33	0 45	5 32	0 15	14 26	7 03	16 23
7	1 18	16 32	0 45	5 30	0 15	14 26	7 03	16 23
9	1 18	16 31	0 45	5 29	0 15	14 26	7 03	16 23
11	1 17	16 29	0 45	5 27	0 15	14 25	7 03	16 23
13	1 17	16 28	0 45	5 26	0 15	14 25	7 03	16 23
15	1 17	16 26	0 45	5 25	0 15	14 25	7 03	16 23
17	1 17	16 24	0 46	5 23	0 15	14 25	7 03	16 23
19	1 17	16 22	0 46	5 22	0 15	14 25	7 03	16 23
21	1 17	16 20	0 46	5 21	0 15	14 24	7 03	16 23
23	1 17	16 18	0 46	5 20	0 15	14 24	7 03	16 23
25	1 17	16 16	0 46	5 19	0 15	14 25	7 03	16 23
27	1 17	16 13	0 46	5 18	0 15	14 25	7 03	16 23
29	1 16	16 11	0 46	5 17	0 15	14 25	7 03	16 23
31	1N16	16N08	0S46	5S16	0S16	14S25	7N03	16S23

Mutual Aspects

1 ♀△♆. ♂‖♅.
2 ☿#♆.
3 ☉☌☿. ☉±♃. ☿±♃. ☿⚼♇. ☉‖☿.
4 ☉⚼♇. ♂⚺♆. ☿‖♄. ☿#♇.
5 ☿⚻♃. ☿□♄. ☿⚹♅.
6 ♃△♄. ☉‖♄. ☉#♇.
7 ☿□♆. ☿±♇. ♀☍♇.
8 ☉⚹♅. ☿⊥♀. ♂±♄.
9 ☉⚻♃. ☉□♄. ☿⚹♂.
10 ☿⚻♇.
11 ☿Q♅. ♀∠♄. ♃□♅.
12 ♂⊥♆. ☿#♃.
13 ☉□♆. ☉±♇. ♂□♇.
14 ☿Q♄. ♀⚼♆.
15 ☿⚺♀. 18 ☿Q♂.
19 ☉⚻♇. ♄#♇.
20 ☿☍♃. ☿□♅. ♀⊥♄. ♂⚼♄.
21 ☉Q♅. ☿⚹♄.
22 ☿‖♀.
23 ☿△♆. ♀⚻♃. ♀±♆.
24 ♂∠♆.
25 ♀△♅. ♆Stat.
26 ♀⚺♄. 27 ☿☍♇.
28 ♀±♃. ♀⚻♆.
29 ☉Q♄. 30 ☉∠♀.
31 ☉#♃.

LAST QUARTER–May 10,04h.27m. (19°♒09′)

NEW MOON–June15,03h.13m. (23° ♊ 41′)

D M	D W	Sidereal Time	☉ Long.	☉ Dec.	☽ Long.	☽ Lat.	☽ Dec.	☽ Node	24h. ☽ Long.	24h. ☽ Dec.
		h m s	° ′ ″	° ′	° ′ ″	° ′	° ′	° ′	° ′ ″	° ′
1	F	4 38 22	10 ♊ 37 59	22 N03	15 ♐ 50 15	4 S 59	27 S 38	11 ♓ 39	22 ♐ 04 05	28 S 06
2	S	4 42 19	11 35 28	22 11	28 20 36	4 47	28 13	11 36	4 ♑ 39 49	27 57
3	Su	4 46 16	12 32 56	22 18	11 ♑ 01 45	4 21	27 19	11 32	17 26 28	26 19
4	M	4 50 12	13 30 23	22 25	23 53 59	3 41	24 57	11 29	0 ♒ 24 24	23 16
5	T	4 54 09	14 27 49	22 32	6 ♒ 57 49	2 49	21 15	11 26	13 34 20	18 58
6	W	4 58 05	15 25 14	22 39	20 14 08	1 47	16 26	11 23	26 57 22	13 40
7	Th	5 02 02	16 22 39	22 45	3 ♓ 44 13	0 S 38	10 44	11 20	10 ♓ 34 51	7 38
8	F	5 05 58	17 20 03	22 50	17 29 24	0 N35	4 S 25	11 17	24 27 58	1 S 07
9	S	5 09 55	18 17 27	22 55	1 ♈ 30 36	1 47	2 N14	11 13	8 ♈ 37 13	5 N35
10	Su	5 13 51	19 14 50	23 00	15 47 42	2 53	8 53	11 10	23 01 43	12 06
11	M	5 17 48	20 12 12	23 05	0 ♉ 18 52	3 50	15 10	11 07	7 ♉ 38 35	18 02
12	T	5 21 45	21 09 35	23 09	15 00 10	4 32	20 40	11 04	22 22 46	22 58
13	W	5 25 41	22 06 56	23 12	29 45 27	4 56	24 55	11 01	7 ♊ 07 15	26 26
14	Th	5 29 38	23 04 17	23 16	14 ♊ 27 07	5 00	27 30	10 57	21 44 04	28 05
15	F	5 33 34	24 01 38	23 18	28 57 10	4 45	28 11	10 54	6 ♋ 05 35	27 49
16	S	5 37 31	24 58 58	23 21	13 ♋ 08 39	4 13	26 59	10 51	20 05 49	25 45
17	Su	5 41 27	25 56 17	23 23	26 56 43	3 26	24 08	10 48	3 ♌ 41 10	22 13
18	M	5 45 24	26 53 36	23 24	10 ♌ 19 08	2 29	20 03	10 45	16 50 46	17 40
19	T	5 49 20	27 50 53	23 25	23 16 19	1 26	15 07	10 42	29 36 08	12 27
20	W	5 53 17	28 48 10	23 26	5 ♍ 50 43	0 N21	9 41	10 38	12 ♍ 00 36	6 52
21	Th	5 57 14	29 ♊ 45 26	23 26	18 06 23	0 S 45	4 N01	10 35	24 08 43	1 N10
22	F	6 01 10	0 ♋ 42 41	23 26	0 ♎ 08 14	1 46	1 S 41	10 32	6 ♎ 05 37	4 S 30
23	S	6 05 07	1 39 56	23 26	12 01 32	2 43	7 15	10 29	17 56 38	9 57
24	Su	6 09 03	2 37 10	23 25	23 51 34	3 32	12 33	10 26	29 46 55	15 02
25	M	6 13 00	3 34 23	23 24	5 ♏ 43 15	4 12	17 24	10 22	11 ♏ 41 06	19 36
26	T	6 16 56	4 31 36	23 22	17 40 55	4 42	21 37	10 19	23 43 06	23 25
27	W	6 20 53	5 28 48	23 20	29 48 02	4 59	24 59	10 16	5 ♐ 55 58	26 16
28	Th	6 24 49	6 26 00	23 17	12 ♐ 07 08	5 03	27 15	10 13	18 21 42	27 54
29	F	6 28 46	7 23 12	23 14	24 39 44	4 52	28 12	10 10	1 ♑ 01 16	28 07
30	S	6 32 43	8 ♋ 20 24	23 N11	7 ♑ 26 17	4 S 27	27 S 40	10 ♓ 07	13 ♑ 54 43	26 S 50

D M	Mercury Lat.	Mercury Dec.		Venus Lat.	Venus Dec.		Mars Lat.	Mars Dec.		Jupiter Lat.	Jupiter Dec.
	° ′	° ′	° ′	° ′	° ′	° ′	° ′	° ′	° ′	° ′	° ′
1	1 N48	25 N11	25 N 02	2 N 37	23 N34	23 N21	1 S 31	3 N38	3 N 55	0 N 42	21 S 57
3	1 33	24 52	24 40	2 34	23 07	22 53	1 31	4 13	4 30	0 42	21 55
5	1 14	24 28	24 14	2 30	22 39	22 24	1 31	4 47	5 04	0 42	21 54
7	0 52	24 01	23 46	2 26	22 09	21 53	1 31	5 21	5 39	0 42	21 52
9	0 N27	23 31	23 15	2 21	21 37	21 21	1 31	5 55	6 12	0 41	21 51
11	0 00	23 00	22 43	2 15	21 04	20 47	1 31	6 29	6 46	0 41	21 49
13	0 S 30	22 27	22 11	2 09	20 30	20 12	1 31	7 03	7 19	0 41	21 48
15	1 02	21 54	21 38	2 02	19 54	19 36	1 30	7 36	7 52	0 41	21 46
17	1 35	21 22	21 06	1 54	19 17	18 59	1 30	8 08	8 24	0 40	21 45
19	2 09	20 50	20 35	1 45	18 40	18 20	1 30	8 40	8 56	0 40	21 44
21	2 42	20 20	20 06	1 36	18 01	17 41	1 29	9 12	9 28	0 40	21 42
23	3 13	19 53	19 41	1 26	17 21	17 01	1 29	9 44	9 59	0 39	21 41
25	3 41	19 29	19 19	1 14	16 41	16 21	1 28	10 15	10 30	0 39	21 39
27	4 05	19 09	19 01	1 02	16 00	15 40	1 28	10 45	11 00	0 39	21 38
29	4 24	18 53	18 N 47	0 49	15 20	14 N59	1 27	11 15	11 N 30	0 38	21 37
31	4 S 38	18 N43		0 N 36	14 N38		1 S 27	11 N45		0 N 38	21 S 35

FIRST QUARTER–June22,13h.15m. (0° ♎ 46′)

FULL MOON–June 1,01h.04m. (10°♐ 12′) & June30,13h.49m. (8°♑25′)

EPHEMERIS]				JUNE	2007												13
D	☿	♀	♂	♃	♄	♅	♆	♇	Lunar Aspects								
M	Long.	Long.	Long.	Long.	Long.	Long.	Long.	Long.	☉	☿	♀	♂	♃	♄	♅	♆	♇
	° ′	° ′	° ′	° ′	° ′	° ′	° ′	° ′									
1	3♋54	25♋46	12♈45	15♐29	19♌43	18♓30	22♒01	28♐06	☍		⚼	△	☌	△	□	⚹	
2	4 54	26 47	13 30	15R 21	19 47	18 31	22R 01	28R 04									☌
3	5 50	27 47	14 15	15 13	19 51	18 32	22 01	28 03		☍		□	⚺	⚼		∠	
4	6 42	28 46	14 59	15 06	19 56	18 33	22 00	28 01	⚼		☍		∠		⚹	⚺	⚺
5	7 30	29♋45	15 44	14 58	20 00	18 34	22 00	28 00							∠		∠
6	8 14	0♌44	16 29	14 51	20 05	18 34	22 00	27 58	△	⚼		⚹	⚹	☍	⚺	☌	
7	8 53	1 42	17 13	14 43	20 10	18 35	21 59	27 57		△		∠					⚹
8	9 29	2 40	17 58	14 35	20 14	18 36	21 59	27 55	□		⚼	⚺	□		☌	⚺	
9	10 01	3 38	18 42	14 28	20 19	18 37	21 58	27 54			△			⚼		∠	□
10	10 28	4 35	19 27	14 20	20 24	18 37	21 58	27 52	⚹	□		☌	△	△	⚺	⚹	
11	10 50	5 32	20 11	14 12	20 29	18 38	21 57	27 51	∠		□		⚼		∠		△
12	11 08	6 28	20 56	14 05	20 34	18 39	21 57	27 49	⚺	⚹		⚺		□	⚹	□	⚼
13	11 22	7 24	21 40	13 57	20 39	18 39	21 56	27 48		∠		∠					
14	11 31	8 19	22 24	13 50	20 44	18 40	21 55	27 46		⚺	⚹		☍	⚹	□		
15	11 35	9 14	23 08	13 42	20 49	18 40	21 55	27 44	☌		∠	⚹		∠		△	☍
16	11R 35	10 08	23 53	13 35	20 55	18 40	21 54	27 43		☌	⚺				△	⚼	
17	11 31	11 01	24 37	13 28	21 00	18 41	21 53	27 41	⚺			□	⚼	⚺	⚼		
18	11 22	11 54	25 21	13 20	21 06	18 41	21 53	27 40	∠	⚺	●		△				⚼
19	11 09	12 47	26 04	13 13	21 11	18 41	21 52	27 38	⚹	∠		△		●		☍	△
20	10 52	13 38	26 48	13 06	21 17	18 41	21 51	27 37		⚹							
21	10 31	14 29	27 32	12 59	21 22	18 41	21 50	27 35			⚺	⚼	□	⚺	☍		
22	10 06	15 20	28 16	12 52	21 28	18 42	21 49	27 33	□		∠						□
23	9 39	16 09	28 59	12 45	21 34	18 42	21 49	27 32		□	⚹		⚹	∠		⚼	
24	9 09	16 58	29♈43	12 38	21 40	18R 42	21 48	27 30					∠	⚹		△	⚹
25	8 36	17 47	0♉26	12 31	21 46	18 41	21 47	27 29	△	△		☍			⚼		
26	8 02	18 34	1 10	12 25	21 52	18 41	21 46	27 27	⚼	⚼	□		⚺	□	△	□	∠
27	7 27	19 21	1 53	12 18	21 58	18 41	21 45	27 26									⚺
28	6 52	20 06	2 36	12 12	22 04	18 41	21 44	27 24				⚼	☌				
29	6 16	20 51	3 20	12 05	22 10	18 41	21 43	27 23			△			△	□	⚹	☌
30	5♋41	21♌35	4♉03	11♐59	22♌16	18♓40	21♒42	27♐21	☍	☍	⚼	△	⚺	⚼		∠	

D	Saturn		Uranus		Neptune		Pluto	
M	Lat.	Dec.	Lat.	Dec.	Lat.	Dec.	Lat.	Dec.
	° ′	° ′	° ′	° ′	° ′	° ′	° ′	° ′
1	1N16	16N07	0S46	5S15	0S16	14S25	7N03	16S23
3	1 16	16 04	0 46	5 15	0 16	14 25	7 03	16 23
5	1 16	16 01	0 46	5 14	0 16	14 25	7 03	16 23
7	1 16	15 58	0 46	5 13	0 16	14 26	7 03	16 23
9	1 16	15 55	0 46	5 13	0 16	14 26	7 03	16 23
11	1 16	15 52	0 46	5 13	0 16	14 26	7 03	16 23
13	1 16	15 48	0 47	5 12	0 16	14 27	7 02	16 23
15	1 16	15 45	0 47	5 12	0 16	14 27	7 02	16 23
17	1 16	15 42	0 47	5 12	0 16	14 28	7 02	16 23
19	1 16	15 38	0 47	5 12	0 16	14 28	7 02	16 23
21	1 16	15 34	0 47	5 12	0 16	14 29	7 02	16 23
23	1 16	15 31	0 47	5 12	0 16	14 29	7 01	16 24
25	1 15	15 27	0 47	5 12	0 16	14 30	7 01	16 24
27	1 15	15 23	0 47	5 12	0 16	14 31	7 01	16 24
29	1 15	15 19	0 47	5 12	0 16	14 31	7 01	16 24
31	1N15	15N15	0S47	5S12	0S16	14S32	7N00	16S24

Mutual Aspects

2 ☿∠♄.
3 ♀⊼♇.
4 ☿⚼♆. ♂△♃.
5 ☉☍♃. ♀⚼♃. ☉∥♀.
7 ♂⋕♅. 8 ♀⋕♃.
9 ☉□♅. ♀⚼♅. ♀±♇. ♂⚺♅.
11 ☉⚹♂. ☉⚹♄. ♂△♄. ☉∥☿.
13 ☉△♆. ♂⚹♆.
15 ☿⋕♃. ☿Stat.
17 ☿⚺♀. ♂⊥♅.
18 ☉∠♀.
19 ☉☍♇. ♀△♃. ♀±♅. ♀⚼♇.
21 ♂△♇.
22 ☿Q♂. ♂⚼♃.
23 ☿⊥♀. ♅Stat.
25 ♄☍♆.
26 ♀⊼♅. ♀⋕♇.
28 ☉☌☿. ☉⚼♆. ☿∠♄. ☿⚼♆.
29 ☉∠♄. ☿∠♀. ♂∠♅. ♀∥♄.
30 ♀☍♆. ♂Q♆.

LAST QUARTER–June 8,11h.43m. (17°♓19′)

NEW MOON–July14,12h.04m. (21°♋41′)

D M	D W	Sidereal Time	☉ Long.	☉ Dec.	☽ Long.	☽ Lat.	☽ Dec.	☽ Node	24h. ☽ Long.	24h. ☽ Dec.
		h m s	° ′ ″	° ′	° ′ ″	° ′	° ′	° ′	° ′ ″	° ′
1	Su	6 36 39	9 ♋ 17 35	23 N07	20 ♑ 26 27	3 S 47	25 S 38	10 ♓ 03	27 ♑ 01 23	24 S 04
2	M	6 40 36	10 14 46	23 03	3 ♒ 39 20	2 55	22 10	10 00	10 ♒ 20 10	19 58
3	T	6 44 32	11 11 57	22 58	17 03 46	1 52	17 30	9 57	23 49 58	14 48
4	W	6 48 29	12 09 09	22 53	0 ♓ 38 42	0 S 42	11 54	9 54	7 ♓ 29 50	8 50
5	Th	6 52 25	13 06 20	22 48	14 23 20	0 N 32	5 S 39	9 51	21 19 07	2 S 24
6	F	6 56 22	14 03 32	22 42	28 17 08	1 44	0 N 55	9 48	5 ♈ 17 19	4 N 14
7	S	7 00 18	15 00 44	22 36	12 ♈ 19 37	2 52	7 30	9 44	19 23 53	10 42
8	Su	7 04 15	15 57 56	22 29	26 29 59	3 49	13 46	9 41	3 ♉ 37 41	16 41
9	M	7 08 12	16 55 09	22 22	10 ♉ 46 43	4 32	19 22	9 38	17 56 41	21 47
10	T	7 12 08	17 52 22	22 15	25 07 10	4 59	23 53	9 35	2 ♊ 17 38	25 36
11	W	7 16 05	18 49 36	22 07	9 ♊ 27 32	5 07	26 55	9 32	16 36 13	27 48
12	Th	7 20 01	19 46 50	21 59	23 43 03	4 56	28 13	9 28	0 ♋ 47 23	28 10
13	F	7 23 58	20 44 04	21 50	7 ♋ 48 34	4 27	27 39	9 25	14 46 03	26 42
14	S	7 27 54	21 41 19	21 42	21 39 19	3 42	25 22	9 22	28 27 57	23 40
15	Su	7 31 51	22 38 34	21 32	5 ♌ 11 38	2 46	21 40	9 19	11 ♌ 50 09	19 24
16	M	7 35 47	23 35 50	21 23	18 23 26	1 43	16 57	9 16	24 51 29	14 19
17	T	7 39 44	24 33 05	21 13	1 ♍ 14 28	0 N 35	11 35	9 13	7 ♍ 32 34	8 45
18	W	7 43 41	25 30 21	21 02	13 46 08	0 S 33	5 53	9 09	19 55 33	2 N 59
19	Th	7 47 37	26 27 36	20 52	26 01 17	1 38	0 N 05	9 06	2 ♎ 03 52	2 S 47
20	F	7 51 34	27 24 52	20 41	8 ♎ 03 50	2 37	5 S 36	9 03	14 01 47	8 22
21	S	7 55 30	28 22 09	20 29	19 58 20	3 29	11 02	9 00	25 54 06	13 36
22	Su	7 59 27	29 ♋ 19 25	20 18	1 ♏ 49 43	4 12	16 03	8 57	7 ♏ 45 49	18 21
23	M	8 03 23	0 ♌ 16 42	20 06	13 43 00	4 44	20 28	8 54	19 41 51	22 24
24	T	8 07 20	1 13 59	19 53	25 42 55	5 04	24 07	8 50	1 ♐ 46 42	25 34
25	W	8 11 16	2 11 17	19 40	7 ♐ 53 42	5 11	26 44	8 47	14 04 18	27 36
26	Th	8 15 13	3 08 35	19 27	20 18 51	5 03	28 08	8 44	26 37 37	28 18
27	F	8 19 10	4 05 53	19 14	3 ♑ 00 48	4 41	28 05	8 41	9 ♑ 28 31	27 30
28	S	8 23 06	5 03 13	19 00	16 00 48	4 04	26 31	8 38	22 37 35	25 09
29	Su	8 27 03	6 00 32	18 46	29 18 45	3 12	23 26	8 34	6 ♒ 04 06	21 22
30	M	8 30 59	6 57 53	18 32	12 ♒ 53 21	2 09	19 01	8 31	19 46 11	16 23
31	T	8 34 56	7 ♌ 55 14	18 N17	26 ♒ 42 15	0 S 57	13 S 31	8 ♓ 28	3 ♓ 41 09	10 S 27

D M	Mercury Lat.	Mercury Dec.		Venus Lat.	Venus Dec.		Mars Lat.	Mars Dec.		Jupiter Lat.	Jupiter Dec.
	° ′	° ′	° ′	° ′	° ′	° ′	° ′	° ′	° ′	° ′	° ′
1	4 S 38	18 N43	18 N 40	0 N 36	14 N38	14 N18	1 S 27	11 N45	11 N 59	0 N 38	21 S 35
3	4 45	18 38	18 37	0 21	13 57	13 37	1 26	12 14	12 28	0 38	21 34
5	4 46	18 38	18 40	0 N 05	13 16	12 56	1 25	12 42	12 56	0 37	21 33
7	4 41	18 44	18 48	0 S 12	12 35	12 15	1 25	13 10	13 24	0 37	21 32
9	4 31	18 54	19 01	0 29	11 55	11 35	1 24	13 38	13 51	0 36	21 31
11	4 16	19 09	19 18	0 48	11 15	10 56	1 23	14 05	14 18	0 36	21 30
13	3 57	19 28	19 38	1 08	10 36	10 17	1 22	14 31	14 44	0 36	21 29
15	3 34	19 49	20 00	1 29	9 58	9 40	1 21	14 57	15 09	0 35	21 28
17	3 09	20 12	20 23	1 51	9 22	9 04	1 20	15 22	15 34	0 35	21 27
19	2 43	20 35	20 46	2 14	8 47	8 30	1 19	15 46	15 58	0 34	21 27
21	2 15	20 57	21 07	2 38	8 13	7 57	1 18	16 10	16 22	0 34	21 26
23	1 46	21 17	21 25	3 03	7 42	7 27	1 17	16 33	16 44	0 34	21 26
25	1 17	21 33	21 38	3 28	7 13	6 59	1 16	16 56	17 07	0 33	21 26
27	0 49	21 43	21 46	3 55	6 46	6 34	1 14	17 17	17 28	0 33	21 25
29	0 S 21	21 46	21 N 45	4 21	6 23	6 N12	1 13	17 39	17 N 49	0 32	21 25
31	0 N04	21 N41		4 S 48	6 N02		1 S 12	17 N59		0 N 32	21 S 25

FIRST QUARTER–July22,06h.29m. (29°♎06′)

FULL MOON–July30,00h.48m. (6°♒31′)

D M	☿ Long.	♀ Long.	♂ Long.	♃ Long.	♄ Long.	♅ Long.	♆ Long.	♇ Long.
	° ′	° ′	° ′	° ′	° ′	° ′	° ′	° ′
1	5♋08	22♌18	4♉46	11♐53	22♌22	18♓40	21♒41	27♐20
2	4R 36	23 00	5 29	11R 47	22 28	18R 40	21R 40	27R 18
3	4 07	23 41	6 11	11 41	22 35	18 39	21 38	27 17
4	3 41	24 21	6 54	11 36	22 41	18 39	21 37	27 15
5	3 18	25 00	7 37	11 30	22 48	18 38	21 36	27 14
6	3 00	25 38	8 20	11 25	22 54	18 38	21 35	27 12
7	2 45	26 14	9 02	11 19	23 01	18 37	21 34	27 11
8	2 35	26 50	9 45	11 14	23 07	18 36	21 32	27 09
9	2 29	27 24	10 27	11 09	23 14	18 36	21 31	27 08
10	2D 29	27 56	11 09	11 04	23 21	18 35	21 30	27 06
11	2 33	28 28	11 51	10 59	23 27	18 34	21 29	27 05
12	2 43	28 58	12 34	10 55	23 34	18 33	21 27	27 03
13	2 58	29 26	13 16	10 50	23 41	18 32	21 26	27 02
14	3 19	29♌53	13 57	10 46	23 48	18 31	21 25	27 01
15	3 45	0♍18	14 39	10 42	23 55	18 30	21 23	26 59
16	4 16	0 42	15 21	10 38	24 02	18 29	21 22	26 58
17	4 53	1 04	16 03	10 34	24 09	18 28	21 20	26 57
18	5 35	1 24	16 44	10 31	24 16	18 27	21 19	26 55
19	6 22	1 43	17 25	10 27	24 23	18 26	21 18	26 54
20	7 14	1 59	18 07	10 24	24 30	18 25	21 16	26 53
21	8 12	2 14	18 48	10 21	24 37	18 23	21 15	26 51
22	9 14	2 27	19 29	10 18	24 44	18 22	21 13	26 50
23	10 22	2 37	20 10	10 15	24 51	18 21	21 12	26 49
24	11 35	2 45	20 51	10 13	24 58	18 19	21 10	26 48
25	12 52	2 52	21 31	10 10	25 05	18 18	21 09	26 46
26	14 14	2 56	22 12	10 08	25 13	18 17	21 07	26 45
27	15 41	2 57	22 52	10 06	25 20	18 15	21 06	26 44
28	17 12	2R 57	23 33	10 04	25 27	18 14	21 04	26 43
29	18 47	2 54	24 13	10 03	25 35	18 12	21 03	26 42
30	20 27	2 48	24 53	10 01	25 42	18 10	21 01	26 41
31	22♋10	2♍41	25♉33	10♐00	25♌49	18♓09	20♒59	26♐40

D M	Lunar Aspects ☉	☿	♀	♂	♃	♄	♅	♆	♇
1					∠		✱	⚺	
2				□			∠		⚺
3		⚼			✱	☍	⚺	☌	∠
4	⚼	△	☍	✱					✱
5	△				□		☌		
6		□		∠				⚺	□
7	□		⚼	⚺	△	⚼	⚺	∠	
8		✱	△		⚼	△	∠	✱	△
9	✱	∠		☌					⚼
10			□			□	✱	□	
11	∠	⚺		⚺	☍				
12	⚺		✱	∠		✱	□	△	☍
13		☌	∠	✱		∠		⚼	
14	☌				⚼	⚺	△		
15		⚺	⚺		△		⚼		
16	⚺	∠		□		●		☍	⚼
17		✱	☌						△
18	∠			△	□		☍		
19	✱		⚺			⚺			□
20		□		⚼	✱	∠		⚼	
21			∠		∠	✱		△	
22	□		✱				⚼		✱
23		△			⚺		△		∠
24	△	⚼		☍		□		□	⚺
25			□		☌				
26	⚼					△	□	✱	
27			△	⚼				∠	☌
28		☍	⚼		⚺	⚼	✱	⚺	
29				△	∠		∠		⚺
30	☍				✱		⚺		∠
31			☍	□		☍		☌	✱

D M	Saturn Lat.	Saturn Dec.	Uranus Lat.	Uranus Dec.	Neptune Lat.	Neptune Dec.	Pluto Lat.	Pluto Dec.
	° ′	° ′	° ′	° ′	° ′	° ′	° ′	° ′
1	1N15	15N15	0S47	5S12	0S16	14S32	7N00	16S24
3	1 15	15 11	0 47	5 13	0 16	14 33	7 00	16 25
5	1 15	15 06	0 47	5 13	0 16	14 34	7 00	16 25
7	1 15	15 02	0 47	5 14	0 16	14 34	6 59	16 25
9	1 15	14 58	0 47	5 14	0 16	14 35	6 59	16 26
11	1 15	14 53	0 48	5 15	0 16	14 36	6 59	16 26
13	1 15	14 49	0 48	5 16	0 16	14 37	6 58	16 26
15	1 15	14 44	0 48	5 17	0 16	14 38	6 58	16 27
17	1 15	14 40	0 48	5 18	0 16	14 39	6 58	16 27
19	1 15	14 35	0 48	5 19	0 16	14 40	6 57	16 27
21	1 15	14 30	0 48	5 20	0 16	14 41	6 57	16 28
23	1 15	14 25	0 48	5 21	0 16	14 42	6 56	16 28
25	1 16	14 21	0 48	5 22	0 16	14 43	6 56	16 28
27	1 16	14 16	0 48	5 23	0 17	14 44	6 55	16 29
29	1 16	14 11	0 48	5 24	0 17	14 45	6 55	16 29
31	1N16	14N06	0S48	5S26	0S17	14S46	6N54	16S30

Mutual Aspects

1 ☿✱♂. ♀☌♄. ♀∥Ψ.
2 ♂±♃. 3 ☉∇♃.
6 ♀∥♂.
8 ☉±Ψ.
9 ☉±♃. ☉⊥♄. ♀△♇.
10 ♂∇♃. ☿Stat.
11 ☉△♅. ♂⚼♇.
13 ♂∥Ψ.
14 ☉∇Ψ. ♂∥♄.
15 ☉∥♃.
17 ☉⚺♄. ♄∥Ψ.
18 ☉⊥♀. ☉⚼♃.
19 ☉∇♇. ☿⚼Ψ.
20 ♂✱♅. ☉∥☿.
22 ☿∠♄.
23 ☿∇♃. ♂∥♇.
24 ♂□Ψ. ♂±♇. ☿∥♃.
26 ☉⚺♀. ☉⚼♅. ☉±♇.
27 ☿±♃. ☿±Ψ. ♀Stat.
28 ☿∠♀. 29 ☿△♅.
30 ☉Q♂. ☿⊥♄. ☿∇Ψ.
31 ♂□♄.

LAST QUARTER–July 7,16h.54m. (15°♈12′)

NEW MOON – Aug.12,23h.02m. (19° ♌ 51′)

D M	D W	Sidereal Time	☉ Long.	☉ Dec.	☽ Long.	☽ Lat.	☽ Dec.	☽ Node	24h. ☽ Long.	24h. ☽ Dec.
		h m s	° ′ ″	° ′	° ′ ″	° ′	° ′	° ′	° ′ ″	° ′
1	W	8 38 52	8 ♌ 52 36	18 N02	10 ♓ 42 27	0 N19	7 S 15	8 ♓ 25	17 ♓ 45 46	3 S 57
2	Th	8 42 49	9 49 59	17 47	24 50 41	1 35	0 S 35	8 22	1 ♈ 56 49	2 N47
3	F	8 46 45	10 47 23	17 32	9 ♈ 03 46	2 46	6 N08	8 19	16 11 12	9 24
4	S	8 50 42	11 44 48	17 16	23 18 47	3 47	12 34	8 15	0 ♉ 26 13	15 33
5	Su	8 54 39	12 42 14	17 00	7 ♉ 33 11	4 33	18 20	8 12	14 39 27	20 51
6	M	8 58 35	13 39 42	16 44	21 44 42	5 03	23 04	8 09	28 48 42	24 57
7	T	9 02 32	14 37 11	16 27	5 ♊ 51 09	5 14	26 26	8 06	12 ♊ 51 49	27 31
8	W	9 06 28	15 34 42	16 10	19 50 24	5 07	28 09	8 03	26 46 38	28 20
9	Th	9 10 25	16 32 14	15 53	3 ♋ 40 14	4 42	28 05	8 00	10 ♋ 30 58	27 24
10	F	9 14 21	17 29 47	15 35	17 18 33	4 01	26 18	7 56	24 02 45	24 50
11	S	9 18 18	18 27 21	15 18	0 ♌ 43 24	3 07	23 02	7 53	7 ♌ 20 17	20 58
12	Su	9 22 14	19 24 57	15 00	13 53 18	2 04	18 39	7 50	20 22 22	16 08
13	M	9 26 11	20 22 33	14 42	26 47 28	0 N56	13 28	7 47	3 ♍ 08 37	10 41
14	T	9 30 08	21 20 11	14 23	9 ♍ 25 54	0 S 13	7 50	7 44	15 39 29	4 N56
15	W	9 34 04	22 17 50	14 05	21 49 35	1 21	2 N00	7 40	27 56 25	0 S 55
16	Th	9 38 01	23 15 30	13 46	4 ♎ 00 21	2 24	3 S 47	7 37	10 ♎ 01 44	6 37
17	F	9 41 57	24 13 11	13 27	16 00 58	3 19	9 22	7 34	21 58 31	12 01
18	S	9 45 54	25 10 53	13 08	27 54 53	4 06	14 33	7 31	3 ♏ 50 35	16 57
19	Su	9 49 50	26 08 36	12 48	9 ♏ 46 09	4 41	19 11	7 28	15 42 11	21 14
20	M	9 53 47	27 06 21	12 29	21 39 14	5 05	23 05	7 25	27 37 53	24 42
21	T	9 57 43	28 04 06	12 09	3 ♐ 38 44	5 16	26 03	7 21	9 ♐ 42 21	27 07
22	W	10 01 40	29 01 53	11 49	15 49 17	5 13	27 52	7 18	22 00 03	28 18
23	Th	10 05 37	29 ♌ 59 41	11 28	28 15 08	4 56	28 21	7 15	4 ♑ 34 57	28 03
24	F	10 09 33	0 ♍ 57 30	11 08	10 ♑ 59 53	4 23	27 21	7 12	17 30 12	26 17
25	S	10 13 30	1 55 20	10 47	24 06 06	3 36	24 50	7 09	0 ♒ 47 41	23 02
26	Su	10 17 26	2 53 12	10 27	7 ♒ 34 55	2 36	20 54	7 06	14 27 42	18 26
27	M	10 21 23	3 51 05	10 06	21 25 46	1 26	15 43	7 02	28 28 46	12 45
28	T	10 25 19	4 48 59	9 45	5 ♓ 36 12	0 S 08	9 35	6 59	12 ♓ 47 29	6 S 16
29	W	10 29 16	5 46 55	9 24	20 01 59	1 N11	2 S 51	6 56	27 18 57	0 N37
30	Th	10 33 12	6 44 52	9 02	4 ♈ 37 36	2 27	4 N05	6 53	11 ♈ 57 10	7 31
31	F	10 37 09	7 ♍ 42 52	8 N41	19 ♈ 16 51	3 N33	10 N50	6 ♓ 50	26 ♈ 35 54	14 N00

D M	Mercury Lat.	Mercury Dec.		Venus Lat.	Venus Dec.		Mars Lat.	Mars Dec.		Jupiter Lat.	Jupiter Dec.
	° ′	° ′	° ′	° ′	° ′	° ′	° ′	° ′	° ′	° ′	° ′
1	0 N16	21 N35	21 N 27	5 S 02	5 N53	5 N45	1 S 11	18 N09	18 N 19	0 N 32	21 S 25
3	0 39	21 16	21 02	5 28	5 38	5 31	1 10	18 29	18 38	0 31	21 26
5	0 58	20 46	20 26	5 54	5 26	5 22	1 08	18 48	18 57	0 31	21 26
7	1 14	20 05	19 41	6 20	5 18	5 16	1 07	19 06	19 15	0 31	21 26
9	1 27	19 14	18 45	6 43	5 15	5 14	1 05	19 23	19 32	0 30	21 27
11	1 36	18 14	17 41	7 05	5 15	5 16	1 04	19 40	19 48	0 30	21 27
13	1 42	17 06	16 29	7 25	5 19	5 22	1 02	19 56	20 04	0 29	21 28
15	1 45	15 51	15 12	7 41	5 27	5 32	1 00	20 12	20 19	0 29	21 29
17	1 45	14 31	13 49	7 55	5 38	5 45	0 59	20 27	20 34	0 29	21 30
19	1 43	13 07	12 23	8 05	5 52	6 00	0 57	20 41	20 47	0 28	21 31
21	1 38	11 39	10 54	8 12	6 09	6 18	0 55	20 54	21 00	0 28	21 32
23	1 32	10 09	9 23	8 15	6 28	6 38	0 53	21 07	21 13	0 27	21 33
25	1 23	8 38	7 52	8 15	6 49	6 59	0 51	21 19	21 25	0 27	21 34
27	1 13	7 05	6 19	8 12	7 10	7 21	0 49	21 30	21 36	0 27	21 36
29	1 02	5 33	4 N 47	8 05	7 32	7 N43	0 47	21 41	21 N 46	0 26	21 37
31	0 N49	4 N01		7 S 56	7 N54		0 S 45	21 N51		0 N 26	21 S 39

FIRST QUARTER – Aug.20,23h.54m. (27° ♏ 35′)

FULL MOON–Aug.28,10h.35m. (4°♓46′)

EPHEMERIS]				AUGUST 2007													17
D	☿	♀	♂	♃	♄	♅	♆	♇	Lunar Aspects								
M	Long.	Long.	Long.	Long.	Long.	Long.	Long.	Long.	☉	☿	♀	♂	♃	♄	♅	♆	♇
	° ′	° ′	° ′	° ′	° ′	° ′	° ′	° ′									
1	23♋56	2♍30	26♉13	9♐59	25♌57	18♓07	20♒58	26♐39		⚼			□				
2	25 46	2R 18	26 53	9R 58	26 04	18R 05	20R 56	26R 38	⚼	△		✱			☌	⚺	□
3	27 39	2 03	27 32	9 57	26 12	18 04	20 55	26 37	△			∠	△	⚼		∠	
4	29♋34	1 46	28 12	9 56	26 19	18 02	20 53	26 36			⚼	⚺	⚼	△	⚺	✱	△
5	1♌32	1 26	28 51	9 56	26 27	18 00	20 51	26 35	□	□	△				∠		⚼
6	3 32	1 05	29♉31	9 56	26 34	17 58	20 50	26 34						□	✱	□	
7	5 33	0 41	0♊10	9D 56	26 42	17 57	20 48	26 33		✱	□	☌	☍				
8	7 35	0♍15	0 49	9 56	26 49	17 55	20 47	26 32	✱	∠					□	△	☍
9	9 38	29♌47	1 28	9 56	26 57	17 53	20 45	26 31	∠		✱	⚺		✱		⚼	
10	11 41	29 18	2 06	9 57	27 04	17 51	20 43	26 30	⚺	⚺	∠	∠		∠	△		
11	13 45	28 47	2 45	9 58	27 12	17 49	20 42	26 29			⚺	✱	⚼	⚺	⚼		
12	15 49	28 14	3 23	9 59	27 19	17 47	20 40	26 29	☌	●			△				⚼
13	17 52	27 40	4 01	10 00	27 27	17 45	20 38	26 28			☌			●		☍	△
14	19 55	27 05	4 40	10 01	27 35	17 43	20 37	26 27				□	□				
15	21 57	26 29	5 17	10 02	27 42	17 41	20 35	26 26	⚺	⚺	⚺			⚺	☍		□
16	23 58	25 52	5 55	10 04	27 50	17 39	20 34	26 26	∠	∠		△				⚼	
17	25 58	25 15	6 33	10 06	27 58	17 36	20 32	26 25			∠	⚼	✱	∠		△	
18	27 57	24 38	7 10	10 08	28 05	17 34	20 30	26 24	✱	✱	✱		∠	✱	⚼		✱
19	29♌55	24 01	7 48	10 10	28 13	17 32	20 29	26 24					⚺				∠
20	1♍52	23 24	8 25	10 12	28 20	17 30	20 27	26 23	□		□				△	□	⚺
21	3 47	22 47	9 02	10 15	28 28	17 28	20 25	26 23		□		☍		□			
22	5 41	22 12	9 38	10 18	28 36	17 25	20 24	26 22			△		☌		□	✱	
23	7 34	21 37	10 15	10 21	28 43	17 23	20 22	26 22	△					△			☌
24	9 25	21 03	10 51	10 24	28 51	17 21	20 21	26 21	⚼	△	⚼		⚺	⚼	✱	∠	
25	11 15	20 31	11 28	10 27	28 59	17 19	20 19	26 21		⚼		⚼	∠			⚺	⚺
26	13 04	20 00	12 04	10 30	29 06	17 16	20 17	26 20				△	✱		∠		∠
27	14 52	19 31	12 39	10 34	29 14	17 14	20 16	26 20			☍				⚺	☌	✱
28	16 38	19 04	13 15	10 38	29 21	17 12	20 14	26 20	●☍				□	☍			
29	18 22	18 39	13 51	10 42	29 29	17 09	20 13	26 19		☍		□			☌	⚺	□
30	20 06	18 16	14 26	10 46	29 37	17 07	20 11	26 19			⚼		△			∠	
31	21♍48	17♌56	15♊01	10♐50	29♌44	17♓05	20♒10	26♐19	⚼		△	✱	⚼	⚼	⚺	✱	△

D	Saturn		Uranus		Neptune		Pluto	
M	Lat.	Dec.	Lat.	Dec.	Lat.	Dec.	Lat.	Dec.
	° ′	° ′	° ′	° ′	° ′	° ′	° ′	° ′
1	1N16	14N03	0S48	5S26	0S17	14S46	6N54	16S30
3	1 16	13 59	0 48	5 28	0 17	14 47	6 53	16 30
5	1 16	13 53	0 48	5 29	0 17	14 48	6 53	16 31
7	1 16	13 48	0 48	5 31	0 17	14 49	6 52	16 31
9	1 16	13 43	0 48	5 32	0 17	14 50	6 52	16 32
11	1 16	13 38	0 48	5 34	0 17	14 52	6 51	16 32
13	1 16	13 33	0 48	5 35	0 17	14 53	6 51	16 33
15	1 16	13 28	0 49	5 37	0 17	14 54	6 50	16 34
17	1 17	13 23	0 49	5 39	0 17	14 55	6 50	16 34
19	1 17	13 18	0 49	5 40	0 17	14 56	6 49	16 35
21	1 17	13 12	0 49	5 42	0 17	14 57	6 48	16 35
23	1 17	13 07	0 49	5 44	0 17	14 58	6 48	16 36
25	1 17	13 02	0 49	5 46	0 17	14 59	6 47	16 36
27	1 17	12 57	0 49	5 47	0 17	15 00	6 47	16 37
29	1 17	12 52	0 49	5 49	0 17	15 01	6 46	16 38
31	1N18	12N46	0S49	5S51	0S17	15S02	6N45	16S38

Mutual Aspects

1 ☉∥♂.
2 ☉△♃. ☿⊥♀. ☿⚼♃. ☿⚺♄. ☿⚻♇.
♂⚻♇. ☿#♃.
3 ☿✱♂.
4 ☉±♅. ☉⚼♇.
5 ☿⚺♀. ♀#♅.
6 ☿⚼♅. ☿±♇. ♄△♇.
7 ♀□♂. ♂Q♅. ☉#♇. ♃Stat.
9 ☿△♃. ☿∥♂.
10 ☉⚻♅. ☿±♅. ☿⚼♇.
12 ☿Q♂. ☉#♆.
13 ☉☍♆. ☿⚻♅. ♀☌♄.
14 ☿☍♆. ☿#♇.
15 ☉☌☿. ♀△♇.
16 ☿#♆.
17 ☿☌♀. ☿△♇. ☉∥♄. ♀#♅.
18 ☉☌♀. ☿☌♄.
19 ☉△♇. ☿∥♄.
20 ☉∥☿. 21 ☉☌♄.
22 ♀Q♂.
23 ♂☍♃.
25 ☿□♂. ☿□♃. ♀☍♆.
27 ☿∥♀.
28 ☿☍♅. ♂#♃.
29 ☿⚺♀. ☿#♅.
30 ☿⚻♆.

LAST QUARTER–Aug. 5,21h.20m. (13°♉05′)

NEW MOON – Sep.11,12h.44m. (18°♍25′)

D M	D W	Sidereal Time	☉ Long.	☉ Dec.	☽ Long.	☽ Lat.	☽ Dec.	☽ Node	24h. ☽ Long.	24h. ☽ Dec.
		h m s	° ′ ″	° ′	° ′ ″	° ′	° ′	° ′	° ′ ″	° ′
1	S	10 41 06	8♍40 53	8 N19	3♉53 37	4 N26	16 N59	6♓46	11♉09 23	19 N41
2	Su	10 45 02	9 38 56	7 57	18 22 37	5 00	22 06	6 43	25 32 53	24 10
3	M	10 48 59	10 37 01	7 35	2♊39 49	5 16	25 51	6 40	9♊43 07	27 08
4	T	10 52 55	11 35 08	7 13	16 42 37	5 13	27 58	6 37	23 38 10	28 21
5	W	10 56 52	12 33 17	6 51	0♋29 43	4 51	28 17	6 34	7♋17 17	27 48
6	Th	11 00 48	13 31 28	6 29	14 00 54	4 14	26 54	6 31	20 40 37	25 38
7	F	11 04 45	14 29 41	6 06	27 16 33	3 23	24 02	6 27	3♌48 47	22 07
8	S	11 08 41	15 27 56	5 44	10♌17 28	2 23	19 58	6 24	16 42 43	17 35
9	Su	11 12 38	16 26 13	5 21	23 04 40	1 17	15 02	6 21	29 23 25	12 21
10	M	11 16 35	17 24 32	4 58	5♍39 08	0 N08	9 34	6 18	11♍51 57	6 42
11	T	11 20 31	18 22 52	4 36	18 02 01	1 S00	3 N49	6 15	24 09 30	0 N54
12	W	11 24 28	19 21 15	4 13	0♎14 34	2 04	2 S00	6 11	6♎17 24	4 S52
13	Th	11 28 24	20 19 39	3 50	12 18 15	3 02	7 40	6 08	18 17 21	10 23
14	F	11 32 21	21 18 05	3 27	24 14 59	3 52	13 00	6 05	0♏11 28	15 29
15	S	11 36 17	22 16 32	3 04	6♏07 08	4 31	17 49	6 02	12 02 21	19 59
16	Su	11 40 14	23 15 02	2 41	17 57 33	4 58	21 57	5 59	23 53 11	23 42
17	M	11 44 10	24 13 33	2 18	29 49 42	5 13	25 12	5 56	5♐47 38	26 27
18	T	11 48 07	25 12 06	1 54	11♐47 31	5 14	27 23	5 52	17 49 53	28 01
19	W	11 52 04	26 10 40	1 31	23 55 18	5 01	28 19	5 49	0♑04 19	28 16
20	Th	11 56 00	27 09 16	1 08	6♑17 32	4 35	27 52	5 46	12 35 27	27 06
21	F	11 59 57	28 07 54	0 45	18 58 36	3 54	25 58	5 43	25 27 26	24 28
22	S	12 03 53	29♍06 34	0 N21	2♒02 22	3 01	22 38	5 40	8♒43 41	20 29
23	Su	12 07 50	0♎05 15	0 S02	15 31 37	1 55	18 01	5 37	22 26 14	15 17
24	M	12 11 46	1 03 58	0 25	29 27 29	0 S41	12 18	5 33	6♓35 08	9 08
25	T	12 15 43	2 02 43	0 49	13♓48 48	0 N37	5 S47	5 30	21 07 54	2 S20
26	W	12 19 39	3 01 29	1 12	28 31 42	1 56	1 N11	5 27	5♈59 17	4 N43
27	Th	12 23 36	4 00 17	1 36	13♈29 39	3 07	8 12	5 24	21 01 38	11 35
28	F	12 27 33	4 59 08	1 59	28 34 06	4 06	14 47	5 21	6♉05 51	17 47
29	S	12 31 29	5 58 01	2 22	13♉35 45	4 47	20 29	5 17	21 02 45	22 51
30	Su	12 35 26	6♎56 56	2 S46	28♉25 56	5 N09	24 N50	5♓14	5♊44 33	26 N23

D M	Mercury Lat.	Mercury Dec.		Venus Lat.	Venus Dec.		Mars Lat.	Mars Dec.		Jupiter Lat.	Jupiter Dec.
	° ′	° ′	° ′	° ′	° ′	° ′	° ′	° ′	° ′	° ′	° ′
1	0 N43	3 N15	2 N29	7 S 50	8 N05	8 N15	0 S 44	21 N56	22 N 01	0 N 26	21 S 39
3	0 29	1 44	0 N 58	7 37	8 26	8 36	0 41	22 06	22 10	0 25	21 41
5	0 N15	0 N13	0 S 31	7 23	8 45	8 55	0 39	22 14	22 18	0 25	21 43
7	0 00	1 S15	1 59	7 07	9 04	9 12	0 37	22 22	22 26	0 25	21 45
9	0 S16	2 42	3 25	6 50	9 21	9 28	0 34	22 30	22 34	0 24	21 47
11	0 32	4 07	4 49	6 31	9 35	9 42	0 32	22 37	22 40	0 24	21 48
13	0 48	5 30	6 11	6 13	9 48	9 54	0 29	22 44	22 47	0 24	21 50
15	1 04	6 51	7 30	5 53	9 59	10 04	0 27	22 50	22 52	0 23	21 53
17	1 20	8 09	8 47	5 34	10 08	10 11	0 24	22 55	22 58	0 23	21 55
19	1 36	9 24	10 00	5 14	10 14	10 16	0 21	23 00	23 03	0 23	21 57
21	1 51	10 36	11 10	4 54	10 18	10 19	0 19	23 05	23 07	0 22	21 59
23	2 07	11 44	12 17	4 35	10 20	10 20	0 16	23 09	23 11	0 22	22 01
25	2 21	12 48	13 19	4 15	10 19	10 18	0 13	23 13	23 15	0 22	22 04
27	2 35	13 49	14 17	3 56	10 16	10 14	0 10	23 17	23 18	0 21	22 06
29	2 48	14 44	15 S 09	3 37	10 11	10 N07	0 06	23 20	23 N 21	0 21	22 08
31	3 S00	15 S33		3 S 19	10 N03		0 S 03	23 N23		0 N 21	22 S 11

FIRST QUARTER – Sep.19,16h.48m. (26°♐22′)

FULL MOON – Sep.26,19h.45m. (3°♈20′)

EPHEMERIS]				SEPTEMBER 2007													19
D	☿	♀	♂	♃	♄	♅	♆	♇	Lunar Aspects								
M	Long.	Long.	Long.	Long.	Long.	Long.	Long.	Long.	☉	☿	♀	♂	♃	♄	♅	♆	♇
	° ′	° ′	° ′	° ′	° ′	° ′	° ′	° ′									
1	23♍29	17♌37	15♊36	10♐54	29♌52	17♓02	20♒08	26♐19	△	⚼		∠		△	∠		
2	25 08	17R 21	16 11	10 59	29♌59	17R 00	20R 06	26R 19			□	⊻			⚹	□	⚼
3	26 47	17 08	16 45	11 04	0♍07	16 58	20 05	26 18		△				□			
4	28♍24	16 56	17 19	11 09	0 15	16 55	20 03	26 18	□		⚹	☌	☍		□	△	
5	0♎00	16 47	17 54	11 14	0 22	16 53	20 02	26 18		□	∠			⚹		⚼	☍
6	1 35	16 41	18 27	11 19	0 30	16 51	20 01	26 18	⚹		⊻	⊻		∠	△		
7	3 08	16 37	19 01	11 24	0 37	16 48	19 59	26 18	∠				⚼	⊻	⚼		
8	4 41	16 35	19 34	11 30	0 45	16 46	19 58	26D 18	⊻	⚹	☌	∠	△				⚼
9	6 12	16D 36	20 08	11 36	0 52	16 43	19 56	26 18		∠		⚹				☍	△
10	7 42	16 39	20 40	11 42	1 00	16 41	19 55	26 18		⊻			□	●			
11	9 10	16 45	21 13	11 48	1 07	16 39	19 53	26 18	●		⊻	□			☍		
12	10 38	16 52	21 46	11 54	1 14	16 36	19 52	26 18			∠			⊻		⚼	□
13	12 04	17 02	22 18	12 00	1 22	16 34	19 51	26 19		☌	⚹		⚹	∠			
14	13 30	17 14	22 50	12 07	1 29	16 31	19 49	26 19	⊻			△	∠			△	⚹
15	14 53	17 28	23 21	12 13	1 36	16 29	19 48	26 19	∠			⚼		⚹	⚼		∠
16	16 16	17 44	23 53	12 20	1 44	16 27	19 47	26 19	⚹	⊻	□		⊻		△	□	
17	17 37	18 02	24 24	12 27	1 51	16 24	19 45	26 20		∠				□			⊻
18	18 57	18 21	24 55	12 34	1 58	16 22	19 44	26 20					☌		□		
19	20 16	18 43	25 25	12 41	2 05	16 19	19 43	26 20	□	⚹	△	☍				⚹	☌
20	21 33	19 06	25 55	12 49	2 13	16 17	19 42	26 21			⚼			△		∠	
21	22 49	19 31	26 25	12 56	2 20	16 15	19 40	26 21		□			⊻	⚼	⚹	⊻	
22	24 03	19 58	26 55	13 04	2 27	16 12	19 39	26 22	△				∠		∠		⊻
23	25 15	20 26	27 24	13 11	2 34	16 10	19 38	26 22	⚼		☍	⚼	⚹		⊻	☌	∠
24	26 26	20 56	27 53	13 19	2 41	16 08	19 37	26 23		△		△		☍			⚹
25	27 35	21 28	28 22	13 27	2 48	16 06	19 36	26 23		⚼			□		☌	⊻	
26	28 41	22 00	28 50	13 36	2 55	16 03	19 35	26 24	☍			□				∠	□
27	29♎46	22 35	29 19	13 44	3 02	16 01	19 34	26 24			⚼		△	⚼	⊻	⚹	
28	0♏48	23 10	29♊46	13 52	3 09	15 59	19 33	26 25		☍	△	⚹	⚼	△	∠		△
29	1 48	23 47	0♋14	14 01	3 16	15 57	19 32	26 26				∠			⚹	□	⚼
30	2♏46	24♌25	0♋41	14♐09	3♍23	15♓54	19♒31	26♐26	⚼		□	⊻		□			

D	Saturn		Uranus		Neptune		Pluto	
M	Lat.	Dec.	Lat.	Dec.	Lat.	Dec.	Lat.	Dec.
	° ′	° ′	° ′	° ′	° ′	° ′	° ′	° ′
1	1N18	12N44	0S49	5S52	0S17	15S02	6N45	16S38
3	1 18	12 39	0 49	5 54	0 17	15 03	6 44	16 39
5	1 18	12 34	0 49	5 56	0 17	15 04	6 44	16 40
7	1 18	12 28	0 49	5 58	0 17	15 05	6 43	16 40
9	1 18	12 23	0 49	5 59	0 17	15 06	6 43	16 41
11	1 19	12 18	0 49	6 01	0 17	15 07	6 42	16 42
13	1 19	12 13	0 49	6 03	0 17	15 08	6 41	16 42
15	1 19	12 08	0 49	6 05	0 17	15 09	6 41	16 43
17	1 19	12 03	0 49	6 07	0 17	15 10	6 40	16 44
19	1 20	11 58	0 49	6 09	0 17	15 10	6 39	16 44
21	1 20	11 53	0 49	6 10	0 17	15 11	6 39	16 45
23	1 20	11 48	0 49	6 12	0 17	15 12	6 38	16 46
25	1 20	11 44	0 49	6 14	0 17	15 13	6 37	16 46
27	1 21	11 39	0 49	6 16	0 17	15 13	6 37	16 47
29	1 21	11 34	0 49	6 17	0 17	15 14	6 36	16 47
31	1N21	11N29	0S49	6S19	0S17	15S15	6N36	16S48

Mutual Aspects

1 ☿⊥♀. ☉∥♀.
3 ☿±♆. ☿□♇. ♀⚹♂. ♂□♅.
4 ☉□♃. ☿Q♃. ♀∇♅.
5 ☿⊻♄.
6 ☿∠♀. ♂Q♄.
7 ☉#♅. ♇Stat.
8 ☿⚼♆. ♀Stat.
9 ☉⊻♀. ☉☍♅. ☿⊥♄. ♂△♆.
10 ♀∇♅. 11 ☉#☿.
13 ☉∇♆. ☿⚹♃.
14 ☿∥♅. 15 ☿Q♇.
16 ☿∠♄. ☿∇♅.
17 ☉⊥♀. ☉□♂. ☿⚹♀.
19 ☉±♆. ☉□♇. ☿△♆.
20 ☿#♀.
21 ☿±♅. ♀☍♆. ♂☍♇.
23 ☿#♄.
24 ☉Q♃. ☿⚹♇.
26 ☉⊻♄. ☿△♂. ☿∠♃.
28 ☉⚼♆. ☿⚼♅.
30 ☿∥♆.

LAST QUARTER – Sep. 4,02h.32m. (11°♊12′)

NEW MOON – Oct.11,05h.01m. (17°♎30′)

D M	D W	Sidereal Time	☉ Long.	☉ Dec.	☽ Long.	☽ Lat.	☽ Dec.	☽ Node	24h. ☽ Long.	24h. ☽ Dec.
		h m s	° ′ ″	° ′	° ′ ″	° ′	° ′	° ′	° ′ ″	° ′
1	M	12 39 22	7 ♎ 55 53	3 S 09	12 ♊ 57 58	5 N 11	27 N 29	5 ♓ 11	20 ♊ 05 47	28 N 07
2	T	12 43 19	8 54 53	3 32	27 07 45	4 53	28 17	5 08	4 ♋ 03 46	28 00
3	W	12 47 15	9 53 55	3 55	10 ♋ 53 52	4 19	27 17	5 05	17 38 12	26 11
4	Th	12 51 12	10 52 59	4 18	24 17 00	3 31	24 43	5 02	0 ♌ 50 36	22 57
5	F	12 55 08	11 52 06	4 42	7 ♌ 19 21	2 33	20 55	4 58	13 43 37	18 39
6	S	12 59 05	12 51 15	5 05	20 03 49	1 30	16 13	4 55	26 20 20	13 37
7	Su	13 03 02	13 50 26	5 28	2 ♍ 33 33	0 N 23	10 55	4 52	8 ♍ 43 49	8 08
8	M	13 06 58	14 49 39	5 51	14 51 29	0 S 44	5 N 17	4 49	20 56 52	2 N 25
9	T	13 10 55	15 48 55	6 13	27 00 14	1 48	0 S 28	4 46	3 ♎ 01 52	3 S 19
10	W	13 14 51	16 48 12	6 36	9 ♎ 01 58	2 46	6 08	4 43	15 00 46	8 52
11	Th	13 18 48	17 47 32	6 59	20 58 28	3 37	11 32	4 39	26 55 17	14 04
12	F	13 22 44	18 46 54	7 22	2 ♏ 51 24	4 17	16 29	4 36	8 ♏ 47 01	18 44
13	S	13 26 41	19 46 18	7 44	14 42 22	4 46	20 48	4 33	20 37 41	22 40
14	Su	13 30 37	20 45 43	8 06	26 33 15	5 03	24 18	4 30	2 ♐ 29 20	25 40
15	M	13 34 34	21 45 11	8 29	8 ♐ 26 17	5 07	26 46	4 27	14 24 28	27 34
16	T	13 38 31	22 44 41	8 51	20 24 17	4 58	28 03	4 23	26 26 11	28 11
17	W	13 42 27	23 44 12	9 13	2 ♑ 30 38	4 35	28 00	4 20	8 ♑ 38 09	27 28
18	Th	13 46 24	24 43 45	9 35	14 49 17	3 59	26 35	4 17	21 04 34	25 21
19	F	13 50 20	25 43 20	9 57	27 24 33	3 11	23 48	4 14	3 ♒ 49 48	21 56
20	S	13 54 17	26 42 57	10 18	10 ♒ 20 51	2 12	19 46	4 11	16 58 10	17 20
21	Su	13 58 13	27 42 35	10 40	23 42 10	1 S 04	14 38	4 08	0 ♓ 33 09	11 43
22	M	14 02 10	28 42 15	11 01	7 ♓ 31 19	0 N 09	8 36	4 04	14 36 42	5 S 20
23	T	14 06 06	29 ♎ 41 57	11 22	21 49 10	1 25	1 S 57	4 01	29 08 20	1 N 31
24	W	14 10 03	0 ♏ 41 40	11 43	6 ♈ 33 39	2 37	5 N 01	3 58	14 ♈ 04 18	8 28
25	Th	14 14 00	1 41 26	12 04	21 39 16	3 40	11 50	3 55	29 17 21	15 03
26	F	14 17 56	2 41 13	12 24	6 ♉ 57 13	4 28	18 03	3 52	14 ♉ 37 24	20 45
27	S	14 21 53	3 41 02	12 45	22 16 27	4 57	23 07	3 49	29 52 58	25 03
28	Su	14 25 49	4 40 54	13 05	7 ♊ 25 39	5 04	26 33	3 45	14 ♊ 53 21	27 33
29	M	14 29 46	5 40 47	13 25	22 15 09	4 51	28 03	3 42	29 30 22	28 04
30	T	14 33 42	6 40 43	13 45	6 ♋ 38 31	4 19	27 35	3 39	13 ♋ 39 23	26 41
31	W	14 37 39	7 ♏ 40 41	14 S 04	20 ♋ 32 56	3 N 33	25 N 23	3 ♓ 36	27 ♋ 19 18	23 N 44

D M	Mercury Lat.	Mercury Dec.		Venus Lat.	Venus Dec.		Mars Lat.	Mars Dec.		Jupiter Lat.	Jupiter Dec.
	° ′	° ′	° ′	° ′	° ′	° ′	° ′	° ′	° ′	° ′	° ′
1	3 S 00	15 S 33	15 S 56	3 S 19	10 N 03	9 N 58	0 S 03	23 N 23	23 N 24	0 N 21	22 S 11
3	3 10	16 17	16 36	3 00	9 52	9 46	0 00	23 26	23 27	0 20	22 13
5	3 18	16 53	17 08	2 43	9 40	9 33	0 N 03	23 28	23 29	0 20	22 15
7	3 24	17 21	17 31	2 25	9 25	9 17	0 07	23 30	23 31	0 20	22 18
9	3 27	17 39	17 44	2 08	9 08	8 59	0 11	23 32	23 34	0 19	22 20
11	3 25	17 45	17 44	1 52	8 49	8 38	0 14	23 34	23 35	0 19	22 22
13	3 20	17 38	17 29	1 36	8 27	8 16	0 18	23 36	23 37	0 19	22 25
15	3 08	17 15	16 57	1 20	8 04	7 52	0 22	23 38	23 39	0 19	22 27
17	2 50	16 35	16 08	1 06	7 39	7 25	0 26	23 40	23 41	0 18	22 29
19	2 24	15 37	15 01	0 51	7 11	6 57	0 30	23 42	23 43	0 18	22 32
21	1 52	14 22	13 40	0 37	6 42	6 27	0 34	23 44	23 45	0 18	22 34
23	1 14	12 55	12 10	0 24	6 11	5 55	0 39	23 46	23 47	0 18	22 36
25	0 S 33	11 24	10 40	0 S 11	5 39	5 22	0 43	23 48	23 50	0 17	22 39
27	0 N 08	9 59	9 21	0 N 01	5 04	4 46	0 48	23 51	23 52	0 17	22 41
29	0 45	8 48	8 S 20	0 13	4 28	4 N 10	0 52	23 53	23 N 55	0 17	22 43
31	1 N 17	7 S 58		0 N 25	3 N 51		0 N 57	23 N 56		0 N 17	22 S 45

FIRST QUARTER – Oct.19,08h.33m. (25°♑35′)

FULL MOON-Oct.26,04h.52m. (2°♉23′)

D M	☿ Long.	♀ Long.	♂ Long.	♃ Long.	♄ Long.	♅ Long.	♆ Long.	♇ Long.	☉	☿	♀	♂	♃	♄	♅	♆	♇
	° ′	° ′	° ′	° ′	° ′	° ′	° ′	° ′									
1	3♏40	25♌04	1♋08	14♐18	3♍29	15♓52	19♒30	26♐27	△	⚼			☍		□	△	
2	4 32	25 45	1 34	14 27	3 36	15R 50	19R 29	26 28			✱	☌		✱			☍
3	5 20	26 27	2 00	14 36	3 43	15 48	19 28	26 29	□	△	∠				△	⚼	
4	6 05	27 09	2 26	14 45	3 49	15 46	19 27	26 30			⚺		⚼	∠	⚼		
5	6 45	27 53	2 51	14 54	3 56	15 44	19 26	26 30	✱	□		⚺		⚺			⚼
6	7 21	28 38	3 16	15 04	4 02	15 42	19 25	26 31				∠	△			☍	
7	7 53	29♌23	3 40	15 13	4 09	15 40	19 25	26 32	∠	✱	☌	✱		•			△
8	8 19	0♍10	4 04	15 23	4 15	15 38	19 24	26 33	⚺				□		☍		
9	8 40	0 58	4 28	15 33	4 22	15 36	19 23	26 34		∠	⚺						□
10	8 55	1 46	4 51	15 42	4 28	15 34	19 22	26 35		⚺		□		⚺		⚼	
11	9 03	2 35	5 14	15 52	4 34	15 32	19 22	26 36	☌		∠		✱	∠		△	✱
12	9R 04	3 25	5 36	16 02	4 41	15 30	19 21	26 37			✱	△	∠	✱	⚼		
13	8 58	4 16	5 58	16 12	4 47	15 28	19 20	26 38	⚺	☌			⚺		△	□	∠
14	8 44	5 07	6 19	16 23	4 53	15 26	19 20	26 40				⚼					⚺
15	8 21	5 59	6 40	16 33	4 59	15 24	19 19	26 41	∠	⚺	□			□			
16	7 50	6 52	7 00	16 43	5 05	15 23	19 19	26 42	✱	∠			☌		□	✱	
17	7 11	7 46	7 20	16 54	5 11	15 21	19 18	26 43		✱	△	☍		△		∠	☌
18	6 23	8 40	7 39	17 05	5 17	15 19	19 18	26 44					⚺	⚼	✱	⚺	
19	5 28	9 35	7 58	17 15	5 23	15 18	19 17	26 46	□		⚼		∠		∠		⚺
20	4 25	10 30	8 16	17 26	5 28	15 16	19 17	26 47		□					⚺		∠
21	3 17	11 26	8 34	17 37	5 34	15 14	19 17	26 48	△			⚼	✱			☌	✱
22	2 04	12 23	8 51	17 48	5 39	15 13	19 16	26 50	⚼	△	☍	△		☍			
23	0♏49	13 20	9 08	17 59	5 45	15 11	19 16	26 51		⚼			□		☌	⚺	□
24	29♎34	14 17	9 24	18 10	5 50	15 10	19 16	26 52				□				∠	
25	28 21	15 16	9 39	18 21	5 56	15 08	19 16	26 54		☍			△	⚼	⚺	✱	△
26	27 12	16 14	9 54	18 33	6 01	15 07	19 15	26 55	☍		⚼	✱	⚼	△	∠		⚼
27	26 09	17 13	10 09	18 44	6 06	15 06	19 15	26 57			△	∠			✱	□	
28	25 15	18 13	10 22	18 56	6 12	15 04	19 15	26 58		⚼		⚺		□			
29	24 30	19 13	10 35	19 07	6 17	15 03	19 15	27 00	⚼	△	□		☍		□	△	☍
30	23 56	20 13	10 48	19 19	6 22	15 02	19 15	27 01	△			☌		✱		⚼	
31	23♎34	21♍14	10♋59	19♐31	6♍27	15♓01	19♒15	27♐03		□	✱			∠	△		

D M	Saturn Lat.	Saturn Dec.	Uranus Lat.	Uranus Dec.	Neptune Lat.	Neptune Dec.	Pluto Lat.	Pluto Dec.
	° ′	° ′	° ′	° ′	° ′	° ′	° ′	° ′
1	1N21	11N29	0S49	6S19	0S17	15S15	6N36	16S48
3	1 21	11 25	0 48	6 21	0 17	15 15	6 35	16 49
5	1 22	11 20	0 48	6 22	0 17	15 16	6 34	16 49
7	1 22	11 16	0 48	6 24	0 17	15 16	6 34	16 50
9	1 22	11 11	0 48	6 25	0 17	15 17	6 33	16 51
11	1 23	11 07	0 48	6 27	0 17	15 17	6 33	16 51
13	1 23	11 03	0 48	6 28	0 17	15 18	6 32	16 52
15	1 23	10 59	0 48	6 30	0 17	15 18	6 31	16 53
17	1 24	10 55	0 48	6 31	0 17	15 18	6 31	16 53
19	1 24	10 51	0 48	6 32	0 17	15 19	6 30	16 54
21	1 24	10 47	0 48	6 33	0 17	15 19	6 30	16 55
23	1 25	10 43	0 48	6 34	0 17	15 19	6 29	16 55
25	1 25	10 39	0 48	6 36	0 17	15 19	6 29	16 56
27	1 26	10 36	0 48	6 37	0 17	15 19	6 28	16 56
29	1 26	10 32	0 48	6 37	0 17	15 19	6 28	16 57
31	1N26	10N29	0S48	6S38	0S17	15S19	6N27	16S58

Mutual Aspects

1 ☿✱♄.
3 ☉⊥♄. ♀△♇.
5 ☿∥♇. 8 ☉Q♇.
9 ☉✱♃. ☉∇♅. ♂✱♄. ♂⚼♆. ♃□♅.
10 ☉∠♀. ☉∥♅.
12 ☿Stat.
13 ☉∠♄. ☉△♆.
14 ♀☌♄. ☉⋕♀.
15 ☉±♅.
16 ♀✱♂. ☿∥♇.
17 ☿✱♀. ☿△♂.
19 ☿✱♄.
20 ☉✱♇. ☿∥♆.
21 ☿∠♃. ☉⋕♄.
22 ♀⋕♅.
23 ☉☌☿. ☉⚼♅.
24 ☿∠♀. ☿⚼♅. ☉∥☿.
25 ♀☍♅.
26 ☿✱♇. ☿⋕♄.
27 ☉∠♃.
29 ☿⊥♀. ♀□♃. ♀∇♆.
30 ☉✱♄. ♃✱♆.
31 ♆Stat.

LAST QUARTER-Oct. 3,10h.06m. (9°♋49′)

NEW MOON–Nov. 9,23h.03m. (17°♏10′)

D M	D W	Sidereal Time	☉ Long.	☉ Dec.	☽ Long.	☽ Lat.	☽ Dec.	☽ Node	24h. ☽ Long.	24h. ☽ Dec.
		h m s	° ′ ″	° ′	° ′ ″	° ′	° ′	° ′	° ′ ″	° ′
1	Th	14 41 35	8 ♏ 40 41	14 S 24	3 ♌ 58 46	2 N37	21 N48	3 ♓ 33	10 ♌ 31 44	19 N37
2	F	14 45 32	9 40 43	14 43	16 58 43	1 34	17 14	3 29	23 20 13	14 42
3	S	14 49 29	10 40 48	15 02	29 36 50	0 N28	12 03	3 26	5 ♍ 49 09	9 18
4	Su	14 53 25	11 40 54	15 20	11 ♍ 57 43	0 S38	6 30	3 23	18 03 07	3 N39
5	M	14 57 22	12 41 03	15 39	24 05 52	1 40	0 N48	3 20	0 ♎ 06 27	2 S02
6	T	15 01 18	13 41 13	15 57	6 ♎ 05 19	2 38	4 S50	3 17	12 02 52	7 35
7	W	15 05 15	14 41 26	16 15	17 59 29	3 28	10 15	3 14	23 55 27	12 50
8	Th	15 09 11	15 41 40	16 32	29 51 03	4 08	15 17	3 10	5 ♏ 46 31	17 36
9	F	15 13 08	16 41 57	16 50	11 ♏ 42 04	4 38	19 45	3 07	17 37 51	21 42
10	S	15 17 04	17 42 15	17 07	23 34 04	4 55	23 26	3 04	29 30 51	24 55
11	Su	15 21 01	18 42 35	17 23	5 ♐ 28 23	5 00	26 08	3 01	11 ♐ 26 49	27 04
12	M	15 24 58	19 42 56	17 40	17 26 20	4 52	27 41	2 58	23 27 09	27 59
13	T	15 28 54	20 43 19	17 56	29 29 31	4 30	27 56	2 55	5 ♑ 33 43	27 34
14	W	15 32 51	21 43 44	18 12	11 ♑ 40 03	3 56	26 51	2 51	17 48 55	25 48
15	Th	15 36 47	22 44 10	18 27	24 00 42	3 11	24 26	2 48	0 ♒ 15 50	22 46
16	F	15 40 44	23 44 37	18 43	6 ♒ 34 49	2 15	20 48	2 45	12 58 08	18 35
17	S	15 44 40	24 45 06	18 57	19 26 17	1 11	16 07	2 42	25 59 46	13 26
18	Su	15 48 37	25 45 36	19 12	2 ♓ 39 04	0 S02	10 34	2 39	9 ♓ 24 35	7 32
19	M	15 52 33	26 46 07	19 26	16 16 40	1 N09	4 S21	2 35	23 15 34	1 S05
20	T	15 56 30	27 46 40	19 40	0 ♈ 21 20	2 19	2 N16	2 32	7 ♈ 33 54	5 N37
21	W	16 00 27	28 47 13	19 53	14 52 59	3 21	8 57	2 29	22 18 04	12 13
22	Th	16 04 23	29 ♏ 47 48	20 06	29 48 23	4 12	15 20	2 26	7 ♉ 22 58	18 15
23	F	16 08 20	0 ♐ 48 24	20 19	15 ♉ 00 39	4 46	20 53	2 23	22 40 04	23 12
24	S	16 12 16	1 49 02	20 32	0 ♊ 19 47	5 00	25 06	2 20	7 ♊ 58 19	26 33
25	Su	16 16 13	2 49 41	20 44	15 34 12	4 52	27 30	2 16	23 06 05	27 56
26	M	16 20 09	3 50 22	20 55	0 ♋ 32 48	4 24	27 51	2 13	7 ♋ 53 22	27 16
27	T	16 24 06	4 51 04	21 06	15 07 03	3 40	26 13	2 10	22 13 21	24 46
28	W	16 28 02	5 51 47	21 17	29 12 01	2 43	22 59	2 07	6 ♌ 03 01	20 53
29	Th	16 31 59	6 52 33	21 28	12 ♌ 46 29	1 39	18 33	2 04	19 22 45	16 03
30	F	16 35 56	7 ♐ 53 19	21 S 38	25 ♌ 52 14	0 N31	13 N23	2 ♓ 00	2 ♍ 15 28	10 N38

D M	Mercury Lat.	Mercury Dec.		Venus Lat.	Venus Dec.		Mars Lat.	Mars Dec.		Jupiter Lat.	Jupiter Dec.
	° ′	° ′	° ′	° ′	° ′	° ′	° ′	° ′	° ′	° ′	° ′
1	1 N30	7 S 41	7 S 31	0 N 30	3 N32	3 N12	1 N 00	23 N58	23 N 59	0 N 16	22 S 46
3	1 51	7 26	7 27	0 40	2 52	2 32	1 05	24 01	24 03	0 16	22 48
5	2 05	7 33	7 43	0 50	2 12	1 51	1 10	24 05	24 06	0 16	22 50
7	2 13	7 57	8 15	1 00	1 30	1 08	1 15	24 08	24 11	0 16	22 52
9	2 16	8 36	9 00	1 08	0 47	0 N25	1 20	24 13	24 15	0 15	22 54
11	2 14	9 26	9 54	1 17	0 N03	0 S19	1 26	24 17	24 20	0 15	22 56
13	2 09	10 24	10 54	1 24	0 S42	1 04	1 31	24 23	24 25	0 15	22 58
15	2 02	11 26	11 59	1 32	1 27	1 50	1 37	24 28	24 31	0 15	22 59
17	1 52	12 31	13 05	1 38	2 13	2 36	1 43	24 34	24 37	0 15	23 01
19	1 41	13 38	14 11	1 44	3 00	3 23	1 49	24 40	24 44	0 14	23 02
21	1 29	14 45	15 17	1 50	3 47	4 10	1 55	24 47	24 51	0 14	23 04
23	1 16	15 50	16 22	1 55	4 34	4 58	2 01	24 54	24 58	0 14	23 05
25	1 02	16 54	17 25	2 00	5 22	5 46	2 07	25 02	25 05	0 14	23 06
27	0 48	17 55	18 25	2 04	6 10	6 34	2 13	25 09	25 13	0 13	23 08
29	0 34	18 54	19 S 22	2 07	6 58	7 S 22	2 19	25 17	25 N 21	0 13	23 09
31	0 N20	19 S 49		2 N 10	7 S 45		2 N 25	25 N25		0 N 13	23 S 10

FIRST QUARTER–Nov.17,22h.33m. (25°♒12′)

FULL MOON–Nov.24,14h.30m. (1°♊55′)

EPHEMERIS]			NOVEMBER 2007														23
D	☿	♀	♂	♃	♄	♅	♆	♇	Lunar Aspects								
M	Long.	Long.	Long.	Long.	Long.	Long.	Long.	Long.	☉	☿	♀	♂	♃	♄	♅	♆	♇
	° ′	° ′	° ′	° ′	° ′	° ′	° ′	° ′									
1	23♎23	22♍16	11♋10	19♐42	6♍32	15♓00	19♒15	27♐05	□		∠		⚼	⚺	⚼		
2	23D 23	23 18	11 21	19 54	6 36	14R 58	19D 15	27 06				⚺	△			☍	⚼
3	23 35	24 20	11 30	20 06	6 41	14 57	19 15	27 08		⚹	⚺	∠					△
4	23 56	25 22	11 39	20 18	6 46	14 56	19 15	27 09	⚹	∠		⚹		☌	☍		
5	24 28	26 25	11 48	20 30	6 50	14 55	19 15	27 11	∠	⚺	☌		□				□
6	25 08	27 28	11 55	20 42	6 55	14 55	19 15	27 13				□		⚺		⚼	
7	25 56	28 32	12 02	20 55	6 59	14 54	19 16	27 15	⚺				⚹	∠		△	
8	26 51	29♍36	12 08	21 07	7 03	14 53	19 16	27 16		☌	⚺				⚼		⚹
9	27 52	0♎40	12 13	21 19	7 07	14 52	19 16	27 18	☌		∠	△	∠	⚹	△		∠
10	28♎59	1 44	12 17	21 32	7 12	14 51	19 16	27 20				⚼	⚺			□	⚺
11	0♏10	2 49	12 21	21 44	7 16	14 51	19 17	27 22		⚺	⚹			□			
12	1 25	3 54	12 24	21 57	7 20	14 50	19 17	27 24	⚺	∠			☌		□	⚹	
13	2 44	5 00	12 26	22 09	7 23	14 49	19 18	27 25		⚹	□					∠	☌
14	4 05	6 05	12 27	22 22	7 27	14 49	19 18	27 27	∠			☍		△	⚹		
15	5 29	7 11	12R 27	22 35	7 31	14 48	19 19	27 29	⚹				⚺	⚼	∠	⚺	⚺
16	6 55	8 18	12 26	22 47	7 34	14 48	19 19	27 31		□	△		∠				∠
17	8 22	9 24	12 25	23 00	7 38	14 48	19 20	27 33	□		⚼		⚹		⚺	☌	
18	9 51	10 31	12 23	23 13	7 41	14 47	19 20	27 35				⚼		☍			⚹
19	11 21	11 38	12 20	23 26	7 44	14 47	19 21	27 37		△		△			☌	⚺	
20	12 52	12 45	12 16	23 39	7 48	14 47	19 21	27 39	△	⚼			□			∠	□
21	14 24	13 52	12 11	23 52	7 51	14 47	19 22	27 41	⚼		☍	□			⚺	⚹	
22	15 56	15 00	12 05	24 05	7 54	14 47	19 23	27 43					△	⚼	∠		△
23	17 29	16 07	11 59	24 18	7 57	14 46	19 24	27 45		☍		⚹	⚼	△	⚹	□	⚼
24	19 02	17 15	11 51	24 31	7 59	14D 46	19 24	27 47	☍		⚼	∠					
25	20 35	18 24	11 43	24 44	8 02	14 46	19 25	27 49			△	⚺		□	□	△	
26	22 09	19 32	11 34	24 57	8 05	14 47	19 26	27 51					☍			⚼	☍
27	23 43	20 41	11 24	25 11	8 07	14 47	19 27	27 53	⚼	⚼	□	☌		⚹	△		
28	25 17	21 49	11 13	25 24	8 09	14 47	19 28	27 55		△				∠	⚼		
29	26 51	22 58	11 02	25 37	8 12	14 47	19 29	27 57	△			⚺	⚼	⚺			⚼
30	28♏25	24♎07	10♋49	25♐51	8♍14	14♓47	19♒30	27♐59		□	⚹	∠	△			☍	△

D	Saturn		Uranus		Neptune		Pluto	
M	Lat.	Dec.	Lat.	Dec.	Lat.	Dec.	Lat.	Dec.
	° ′	° ′	° ′	° ′	° ′	° ′	° ′	° ′
1	1N27	10N28	0S48	6S39	0S17	15S19	6N27	16S58
3	1 27	10 24	0 48	6 39	0 17	15 19	6 26	16 58
5	1 27	10 21	0 48	6 40	0 17	15 19	6 26	16 59
7	1 28	10 18	0 47	6 41	0 17	15 19	6 25	16 59
9	1 28	10 16	0 47	6 41	0 17	15 19	6 25	17 00
11	1 29	10 13	0 47	6 42	0 17	15 19	6 24	17 01
13	1 29	10 11	0 47	6 42	0 17	15 19	6 24	17 01
15	1 30	10 08	0 47	6 43	0 17	15 18	6 24	17 02
17	1 30	10 06	0 47	6 43	0 17	15 18	6 23	17 02
19	1 31	10 04	0 47	6 43	0 17	15 18	6 23	17 03
21	1 31	10 02	0 47	6 43	0 17	15 17	6 22	17 03
23	1 31	10 00	0 47	6 43	0 17	15 17	6 22	17 03
25	1 32	9 59	0 47	6 43	0 17	15 16	6 22	17 04
27	1 32	9 57	0 47	6 43	0 17	15 16	6 21	17 04
29	1 33	9 56	0 47	6 43	0 17	15 15	6 21	17 05
31	1N33	9N55	0S47	6S42	0S17	15S14	6N21	17S05

Mutual Aspects

1 ☿Stat.
2 ☿⚺♀. ♀Q♂.
4 ☉△♂. ☉∠♇. ♀±♆. ☉∥♆.
6 ♀□♇.
7 ☉⊥♃. ☉△♅.
8 ☿⚹♇. 10 ☉∥♇.
11 ☿⚼♅.
12 ☉Q♄. ☉□♆. ♀⚼♆.
13 ☿#♄. 14 ☉⊥♇.
15 ☉⚺♃. ♀⚺♄. ♂Stat.
16 ☿⚹♄. 17 ☿∠♃.
19 ♀Q♃.
20 ☉∠♀. ☉⚼♂. ☉⚺♇. ☿⚺♀. ☿△♂.
☿∠♇. ♀□♂.
21 ☿△♅. ♀⊥♄.
22 ♀▽♅. ☿∥♆.
23 ♀Q♇.
24 ☿⊥♃. ☿□♆. ♅Stat.
25 ☿Q♄. ☿∥♇.
26 ☿⊥♇. ♀△♆.
27 ☉±♂. ♀±♅.
28 ☿⚺♃. ♀∥♅.
29 ☿⚼♂. ♀∠♄.
30 ☉□♄. ☉Q♆. ☿⚺♇.

LAST QUARTER–Nov. 1,21h.18m. (9°♌04′)

NEW MOON–Dec. 9,17h.40m. (17°♐16′)

D M	D W	Sidereal Time	☉ Long.	☉ Dec.	☽ Long.	☽ Lat.	☽ Dec.	☽ Node	24h. ☽ Long.	24h. ☽ Dec.
		h m s	° ′ ″	° ′	° ′ ″	° ′	° ′	° ′	° ′ ″	° ′
1	S	16 39 52	8 ♐ 54 07	21 S 47	8 ♍ 33 03	0 S 36	7 N 49	1 ♓ 57	14 ♍ 45 38	4 N 57
2	Su	16 43 49	9 54 56	21 56	20 53 52	1 39	2 N 05	1 54	26 58 25	0 S 46
3	M	16 47 45	10 55 47	22 05	2 ♎ 59 55	2 37	3 S 35	1 51	8 ♎ 59 00	6 22
4	T	16 51 42	11 56 40	22 13	14 56 16	3 27	9 04	1 48	20 52 14	11 40
5	W	16 55 38	12 57 33	22 21	26 47 26	4 07	14 10	1 45	2 ♏ 42 18	16 32
6	Th	16 59 35	13 58 28	22 29	8 ♏ 37 15	4 37	18 45	1 41	14 32 36	20 47
7	F	17 03 31	14 59 24	22 36	20 28 41	4 55	22 36	1 38	26 25 43	24 12
8	S	17 07 28	16 00 22	22 42	2 ♐ 23 56	5 00	25 32	1 35	8 ♐ 23 29	26 36
9	Su	17 11 25	17 01 20	22 48	14 24 31	4 52	27 21	1 32	20 27 08	27 48
10	M	17 15 21	18 02 19	22 54	26 31 28	4 30	27 54	1 29	2 ♑ 37 36	27 40
11	T	17 19 18	19 03 20	22 59	8 ♑ 45 38	3 56	27 05	1 26	14 55 43	26 10
12	W	17 23 14	20 04 21	23 04	21 07 57	3 10	24 55	1 22	27 22 33	23 22
13	Th	17 27 11	21 05 22	23 08	3 ♒ 39 42	2 15	21 31	1 19	9 ♒ 59 38	19 25
14	F	17 31 07	22 06 24	23 12	16 22 39	1 12	17 04	1 16	22 49 03	14 31
15	S	17 35 04	23 07 27	23 16	29 19 09	0 S 04	11 46	1 13	5 ♓ 53 20	8 52
16	Su	17 39 00	24 08 30	23 19	12 ♓ 31 56	1 N 06	5 S 50	1 10	19 15 16	2 S 43
17	M	17 42 57	25 09 34	23 21	26 03 40	2 14	0 N 29	1 06	2 ♈ 57 21	3 N 43
18	T	17 46 54	26 10 38	23 23	9 ♈ 56 29	3 16	6 56	1 03	17 01 05	10 07
19	W	17 50 50	27 11 42	23 25	24 11 04	4 07	13 12	1 00	1 ♉ 26 09	16 09
20	Th	17 54 47	28 12 46	23 26	8 ♉ 45 56	4 44	18 54	0 57	16 09 45	21 23
21	F	17 58 43	29 ♐ 13 51	23 26	23 36 49	5 02	23 33	0 54	1 ♊ 06 08	25 20
22	S	18 02 40	0 ♑ 14 57	23 26	8 ♊ 36 38	5 00	26 41	0 51	16 07 07	27 33
23	Su	18 06 36	1 16 02	23 26	23 36 20	4 38	27 54	0 47	1 ♋ 03 05	27 45
24	M	18 10 33	2 17 08	23 25	8 ♋ 26 14	3 56	27 06	0 44	15 44 46	25 59
25	T	18 14 29	3 18 15	23 24	22 57 50	3 01	24 27	0 41	0 ♌ 04 44	22 33
26	W	18 18 26	4 19 22	23 22	7 ♌ 05 02	1 55	20 21	0 38	13 58 25	17 55
27	Th	18 22 23	5 20 29	23 20	20 44 50	0 N 44	15 17	0 35	27 24 20	12 31
28	F	18 26 19	6 21 37	23 17	3 ♍ 57 10	0 S 26	9 39	0 32	10 ♍ 23 41	6 44
29	S	18 30 16	7 22 45	23 14	16 44 20	1 34	3 N 48	0 28	22 59 40	0 N 52
30	Su	18 34 12	8 23 54	23 10	29 10 16	2 35	2 S 02	0 25	5 ♎ 16 44	4 S 53
31	M	18 38 09	9 ♑ 25 03	23 S 06	11 ♎ 19 46	3 S 27	7 S 40	0 ♓ 22	17 ♎ 19 58	10 S 21

D M	Mercury Lat.	Mercury Dec.		Venus Lat.	Venus Dec.		Mars Lat.	Mars Dec.		Jupiter Lat.	Jupiter Dec.
	° ′	° ′	° ′	° ′	° ′	° ′	° ′	° ′	° ′	° ′	° ′
1	0 N 20	19 S 49	20 S 15	2 N 10	7 S 45	8 S 09	2 N 25	25 N 25	25 N 29	0 N 13	23 S 10
3	0 N 06	20 41	21 05	2 13	8 33	8 57	2 30	25 33	25 37	0 13	23 11
5	0 S 07	21 28	21 51	2 15	9 20	9 44	2 36	25 42	25 46	0 13	23 12
7	0 21	22 12	22 32	2 17	10 07	10 31	2 42	25 50	25 54	0 12	23 12
9	0 34	22 51	23 09	2 18	10 54	11 17	2 47	25 58	26 02	0 12	23 13
11	0 46	23 26	23 42	2 18	11 40	12 02	2 53	26 06	26 09	0 12	23 14
13	0 58	23 56	24 09	2 19	12 25	12 47	2 58	26 13	26 17	0 12	23 14
15	1 10	24 21	24 32	2 18	13 09	13 31	3 03	26 20	26 24	0 12	23 15
17	1 21	24 41	24 49	2 18	13 52	14 14	3 07	26 27	26 30	0 11	23 15
19	1 30	24 56	25 01	2 17	14 35	14 55	3 12	26 33	26 36	0 11	23 15
21	1 39	25 05	25 08	2 15	15 16	15 36	3 16	26 38	26 41	0 11	23 15
23	1 47	25 09	25 09	2 14	15 56	16 15	3 19	26 43	26 45	0 11	23 15
25	1 54	25 07	25 04	2 12	16 34	16 53	3 22	26 47	26 49	0 11	23 15
27	2 00	24 59	24 53	2 09	17 11	17 29	3 25	26 51	26 52	0 11	23 15
29	2 05	24 45	24 S 35	2 06	17 46	18 S 03	3 28	26 54	26 N 55	0 10	23 15
31	2 S 08	24 S 25		2 N 03	18 S 20		3 N 30	26 N 56		0 N 10	23 S 14

FIRST QUARTER–Dec.17,10h.17m. (25°♓05′)

FULL MOON–Dec.24,01h.16m. (1°♋50′)

EPHEMERIS]				DECEMBER 2007														25
D	☿	♀	♂	♃	♄	♅	♆	♇	Lunar Aspects									
M	Long.	Long.	Long.	Long.	Long.	Long.	Long.	Long.	☉	☿	♀	♂	♃	♄	♅	♆	♇
	° ′	° ′	° ′	° ′	° ′	° ′	° ′	° ′									
1	29♏59	25♎17	10♋36	26♐04	8♍16	14♓48	19♒31	28♐01	□		∠	✱		☌			
2	1♐33	26 26	10R 22	26 17	8 18	14 48	19 32	28 04					□		☍		
3	3 07	27 36	10 07	26 31	8 20	14 49	19 33	28 06		✱	⚺			⚺		⚼	□
4	4 41	28 46	9 51	26 44	8 21	14 49	19 34	28 08	✱	∠		□				△	
5	6 15	29♎56	9 34	26 58	8 23	14 50	19 35	28 10	∠		☌		✱	∠	⚼		✱
6	7 49	1♏06	9 17	27 11	8 24	14 50	19 36	28 12	⚺	⚺		△	∠	✱			∠
7	9 23	2 16	8 59	27 25	8 26	14 51	19 38	28 14				⚼			△	□	
8	10 57	3 26	8 41	27 39	8 27	14 51	19 39	28 16			⚺		⚺				⚺
9	12 31	4 37	8 22	27 52	8 28	14 52	19 40	28 19	☌	☌	∠			□	□	✱	
10	14 05	5 48	8 02	28 06	8 29	14 53	19 41	28 21					☌				☌
11	15 39	6 58	7 41	28 19	8 30	14 54	19 43	28 23			✱	☍		△	✱	∠	
12	17 13	8 09	7 20	28 33	8 31	14 55	19 44	28 25	⚺	⚺				⚼		⚺	
13	18 47	9 20	6 59	28 47	8 32	14 56	19 45	28 27	∠	∠	□		⚺		∠		⚺
14	20 21	10 31	6 37	29 00	8 33	14 57	19 47	28 30	✱	✱		⚼	∠		⚺	☌	∠
15	21 56	11 42	6 15	29 14	8 33	14 58	19 48	28 32					✱				✱
16	23 30	12 54	5 52	29 28	8 34	14 59	19 50	28 34			△	△		☍	☌		
17	25 05	14 05	5 29	29 42	8 34	15 00	19 51	28 36	□	□	⚼		□			⚺	□
18	26 39	15 17	5 06	29♐55	8 34	15 01	19 53	28 38				□			⚺	∠	
19	28 14	16 28	4 43	0♑09	8 34	15 02	19 54	28 41	△	△			△	⚼	∠	✱	△
20	29♐49	17 40	4 19	0 23	8R 34	15 04	19 56	28 43	⚼	⚼		✱	⚼	△	✱		⚼
21	1♑24	18 52	3 56	0 37	8 34	15 05	19 57	28 45			☍	∠				□	
22	3 00	20 04	3 32	0 50	8 34	15 07	19 59	28 47				⚺		□	□		
23	4 35	21 16	3 08	1 04	8 33	15 08	20 01	28 50								△	☍
24	6 11	22 28	2 45	1 18	8 33	15 09	20 02	28 52	☍	☍	⚼	●	☍	✱	△	⚼	
25	7 47	23 40	2 21	1 32	8 32	15 11	20 04	28 54			△			∠			
26	9 23	24 52	1 58	1 45	8 31	15 13	20 06	28 56				⚺		⚺	⚼		⚼
27	11 00	26 04	1 34	1 59	8 31	15 14	20 07	28 58	⚼	⚼	□	∠	⚼			☍	
28	12 36	27 17	1 11	2 13	8 30	15 16	20 09	29 01	△			✱	△	☌			△
29	14 13	28 29	0 48	2 27	8 29	15 18	20 11	29 03		△					☍		
30	15 50	29♏42	0 26	2 40	8 27	15 19	20 13	29 05			✱	□	□			⚼	□
31	17♑28	0♐54	0♋04	2♑54	8♍26	15♓21	20♒14	29♐07	□		∠			⚺			

D	Saturn		Uranus		Neptune		Pluto	
M	Lat.	Dec.	Lat.	Dec.	Lat.	Dec.	Lat.	Dec.
	° ′	° ′	° ′	° ′	° ′	° ′	° ′	° ′
1	1N33	9N55	0S47	6S42	0S17	15S14	6N21	17S05
3	1 34	9 54	0 46	6 42	0 17	15 14	6 20	17 05
5	1 34	9 53	0 46	6 41	0 17	15 13	6 20	17 06
7	1 35	9 52	0 46	6 41	0 17	15 12	6 20	17 06
9	1 35	9 52	0 46	6 40	0 17	15 12	6 19	17 06
11	1 36	9 52	0 46	6 39	0 17	15 11	6 19	17 07
13	1 36	9 52	0 46	6 39	0 17	15 10	6 19	17 07
15	1 37	9 52	0 46	6 38	0 17	15 09	6 19	17 07
17	1 37	9 52	0 46	6 37	0 17	15 08	6 18	17 08
19	1 38	9 52	0 46	6 36	0 17	15 07	6 18	17 08
21	1 38	9 53	0 46	6 35	0 17	15 06	6 18	17 08
23	1 39	9 53	0 46	6 34	0 17	15 05	6 18	17 08
25	1 39	9 54	0 46	6 32	0 17	15 04	6 18	17 09
27	1 40	9 55	0 46	6 31	0 17	15 03	6 17	17 09
29	1 40	9 57	0 45	6 30	0 17	15 02	6 17	17 09
31	1N41	9N58	0S45	6S28	0S17	15S01	6N17	17S09

Mutual Aspects

2 ☉∇♂. ♀✱♃.
3 ♀✱♇.
4 ☿⊥♀. ☿±♂.
5 ♀⚼♅.
6 ☿□♄. ☿Q♆. ♀#♄.
7 ☉□♅. ☿∇♂.
9 ♂✱♄. ☉∥☿.
10 ☿∥♃.
11 ☿□♅. ♀△♂. ♃☌♇.
12 ☉✱♆. ♀✱♄.
14 ☿✱♆. 15 ☉∥♃.
17 ☉☌☿. ♀∠♇.
18 ♀∠♃. ♀△♅.
19 ☿☌♇. ♂⚼♆. ♄ Stat.
20 ☿☌♃.
21 ☉☌♇. ♀⚼♂. ♀∥♆.
22 ☿☍♂. ☿Q♅. ♀Q♄. ♀□♆.
23 ☉☌♃. ☿∠♆.
24 ☉☍♂. ♀⊥♇.
25 ☉Q♅. ☿△♄.
26 ♂☍♃.
27 ☉∠♆. ☿∠♀. ♀±♂. ♀⊥♃. ♀∥♇.
29 ☿⊥♆. ♀⚺♇. ☉∥♃.
30 ☉△♄. ☿✱♅. ♀∇♂.

LAST QUARTER–Dec. 1,12h.44m. (8°♍56′) & Dec.31,07h.51m. (9°♎14′)

JANUARY

D	☉ ° ′ ″	☽ ° ′ ″	☽Dec. ° ′	☿ ° ′	♀ ° ′	♂ ′
1	1 01 08	13 46 56	0 53	1 35	1 15	43
2	1 01 08	13 32 57	0 51	1 36	1 15	43
3	1 01 08	13 15 55	2 25	1 36	1 15	44
4	1 01 08	12 57 05	3 41	1 36	1 15	44
5	1 01 08	12 38 04	4 35	1 37	1 15	44
6	1 01 08	12 20 28	5 11	1 37	1 15	44
7	1 01 08	12 05 43	5 31	1 38	1 15	44
8	1 01 08	11 54 57	5 40	1 38	1 15	44
9	1 01 08	11 49 00	5 38	1 38	1 15	44
10	1 01 08	11 48 20	5 27	1 39	1 15	44
11	1 01 08	11 53 09	5 06	1 39	1 15	44
12	1 01 08	12 03 15	4 35	1 40	1 15	44
13	1 01 08	12 18 09	3 49	1 40	1 15	44
14	1 01 08	12 36 53	2 47	1 41	1 15	44
15	1 01 08	12 58 09	1 27	1 41	1 15	44
16	1 01 08	13 20 11	0 08	1 41	1 15	44
17	1 01 07	13 41 04	1 50	1 42	1 15	44
18	1 01 07	13 58 56	3 29	1 42	1 15	44
19	1 01 06	14 12 21	4 53	1 42	1 15	44
20	1 01 06	14 20 32	5 56	1 43	1 15	44
21	1 01 05	14 23 32	6 35	1 43	1 15	44
22	1 01 04	14 22 06	6 51	1 43	1 15	44
23	1 01 03	14 17 17	6 45	1 43	1 15	44
24	1 01 02	14 10 13	6 17	1 42	1 15	44
25	1 01 01	14 01 46	5 28	1 42	1 15	44
26	1 01 00	13 52 26	4 20	1 41	1 15	44
27	1 00 59	13 42 24	2 55	1 41	1 15	44
28	1 00 57	13 31 33	1 18	1 40	1 15	44
29	1 00 56	13 19 46	0 23	1 38	1 15	45
30	1 00 55	13 07 00	1 58	1 36	1 15	45
31	1 00 54	12 53 23	3 18	1 34	1 15	45

FEBRUARY

D	☉ ° ′ ″	☽ ° ′ ″	☽Dec. ° ′	☿ ° ′	♀ ° ′	♂ ′
1	1 00 53	12 39 19	4 20	1 31	1 15	45
2	1 00 52	12 25 29	5 02	1 28	1 15	45
3	1 00 51	12 12 39	5 29	1 24	1 15	45
4	1 00 50	12 01 44	5 41	1 20	1 15	45
5	1 00 49	11 53 34	5 42	1 15	1 15	45
6	1 00 48	11 48 56	5 32	1 09	1 14	45
7	1 00 47	11 48 31	5 13	1 02	1 14	45
8	1 00 46	11 52 47	4 44	0 54	1 14	45
9	1 00 45	12 02 00	4 03	0 46	1 14	45
10	1 00 44	12 16 10	3 07	0 37	1 14	45
11	1 00 43	12 34 53	1 56	0 28	1 14	45
12	1 00 42	12 57 20	0 29	0 18	1 14	45
13	1 00 40	13 22 12	1 08	0 07	1 14	45
14	1 00 39	13 47 34	2 49	0 03	1 14	45
15	1 00 38	14 11 14	4 22	0 14	1 14	45
16	1 00 37	14 30 50	5 39	0 24	1 14	45
17	1 00 35	14 44 22	6 34	0 34	1 14	45
18	1 00 33	14 50 36	7 02	0 42	1 14	45
19	1 00 32	14 49 18	7 05	0 50	1 14	45
20	1 00 30	14 41 15	6 41	0 56	1 14	45
21	1 00 28	14 27 59	5 53	1 01	1 14	45
22	1 00 26	14 11 19	4 44	1 04	1 14	45
23	1 00 25	13 52 59	3 18	1 06	1 14	45
24	1 00 23	13 34 27	1 40	1 06	1 14	45
25	1 00 21	13 16 40	0 01	1 04	1 14	45
26	1 00 19	13 00 14	1 36	1 01	1 14	45
27	1 00 17	12 45 23	2 58	0 57	1 14	45
28	1 00 15	12 32 10	4 03	0 51	1 14	45

MARCH

D	☉ ° ′ ″	☽ ° ′ ″	☽Dec. ° ′	☿ ° ′	♀ ° ′	♂ ′
1	1 00 13	12 20 33	4 50	0 45	1 14	45
2	1 00 11	12 10 30	5 21	0 39	1 13	46
3	1 00 09	12 02 04	5 38	0 32	1 13	46
4	1 00 07	11 55 26	5 43	0 25	1 13	46
5	1 00 05	11 50 53	5 37	0 18	1 13	46
6	1 00 04	11 48 47	5 21	0 11	1 13	46
7	1 00 02	11 49 37	4 54	0 05	1 13	46
8	1 00 00	11 53 51	4 15	0 02	1 13	46
9	0 59 59	12 01 57	3 24	0 08	1 13	46
10	0 59 57	12 14 13	2 18	0 14	1 13	46
11	0 59 55	12 30 48	0 59	0 19	1 13	46
12	0 59 54	12 51 29	0 31	0 24	1 13	46
13	0 59 52	13 15 40	2 06	0 29	1 13	46
14	0 59 50	13 42 06	3 40	0 34	1 13	46
15	0 59 49	14 08 55	5 03	0 38	1 13	46
16	0 59 47	14 33 43	6 10	0 42	1 13	46
17	0 59 45	14 53 44	6 55	0 46	1 13	46
18	0 59 43	15 06 25	7 14	0 49	1 12	46
19	0 59 41	15 10 00	7 05	0 52	1 12	46
20	0 59 39	15 04 03	6 28	0 55	1 12	46
21	0 59 37	14 49 32	5 22	0 58	1 12	46
22	0 59 35	14 28 37	3 55	1 01	1 12	46
23	0 59 32	14 04 02	2 12	1 04	1 12	46
24	0 59 30	13 38 24	0 25	1 06	1 12	46
25	0 59 28	13 13 53	1 15	1 08	1 12	46
26	0 59 26	12 51 55	2 41	1 11	1 12	46
27	0 59 23	12 33 20	3 49	1 13	1 12	46
28	0 59 21	12 18 21	4 38	1 15	1 12	46
29	0 59 19	12 06 54	5 12	1 17	1 12	46
30	0 59 16	11 58 39	5 32	1 19	1 12	46
31	0 59 14	11 53 11	5 41	1 20	1 11	46

APRIL

D	☉ ° ′ ″	☽ ° ′ ″	☽Dec. ° ′	☿ ° ′	♀ ° ′	♂ ′
1	0 59 12	11 50 09	5 38	1 22	1 11	46
2	0 59 10	11 49 13	5 25	1 24	1 11	46
3	0 59 08	11 50 16	5 02	1 25	1 11	46
4	0 59 06	11 53 17	4 26	1 27	1 11	46
5	0 59 04	11 58 28	3 37	1 29	1 11	46
6	0 59 02	12 06 08	2 35	1 30	1 11	46
7	0 59 00	12 16 39	1 21	1 32	1 11	46
8	0 58 59	12 30 25	0 04	1 34	1 11	46
9	0 58 57	12 47 41	1 34	1 35	1 11	46
10	0 58 55	13 08 25	3 02	1 37	1 10	46
11	0 58 53	13 32 10	4 24	1 38	1 10	46
12	0 58 52	13 57 52	5 34	1 40	1 10	46
13	0 58 50	14 23 39	6 28	1 41	1 10	46
14	0 58 48	14 46 59	7 01	1 43	1 10	46
15	0 58 46	15 04 52	7 09	1 44	1 10	46
16	0 58 44	15 14 27	6 50	1 46	1 10	46
17	0 58 43	15 13 49	6 00	1 48	1 10	46
18	0 58 41	15 02 44	4 40	1 49	1 10	46
19	0 58 39	14 42 41	2 58	1 51	1 09	46
20	0 58 37	14 16 30	1 04	1 52	1 09	46
21	0 58 34	13 47 31	0 46	1 54	1 09	46
22	0 58 32	13 18 47	2 21	1 56	1 09	46
23	0 58 30	12 52 38	3 36	1 57	1 09	46
24	0 58 28	12 30 31	4 29	1 59	1 09	46
25	0 58 26	12 13 08	5 05	2 00	1 09	46
26	0 58 23	12 00 36	5 27	2 02	1 09	46
27	0 58 21	11 52 37	5 37	2 03	1 08	46
28	0 58 19	11 48 40	5 37	2 05	1 08	46
29	0 58 17	11 48 06	5 27	2 06	1 08	46
30	0 58 16	11 50 14	5 07	2 07	1 08	46

MAY

D	☉ ° ′ ″	☽ ° ′ ″	☽Dec. ° ′	☿ ° ′	♀ ° ′	♂ ′
1	0 58 14	11 54 28	4 35	2 08	1 08	46
2	0 58 12	12 00 18	3 50	2 09	1 08	46
3	0 58 10	12 07 27	2 51	2 09	1 07	46
4	0 58 09	12 15 53	1 38	2 10	1 07	46
5	0 58 07	12 25 44	0 16	2 10	1 07	46
6	0 58 06	12 37 22	1 12	2 10	1 07	46
7	0 58 04	12 51 10	2 38	2 09	1 07	46
8	0 58 03	13 07 29	3 58	2 09	1 07	46
9	0 58 01	13 26 25	5 05	2 08	1 06	46
10	0 58 00	13 47 34	5 59	2 07	1 06	46
11	0 57 59	14 09 53	6 36	2 05	1 06	46
12	0 57 57	14 31 33	6 54	2 03	1 06	46
13	0 57 56	14 50 00	6 49	2 01	1 06	46
14	0 57 55	15 02 20	6 17	1 59	1 05	46
15	0 57 54	15 06 03	5 15	1 56	1 05	46
16	0 57 52	14 59 49	3 44	1 54	1 05	46
17	0 57 51	14 44 01	1 53	1 51	1 05	45
18	0 57 49	14 20 41	0 04	1 48	1 05	45
19	0 57 48	13 52 53	1 51	1 45	1 04	45
20	0 57 46	13 23 53	3 18	1 42	1 04	45
21	0 57 44	12 56 29	4 20	1 39	1 04	45
22	0 57 43	12 32 42	5 02	1 36	1 04	45
23	0 57 41	12 13 44	5 26	1 33	1 03	45
24	0 57 40	12 00 05	5 37	1 29	1 03	45
25	0 57 38	11 51 44	5 38	1 26	1 03	45
26	0 57 37	11 48 20	5 29	1 23	1 02	45
27	0 57 35	11 49 14	5 11	1 19	1 02	45
28	0 57 34	11 53 41	4 43	1 16	1 02	45
29	0 57 33	12 00 48	4 01	1 12	1 02	45
30	0 57 31	12 09 45	3 06	1 09	1 01	45
31	0 57 30	12 19 47	1 56	1 05	1 01	45

JUNE

D	☉ ° ′ ″	☽ ° ′ ″	☽Dec. ° ′	☿ ° ′	♀ ° ′	♂ ′
1	0 57 29	12 30 21	0 34	1 01	1 00	45
2	0 57 28	12 41 09	0 54	0 58	1 00	45
3	0 57 27	12 52 14	2 22	0 54	1 00	45
4	0 57 27	13 03 49	3 42	0 50	0 59	45
5	0 57 26	13 16 20	4 50	0 46	0 59	45
6	0 57 25	13 30 05	5 42	0 42	0 59	45
7	0 57 24	13 45 11	6 19	0 38	0 58	45
8	0 57 24	14 01 12	6 38	0 34	0 58	45
9	0 57 23	14 17 06	6 39	0 29	0 57	44
10	0 57 23	14 31 11	6 17	0 25	0 57	44
11	0 57 22	14 41 18	5 30	0 20	0 56	44
12	0 57 22	14 45 17	4 15	0 16	0 56	44
13	0 57 21	14 41 40	2 36	0 11	0 55	44
14	0 57 21	14 30 03	0 41	0 07	0 55	44
15	0 57 20	14 11 29	1 12	0 02	0 54	44
16	0 57 20	13 48 04	2 51	0 02	0 54	44
17	0 57 19	13 22 26	4 05	0 07	0 53	44
18	0 57 18	12 57 10	4 56	0 11	0 53	44
19	0 57 17	12 34 25	5 26	0 15	0 52	44
20	0 57 16	12 15 40	5 40	0 19	0 51	44
21	0 57 16	12 01 50	5 42	0 23	0 51	44
22	0 57 15	11 53 18	5 34	0 26	0 50	44
23	0 57 14	11 50 02	5 17	0 29	0 49	44
24	0 57 14	11 51 41	4 51	0 31	0 49	44
25	0 57 13	11 57 39	4 13	0 33	0 48	43
26	0 57 13	12 07 07	3 22	0 35	0 47	43
27	0 57 12	12 19 06	2 16	0 35	0 46	43
28	0 57 12	12 32 35	0 57	0 36	0 45	43
29	0 57 12	12 46 33	0 32	0 35	0 44	43
30	0 57 11	13 00 10	2 03	0 34	0 43	43

JULY

D	☉ ° ′ ″	☽ ° ′ ″	☽Dec. ° ′	☿ ° ′	♀ ° ′	♂ ′
1	0 57 11	13 12 52	3 28	0 33	0 43	43
2	0 57 11	13 24 26	4 40	0 30	0 42	43
3	0 57 11	13 34 56	5 36	0 28	0 40	43
4	0 57 11	13 44 38	6 14	0 24	0 39	43
5	0 57 11	13 53 48	6 34	0 21	0 38	43
6	0 57 12	14 02 29	6 35	0 17	0 37	43
7	0 57 12	14 10 22	6 16	0 12	0 36	43
8	0 57 13	14 16 44	5 35	0 08	0 35	42
9	0 57 13	14 20 27	4 31	0 03	0 33	42
10	0 57 14	14 20 22	3 03	0 02	0 32	42
11	0 57 14	14 15 31	1 17	0 07	0 31	42
12	0 57 14	14 05 31	0 34	0 13	0 29	42
13	0 57 15	13 50 45	2 17	0 18	0 28	42
14	0 57 15	13 32 19	3 42	0 23	0 26	42
15	0 57 15	13 11 48	4 43	0 29	0 25	42
16	0 57 15	12 51 02	5 22	0 34	0 23	42
17	0 57 16	12 31 40	5 42	0 39	0 21	42
18	0 57 16	12 15 10	5 48	0 45	0 19	41
19	0 57 16	12 02 32	5 42	0 50	0 17	41
20	0 57 16	11 54 30	5 26	0 55	0 16	41
21	0 57 16	11 51 24	5 01	1 00	0 14	41
22	0 57 17	11 53 17	4 25	1 05	0 12	41
23	0 57 17	11 59 55	3 38	1 10	0 09	41
24	0 57 17	12 10 48	2 38	1 15	0 07	41
25	0 57 18	12 25 09	1 23	1 20	0 05	41
26	0 57 18	12 41 57	0 03	1 24	0 03	41
27	0 57 19	12 59 59	1 35	1 29	0 01	40
28	0 57 19	13 17 57	3 05	1 33	0 02	40
29	0 57 20	13 34 36	4 25	1 37	0 04	40
30	0 57 21	13 48 54	5 30	1 41	0 07	40
31	0 57 22	14 00 12	6 15	1 45	0 09	40

AUGUST

D	☉ ° ′ ″	☽ ° ′ ″	☽Dec. ° ′	☿ ° ′	♀ ° ′	♂ ′
1	0 57 22	14 08 14	6 40	1 48	0 11	40
2	0 57 23	14 13 05	6 44	1 51	0 14	40
3	0 57 25	14 15 01	6 26	1 54	0 16	40
4	0 57 26	14 14 24	5 46	1 57	0 18	39
5	0 57 27	14 11 31	4 44	1 59	0 21	39
6	0 57 29	14 06 27	3 22	2 00	0 23	39
7	0 57 30	13 59 14	1 43	2 02	0 25	39
8	0 57 31	13 49 51	0 04	2 03	0 27	39
9	0 57 33	13 38 18	1 47	2 03	0 29	39
10	0 57 34	13 24 51	3 16	2 04	0 30	39
11	0 57 35	13 09 55	4 24	2 04	0 32	38
12	0 57 36	12 54 10	5 11	2 03	0 33	38
13	0 57 37	12 38 26	5 38	2 03	0 35	38
14	0 57 38	12 23 40	5 50	2 02	0 36	38
15	0 57 39	12 10 47	5 48	2 02	0 36	38
16	0 57 40	12 00 37	5 34	2 01	0 37	38
17	0 57 42	11 53 55	5 11	2 00	0 37	38
18	0 57 43	11 51 16	4 38	1 59	0 37	37
19	0 57 44	11 53 04	3 54	1 57	0 37	37
20	0 57 45	11 59 31	2 58	1 56	0 37	37
21	0 57 46	12 10 33	1 49	1 55	0 36	37
22	0 57 47	12 25 51	0 29	1 53	0 35	37
23	0 57 48	12 44 45	1 00	1 52	0 34	37
24	0 57 50	13 06 13	2 31	1 51	0 33	36
25	0 57 51	13 28 50	3 57	1 49	0 31	36
26	0 57 52	13 50 51	5 11	1 48	0 30	36
27	0 57 54	14 10 25	6 08	1 47	0 28	36
28	0 57 55	14 25 47	6 44	1 45	0 26	36
29	0 57 57	14 35 37	6 57	1 44	0 24	35
30	0 57 58	14 39 15	6 45	1 43	0 22	35
31	0 58 00	14 36 46	6 08	1 42	0 20	35

SEPTEMBER

D	☉	☽	☽Dec.	☿	♀	♂
	° ′ ″	° ′ ″	° ′	° ′	° ′	′
1	0 58 02	14 29 00	5 08	1 40	0 17	35
2	0 58 04	14 17 12	3 45	1 39	0 15	35
3	0 58 06	14 02 48	2 06	1 38	0 12	34
4	0 58 08	13 47 07	0 20	1 37	0 10	34
5	0 58 10	13 31 10	1 23	1 35	0 08	34
6	0 58 12	13 15 39	2 53	1 34	0 05	34
7	0 58 14	13 00 56	4 04	1 33	0 03	34
8	0 58 16	12 47 11	4 55	1 32	0 00	33
9	0 58 18	12 34 29	5 28	1 31	0 02	33
10	0 58 20	12 22 53	5 45	1 29	0 04	33
11	0 58 21	12 12 32	5 49	1 28	0 06	33
12	0 58 23	12 03 42	5 40	1 27	0 09	32
13	0 58 25	11 56 44	5 20	1 26	0 11	32
14	0 58 27	11 52 08	4 49	1 25	0 13	32
15	0 58 29	11 50 26	4 08	1 23	0 15	32
16	0 58 30	11 52 09	3 15	1 22	0 17	31
17	0 58 32	11 57 49	2 11	1 21	0 19	31
18	0 58 34	12 07 47	0 56	1 19	0 21	31
19	0 58 35	12 22 14	0 27	1 18	0 22	30
20	0 58 37	12 41 04	1 54	1 16	0 24	30
21	0 58 39	13 03 46	3 19	1 15	0 26	30
22	0 58 40	13 29 15	4 37	1 13	0 28	30
23	0 58 42	13 55 52	5 43	1 12	0 29	29
24	0 58 44	14 21 19	6 31	1 10	0 31	29
25	0 58 46	14 42 54	6 58	1 08	0 32	29
26	0 58 47	14 57 57	7 01	1 06	0 34	28
27	0 58 49	15 04 28	6 36	1 04	0 35	28
28	0 58 52	15 01 39	5 42	1 01	0 36	28
29	0 58 54	14 50 11	4 21	0 59	0 37	27
30	0 58 56	14 32 02	2 39	0 56	0 39	27

OCTOBER

D	☉	☽	☽Dec.	☿	♀	♂
	° ′ ″	° ′ ″	° ′	° ′	° ′	′
1	0 58 59	14 09 47	0 48	0 53	0 40	27
2	0 59 01	13 46 06	1 00	0 50	0 41	26
3	0 59 03	13 23 09	2 34	0 46	0 42	26
4	0 59 06	13 02 21	3 48	0 43	0 43	25
5	0 59 08	12 44 28	4 42	0 38	0 44	25
6	0 59 10	12 29 44	5 18	0 34	0 45	25
7	0 59 12	12 17 57	5 38	0 29	0 46	24
8	0 59 14	12 08 45	5 45	0 24	0 47	24
9	0 59 17	12 01 43	5 40	0 18	0 48	23
10	0 59 19	11 56 31	5 24	0 12	0 49	23
11	0 59 21	11 52 55	4 57	0 05	0 50	22
12	0 59 23	11 50 58	4 19	0 02	0 50	22
13	0 59 25	11 50 53	3 29	0 10	0 51	22
14	0 59 27	11 53 02	2 28	0 18	0 52	21
15	0 59 29	11 58 00	1 17	0 27	0 53	21
16	0 59 31	12 06 21	0 03	0 35	0 53	20
17	0 59 32	12 18 39	1 25	0 44	0 54	20
18	0 59 34	12 35 16	2 46	0 52	0 54	19
19	0 59 36	12 56 18	4 02	0 59	0 55	19
20	0 59 37	13 21 18	5 08	1 06	0 56	18
21	0 59 39	13 49 09	6 02	1 11	0 56	17
22	0 59 41	14 17 51	6 40	1 14	0 57	17
23	0 59 43	14 44 29	6 57	1 15	0 57	16
24	0 59 44	15 05 37	6 50	1 15	0 58	16
25	0 59 46	15 17 57	6 13	1 11	0 58	15
26	0 59 48	15 19 14	5 04	1 06	0 59	15
27	0 59 50	15 09 11	3 26	0 59	0 59	14
28	0 59 53	14 49 30	1 30	0 50	1 00	13
29	0 59 55	14 23 22	0 28	0 39	1 00	13
30	0 59 57	13 54 25	2 12	0 28	1 01	12
31	0 59 59	13 25 50	3 35	0 17	1 01	11

NOVEMBER

D	☉	☽	☽Dec.	☿	♀	♂
	° ′ ″	° ′ ″	° ′	° ′	° ′	′
1	1 00 01	12 59 57	4 34	0 05	1 02	11
2	1 00 03	12 38 08	5 12	0 06	1 02	10
3	1 00 05	12 20 53	5 33	0 17	1 02	9
4	1 00 07	12 08 08	5 41	0 27	1 03	9
5	1 00 10	11 59 27	5 38	0 36	1 03	8
6	1 00 12	11 54 10	5 25	0 44	1 03	7
7	1 00 13	11 51 34	5 02	0 52	1 04	6
8	1 00 15	11 51 01	4 27	0 58	1 04	6
9	1 00 17	11 52 01	3 41	1 04	1 04	5
10	1 00 19	11 54 19	2 43	1 09	1 05	4
11	1 00 21	11 57 57	1 33	1 13	1 05	3
12	1 00 22	12 03 11	0 15	1 17	1 05	2
13	1 00 24	12 10 33	1 06	1 20	1 06	2
14	1 00 25	12 20 38	2 25	1 23	1 06	1
15	1 00 27	12 34 07	3 38	1 25	1 06	0
16	1 00 28	12 51 28	4 41	1 27	1 06	1
17	1 00 29	13 12 47	5 33	1 28	1 07	2
18	1 00 31	13 37 37	6 13	1 29	1 07	3
19	1 00 32	14 04 40	6 37	1 31	1 07	4
20	1 00 33	14 31 39	6 42	1 31	1 07	4
21	1 00 34	14 55 23	6 22	1 32	1 07	5
22	1 00 36	15 12 16	5 34	1 33	1 08	6
23	1 00 37	15 19 08	4 13	1 33	1 08	7
24	1 00 38	15 14 24	2 24	1 33	1 08	8
25	1 00 40	14 58 36	0 21	1 34	1 08	9
26	1 00 41	14 34 15	1 37	1 34	1 09	10
27	1 00 43	14 04 58	3 15	1 34	1 09	10
28	1 00 44	13 34 28	4 25	1 34	1 09	11
29	1 00 46	13 05 44	5 10	1 34	1 09	12
30	1 00 47	12 40 49	5 34	1 34	1 09	13

DECEMBER

D	☉	☽	☽Dec.	☿	♀	♂
	° ′ ″	° ′ ″	° ′	° ′	° ′	′
1	1 00 49	12 20 49	5 43	1 34	1 09	14
2	1 00 50	12 06 03	5 41	1 34	1 10	15
3	1 00 52	11 56 21	5 28	1 34	1 10	15
4	1 00 53	11 51 11	5 06	1 34	1 10	16
5	1 00 54	11 49 49	4 35	1 34	1 10	17
6	1 00 56	11 51 26	3 51	1 34	1 10	18
7	1 00 57	11 55 15	2 56	1 34	1 10	18
8	1 00 58	12 00 35	1 49	1 34	1 10	19
9	1 00 59	12 06 57	0 32	1 34	1 11	20
10	1 01 00	12 14 10	0 49	1 34	1 11	20
11	1 01 01	12 22 19	2 10	1 34	1 11	21
12	1 01 01	12 31 44	3 24	1 34	1 11	21
13	1 01 02	12 42 57	4 27	1 34	1 11	22
14	1 01 02	12 56 30	5 18	1 34	1 11	22
15	1 01 03	13 12 46	5 56	1 34	1 11	22
16	1 01 03	13 31 44	6 19	1 34	1 11	23
17	1 01 04	13 52 48	6 27	1 35	1 11	23
18	1 01 04	14 14 35	6 16	1 35	1 12	23
19	1 01 04	14 34 52	5 41	1 35	1 12	23
20	1 01 05	14 50 53	4 39	1 35	1 12	24
21	1 01 05	14 59 50	3 08	1 35	1 12	24
22	1 01 05	14 59 42	1 14	1 35	1 12	24
23	1 01 06	14 49 54	0 48	1 36	1 12	24
24	1 01 06	14 31 35	2 39	1 36	1 12	24
25	1 01 07	14 07 12	4 06	1 36	1 12	24
26	1 01 07	13 39 48	5 04	1 36	1 12	23
27	1 01 08	13 12 20	5 38	1 37	1 12	23
28	1 01 08	12 47 10	5 51	1 37	1 12	23
29	1 01 08	12 25 55	5 50	1 37	1 12	23
30	1 01 09	12 09 30	5 38	1 37	1 13	22
31	1 01 09	11 58 14	5 16	1 37	1 13	22

Day	Time	Aspect	
JANUARY			
1 Mo	01 21	☽☍♃	B
	06 53	☽⚼♀	b
	07 06	☽□♅	B
	09 28	♀∠♅	
	18 31	☽△♆	G
	19 08	♀⊻♇	
	20 04	☽☍♂	B
2 Tu	05 11	☿⊻♃	
	05 25	☽✱♄	G
	09 15	☉✱♅	
	10 06	☽☍♇	B
	15 14	☽♋	
	19 12	☿⚼♄	
	20 49	☽⚼♆	b
	23 10	☉⊥♆	
3 We	07 47	☽∠♄	b
	09 32	☽☍☿	B
	11 51	☽△♅	G
	13 57	☽☍☉	B
4 Th	03 31	♀♒	
	05 19	☿✱♅	
	10 01	☽⚼♃	b
	10 45	☽⊻♄	g
	13 58	☿⊥♆	
	15 06	☽⚼♅	b
	16 00	☽#☿	G
	21 14	☽♌	
	23 08	☽☍♀	B
	23 27	☽#♂	B
5 Fr	04 48	☽#☉	G
	09 33	☽⚼♂	b
	13 38	☽#♀	G
	13 46	☽#♃	G
	14 15	☽△♃	G
	15 31	♀∥♃	
	20 03	☽⚼♇	b
	22 16	☉⊥♃	
6 Sa	07 38	☽☍♆	B
	11 46	☿⊥♃	
	13 31	☽#♇	D
	15 48	☽△♂	G
	17 29	♀⊥♇	
	18 13	☽#♆	D
	18 57	☽●♄	B
	22 36	☽∥♄	B
7 Su	00 56	☽△♇	G
	06 05	☉☌☿	
	06 18	☽♍	
	09 38	☽⚼☉	b
	09 50	☽⚼☿	b
8 Mo	01 16	☽□♃	B
	04 46	☽#♅	B
	04 52	☿±♄	
	05 37	☽☍♅	B
	08 45	☿⊻♆	
	17 45	☉±♄	
	18 05	♂△♄	
	18 10	☽△☉	G
	19 07	♀⊥♅	
	20 19	☽△☿	G
9 Tu	00 14	☽⚼♀	b
	01 14	☉⊻♆	
	06 10	☽⊻♄	g
	07 01	☽□♂	B
	12 51	☽□♇	B
	18 15	☽♎	
10 We	01 11	☽⚼♆	b
	02 09	☿∥♂	
	10 14	☽△♀	G
	12 27	☽∠♄	b
	14 50	☽✱♃	G
	23 32	☽∥♅	B
11 Th	07 46	☽△♆	G
	12 45	☽□☉	B
	17 28	☿∇♄	
	18 46	☽✱♄	G
	19 00	☽□☿	B
	21 48	☽∠♃	b
	23 55	☽✱♂	G
12 Fr	00 59	☽⚼♅	b
	01 56	☽✱♇	G
	07 08	☽♏	
	07 23	☽#♄	B
	11 04	☽∥♆	D
	12 45	♀✱♃	
	16 16	☽∥♇	D
	17 19	☿∠♃	
13 Sa	04 16	☽∥♀	G
	04 22	☽⊻♃	g
	05 54	☽□♀	B
	07 07	☽△♅	G
	07 54	☽∠♂	b
	08 01	☽∠♇	b
	10 02	♂☌♇	
	14 42	☿∠♅	
	18 03	♀⊻♅	
	18 25	☽∥♃	G
	18 53	☽∥☉	G
	19 59	☽□♆	B
	21 24	☿⊻♇	
14 Su	02 20	☽∥☿	G
	03 02	♀∠♇	
	04 06	☉∥♃	
	05 50	☿⊻♂	
	06 00	☽✱☉	G
	06 05	☽□♄	B
	07 06	☉∇♄	
	10 34	☽∥♂	B
	13 24	☽⊻♇	g
	15 02	☽⊻♂	g
	15 50	☽✱☿	G
	18 11	☽♐	
15 Mo	01 57	♀∠♂	
	09 25	☿♒	
	13 08	☽∠☉	b
	15 10	☽☌♃	G
	17 04	☽□♅	B
	21 57	☽✱♀	G
16 Tu	00 24	☽∠☿	b
	05 09	☽✱♆	G
	14 12	☽△♄	G
	19 06	☽⊻☉	g
	20 16	☉∠♃	
	20 54	♂♑	
	21 28	☽☌♇	D
17 We	01 49	☽♑	
	02 06	☽☌♂	B
	02 23	♂Q♅	
	04 09	☽∠♀	b
	07 39	☽⊻☿	g
	08 01	☿∥♃	
	08 23	☽∠♆	b
	12 40	☿⊥♇	
	16 54	☉∠♅	
	16 57	☽⚼♄	b
	22 17	☽⊻♃	g
	23 29	☽✱♅	G
18 Th	03 06	☉⊻♇	
	09 17	☽⊻♀	g
	10 49	☽⊻♆	g
19 Fr	00 39	☽∠♃	b
	01 34	☽∠♅	b
	02 04	☿⊥♅	
	02 15	☽⊻♇	g
	02 48	♀☌♆	
	04 01	☽☌☉	D
	05 35	☽∥♂	B
	06 16	☽♒	
	09 25	☽⊻♂	g
	12 38	♀∥♇	
	18 56	☽●☿	G
	19 11	☽∥♃	G
20 Sa	01 33	☽∥☿	G
	01 37	☽∥☉	G
	02 30	☽✱♃	G
	02 44	☉∥☿	
	03 08	☽⊻♅	g
	03 47	☽∠♇	b
	11 01	☉♒	
	12 03	☿⊥♂	
	12 10	☽∠♂	b
	14 02	☽☌♆	D
	17 18	☽●♀	G
	18 06	☽∥♇	D
	20 16	☽∥♀	G
	21 33	☽☍♄	B
	22 49	☽∥♆	D
21 Su	00 38	☽#♄	B
	05 00	☽✱♇	G
	08 48	☽♓	
	10 28	☽⊻☉	g
	14 37	☽✱♂	G
22 Mo	02 03	♂∠♆	
	04 01	☽⊻☿	g
	04 21	☽∥♅	B
	05 20	☽□♃	B
	05 29	☽☌♅	B
	10 12	♀∥♆	
	13 23	☽∠☉	b
	15 38	♀☍♄	
	16 13	☿✱♃	
	16 16	☽⊻♆	g
	16 39	☿⊻♅	
	21 42	♃□♅	
	21 43	☿∠♇	
23 Tu	00 09	☽⊻♀	g
	07 11	☽□♇	B
	07 43	♀#♄	
	08 26	☽∠☿	b
	10 52	☽♈	
	16 22	☽✱☉	G
	17 24	☽∠♆	b
	19 26	☽□♂	B
	19 29	♀Q♃	
24 We	00 21	☽⚼♄	b
	03 41	☽∠♀	b
	05 12	☉⊥♇	
	07 51	☽⊻♅	g
	08 10	☽△♃	G
	09 52	☽#♅	B
	13 03	☽✱☿	G
	18 43	☽✱♆	G
25 Th	01 32	☽△♄	G
	07 28	☽✱♀	G
	09 18	☽∠♅	b
	09 50	☽△♇	G
	09 52	☽⚼♃	b
	10 46	☽#♀	G
	13 28	☽♉	
	14 41	☽∥♄	B
	15 49	☽#♆	D
	20 51	☽#♇	D
	22 51	☽#☿	G
	23 01	☽□☉	B
26 Fr	01 01	☽△♂	G
	06 48	☽#☉	G
	10 59	♀✱♇	
	11 02	☽✱♅	G
	11 32	☽⚼♇	b
	13 20	☿☌♆	
	16 44	☿∥♇	
	21 05	☽#♃	G
	22 06	☽□♆	B
	23 17	☽□☿	B
	23 21	☉⊥♅	
27 Sa	04 18	☽⚼♂	b
	04 39	☽□♄	B
	09 16	☽#♂	B
	10 14	♂⚼♄	
	16 08	☽□♀	B
	17 10	☽♊	
28 Su	03 32	♀♓	
	07 07	☽△☉	G
	14 27	☿∥♆	
	15 28	☽□♅	B
	16 46	☽☍♃	B
	18 07	☿☍♄	
	19 55	☿#♄	
29 Mo	02 47	☽△♆	G
	09 05	☽✱♄	G
	11 16	☽△☿	G
	11 51	☽⚼☉	b
	18 40	☽☍♇	B
	22 16	☽♋	
	23 14	☿∠♂	
	23 32	☉⊻♂	
30 Tu	02 41	☽△♀	G
	05 44	☽⚼♆	b
	11 55	☽∠♄	b
	15 37	☿Q♃	
	16 45	☽☍♂	B
	18 04	☽⚼☿	b
	21 30	☽△♅	G
31 We	08 51	☽⚼♀	b
	15 13	☽⊻♄	g
FEBRUARY			
1 Th	01 17	☽⚼♅	b
	02 33	☿✱♇	
	03 25	☽⚼♃	b
	05 15	☽♌	
	06 49	☽#♂	B
	15 00	♄#♆	
	17 54	☽#♃	G
2 Fr	04 32	☉⊻♅	
	05 45	☽☍☉	B
	05 57	☽⚼♇	b
	08 05	☽△♃	G
	08 18	☉∠♇	
	09 20	☿♓	
	17 47	☽☍♆	B
	20 30	☽#☉	G
	21 25	☽#♇	D
	23 34	☽●♄	B
3 Sa	03 16	☽∥♄	B
	03 33	☽#♆	D
	10 40	☽⚼♂	b
	10 41	♂✱♅	
	10 55	☽△♇	G
	12 18	☉∥♇	
	14 34	☽♍	
	15 47	☉✱♃	
	18 26	☽☍☿	B
	20 46	♂⊥♆	
	23 02	☽#☿	G
4 Su	04 37	☽#♀	G
	08 09	☽☍♀	B
	14 33	☽#♅	B
	16 18	☽☍♅	B
	18 07	☽△♂	G
	19 23	☽□♃	B
5 Mo	07 58	♀Q♇	
	10 18	☽⊻♄	g
	19 30	♂⊻♃	
	22 37	☽□♇	B
6 Tu	02 15	☽♎	
	06 27	☽⚼☉	b
	11 11	☽⚼♆	b
	16 22	☽∠♄	b
7 We	04 31	☽∥♅	B
	05 05	☉#♄	
	08 10	☽∥♀	G
	08 31	♂±♄	
	08 42	☽✱♃	G
	10 28	☽∥☿	G
	10 41	☽□♂	B
	15 45	☽△☉	G
	17 45	☽△♆	G
	18 57	♀☌♅	
	22 39	☽✱♄	G
	22 47	☉∥♆	
	22 55	☽⚼☿	b
8 Th	11 38	☽✱♇	G
	11 39	☽⚼♅	b
	13 31	☽⚼♀	b
	15 09	☽♏	
	15 34	☽∠♃	b
	15 42	☽∥☉	G
	15 52	☉☌♆	
	16 45	☽∥♆	D
	18 07	☽#♄	B
	23 28	☽∥♇	D
9 Fr	02 14	♀∥♅	
	07 46	☽△☿	G
	11 31	♀□♃	
	17 58	☽∠♇	b
	18 03	☽△♅	G
	21 44	☿∥♅	
	22 10	☽⊻♃	g
	23 14	☽△♀	G
10 Sa	03 22	☽✱♂	G
	05 20	☽∥♃	G
	06 28	☽□♆	B
	09 51	☽□☉	B
	10 39	☽□♄	B
	11 37	☽∥♂	B
	18 42	☉☍♄	
	23 45	☽⊻♇	g
11 Su	03 01	☽♐	
	10 46	☽∠♂	b
	21 54	☽□☿	B
12 Mo	04 57	☽□♅	B
	07 36	♂⊻♆	

	09 16	☽☌♃	G
	15 52	☽□♀	B
	16 35	☽✱♆	G
	17 07	☽⊻♂	g
	19 59	☽△♄	G
	23 30	♀⊻♆	
13	00 31	☽✱☉	G
Tu	08 45	☽☌♇	D
	11 42	☽♑	
	20 13	☽∠♆	b
	22 47	♀✱♂	
	23 16	☽⚼♄	b
14	04 38	☿ Stat	
We	06 00	☽∠☉	b
	06 08	☽✱☿	G
	08 17	♀⚻♄	
	12 07	☽✱♅	G
	13 49	♂⚻♄	
	16 29	☽⊻♃	g
	22 53	☽⊻♆	g
15	02 21	☽☌♂	B
Th	03 24	☽✱♀	G
	08 12	☽∠☿	b
	10 19	☽⊻☉	g
	13 55	☽⊻♇	g
	14 17	☽∠♅	b
	16 34	☽♒	
	18 12	♂⊥♃	
	18 40	☽∠♃	b
16	01 08	☽∥♂	B
Fr	02 55	☽∥♃	G
	07 26	☽∠♀	b
	09 09	☽⊻☿	g
	15 15	☽∠♇	b
	15 41	☽⊻♅	g
	20 05	☽✱♃	G
17	01 47	☽☌♆	D
Sa	03 57	☽☍♄	B
	04 06	☽∥♇	D
	07 27	☽#♄	B
	07 41	☽⊻♂	g
	09 55	☽∥♆	D
	10 37	☽⊻♀	g
	12 32	☉Q♃	
	13 07	☉✱♇	
	16 02	☽✱♇	G
	16 14	☽☌☉	D
	18 30	☽♓	
	22 07	☽∥☉	G
	23 40	♀⊥♆	
18	01 13	☿∠♂	
Su	08 43	☽☌☿	G
	09 29	☽∠♂	b
	14 35	♂∥♃	
	15 17	☽∥♅	B
	16 58	☽☌♅	B
	21 13	☽∥☿	G
	21 30	☽□♃	B
	21 41	♀±♄	
19	01 09	☉♓	
Mo	02 46	☽⊻♆	g
	08 29	☽∥♀	G
	11 02	☽✱♂	G
	15 43	☽☌♀	G
	16 43	☽□♇	B
	19 06	☽♈	
	20 24	☽⊻☉	g
	20 59	☽#♀	G
20	03 05	☽∠♆	b
Tu	03 57	♀□♇	
	04 37	☽⚼♄	b
	06 44	☽⊻☿	g
	10 12	☽#☿	G
	15 01	☽#♅	B
	17 43	☽⊻♅	g
	22 32	☽△♃	G
	22 33	☽∠☉	b
21	03 33	☽✱♆	G
We	04 12	☽#☉	G
	04 55	☽△♄	G
	05 40	☽∠☿	b
	08 21	♀♈	
	14 29	☽□♂	B
	17 42	☽△♇	G
	18 24	☽∠♅	b
	19 21	☉⊥♂	
	20 03	☽♉	
	20 36	☽#♆	D
	21 08	☽⊻♀	g
	23 24	☽⚼♃	b
	23 47	☽∥♄	B
22	01 04	☽✱☉	G
Th	02 38	☽#♇	D
	04 47	☽✱☿	G
	18 44	☽⚼♇	b
	19 31	☽✱♅	G
23	00 35	☽∠♀	b
Fr	01 14	☽#♂	B
	04 34	☽#♃	G
	04 45	☉☌☿	
	05 39	☽□♆	B
	06 39	☽□♄	B
	09 18	☿⊥♂	
	19 47	☽△♂	G
	22 42	☽♊	
24	00 22	☿⊻♀	
Sa	04 05	☽□☿	B
	04 47	☽✱♀	G
	05 16	☿∥♅	
	05 49	♂⊻♇	
	07 56	☽□☉	B
	23 28	☽⚼♂	b
	23 29	☽□♅	B
	23 42	♂∠♅	
25	05 11	☽☍♃	B
Su	10 02	☽△♆	G
	10 39	☽✱♄	G
	12 29	♀∠♆	
	18 37	♀⚼♄	
26	01 21	☽☍♇	B
Mo	01 32	♂♒	
	03 48	☽♋	
	05 26	☽△☿	G
	13 13	☽⚼♆	b
	13 36	☽∠♄	b
	15 03	☿⊥♀	
	15 42	☽□♀	B
	15 58	☿⊻♂	
	17 57	☽△☉	G
27	03 00	☿♒	
Tu	06 03	☽△♅	G
	07 02	☽⚼☿	b
	11 29	☉∥☿	
	11 31	☿Q♃	
	17 13	☽⊻♄	g
28	00 11	☽⚼☉	b
We	10 19	☽⚼♅	b
	11 29	☽♌	
	12 01	♄☍♆	
	13 09	☿✱♇	
	15 11	☽☍♂	B
	16 48	☽⚼♃	b
	22 21	☽#♃	G

MARCH

1	06 03	☽△♀	G
Th	07 48	☽#♂	B
	13 46	☽⚼♇	b
	16 47	☉Q♇	
	21 54	☽△♃	G
	21 57	♂∠♃	
2	02 12	☽•♄	B
Fr	02 32	☽☍♆	B
	04 28	☽#♇	D
	06 45	☽∥♄	B
	11 58	☽#♆	D
	14 23	☽⚼♀	b
	15 53	☽☍☿	B
	19 03	☽△♇	G
	21 32	☽♍	
3	00 55	☿∠♀	
Sa	09 51	☽#☿	G
	18 24	☉⊻♀	
	18 46	☉∥♅	
	23 17	●☍☉	B
4	00 08	☽#♅	B
Su	00 30	☽#☉	G
	02 28	☽☍♅	B
	08 13	♂⊥♇	
	08 27	☽∥♀	G
	09 37	☽□♃	B
	13 07	☽⚼♂	b
	13 11	☽⊻♄	g
5	06 56	☽□♇	B
Mo	07 06	♀⊻♅	
	09 25	☽♎	
	15 39	☉☌♅	
	19 14	☽∠♄	b
	20 24	☽⚼♆	b
	21 25	☽△♂	G
6	04 46	☽#♀	G
Tu	05 08	☽∥☉	G
	06 53	☽⚼☿	b
	07 13	☉#♀	
	08 56	☽∥♅	B
	18 48	☽☍♀	B
	22 42	☽✱♃	G
7	01 30	☽✱♄	G
We	02 56	☽△♆	G
	05 21	☽∥☿	G
	13 00	☽△☿	G
	19 51	☽✱♇	G
	21 53	☽⚼♅	b
	22 07	☽∥♆	D
	22 17	☽♏	
8	00 28	♀#♅	
Th	02 37	☽⚼☉	b
	04 30	☽#♄	B
	04 45	☿ Stat	
	05 24	☽∠♃	b
	06 09	☽∥♇	D
	11 16	♀△♃	
	14 30	☽□♂	B
	20 23	☽∥♂	B
9	02 16	☽∠♇	b
Fr	04 24	☽△♅	G
	08 41	♀△♄	
	11 42	☽△☉	G
	11 54	☽⊻♃	g
	13 53	☽□♄	B
	14 11	☽∥♃	G
	14 19	☉□♃	
	15 49	☽□♆	B
	19 30	♂⊥♅	
10	01 51	☽□☿	B
Sa	03 41	♀✱♆	
	08 19	☽⊻♇	g
	10 37	☽♐	
	11 02	♀⊥♅	
	12 21	☉⚻♄	
	23 37	☽⚼♀	b
11	06 20	☽✱♂	G
Su	11 09	♀Q♂	
	14 31	☉⊻♆	
	16 03	☽□♅	B
	23 21	☽☌♃	G
12	00 34	☽△♄	G
Mo	02 52	☽✱♆	G
	03 54	☽□☉	B
	07 47	☽△♀	G
	13 03	☽∠♂	b
	13 42	☽✱☿	G
	18 27	☽☌♇	D
	20 35	☽♑	
13	04 44	☽⚼♄	b
Tu	07 10	☽∠♆	b
	18 35	☽∠☿	b
	18 39	☽⊻♂	g
14	00 30	☽✱♅	G
We	07 23	☽⊻♃	g
	10 30	☽⊻♆	g
	15 45	☽✱☉	G
	20 21	☽□♀	B
	22 35	☽⊻☿	g
15	00 55	☽⊻♇	g
Th	02 52	☽♒	
	03 15	☽∠♅	b
	09 55	☽∠♃	b
	12 13	☽∥♃	G
	19 51	☽∠☉	b
16	02 25	☽☌♂	B
Fr	02 44	☽∠♇	b
	04 21	☉±♄	
	05 04	☽⊻♅	g
	08 13	♂∠♇	
	10 10	☽∥♂	B
	11 31	☽✱♃	G
	11 36	☽☍♄	B
	14 18	☽☌♆	D
	15 15	☽∥♇	D
	15 51	☽#♄	B
	22 06	☽∥♆	D
	22 42	♃△♄	
	22 52	☽⊻☉	g
	23 34	☿✱♇	
17	00 18	♀△♇	
Sa	01 23	☿✱♀	
	03 43	☽✱♇	G
	03 56	☽•☿	G
	04 01	☽✱♀	G
	05 30	☽♓	
	08 20	☽∥☿	G
	11 09	☽#♀	G
	19 52	☉⊥♆	
	22 00	♀♉	
18	04 21	☽∥♅	B
Su	05 57	♀∠♅	
	06 23	☽⊻♂	g
	06 26	☽☌♅	B
	06 29	☽∠♀	b
	07 26	♂⊻♅	
	09 35	☿♓	
	12 36	☽□♃	B
	15 11	☽⊻♆	g
	18 12	☿#♀	
	23 12	☽∥☉	G
19	02 43	☽•●	D
Mo	03 59	☽□♇	B
	04 15	☽#☉	G
	05 42	☽♈	
	06 52	☽⊻☿	g
	07 33	☽∠♂	b
	08 26	☽⊻♀	g
	12 03	☽⚼♄	b
	15 02	☽∠♆	b
	22 14	☉□♇	
	22 46	☿Q♃	
	23 06	☽#♅	B
20	06 14	☽⊻♅	g
Tu	08 02	♀Q♆	
	08 05	☽∠☿	b
	08 33	☽✱♂	G
	11 42	☽△♄	G
	12 20	☽△♃	G
	14 49	☽✱♆	G
	17 11	☽#☿	G
	21 57	☽∥♀	G
21	00 07	☉♈	
We	03 33	☽△♇	G
	04 39	☽#♆	D
	05 15	☽♉	
	05 37	☽⊻☉	g
	06 10	☽∠♅	b
	09 32	☽✱☿	G
	11 11	☽∥♄	B
	11 25	☽#♇	D
	11 49	☽#♂	B
	12 11	☽☌♀	G
	12 18	☽⚼♃	b
	13 41	♀⚼♃	
	22 53	♂∥♇	
22	03 32	♂#♄	
Th	03 41	☽⚼♇	b
	06 25	☽✱♅	G
	07 31	☽∠☉	b
	11 15	☽□♂	B
	11 43	☽□♄	B
	13 34	☽#♃	G
	15 12	☽□♆	B
	19 34	♂☍♄	
23	06 06	☽♊	
Fr	10 07	☽✱☉	G
	14 21	☽□☿	B
	16 01	♂✱♃	
	17 55	☽⊻♀	g
24	08 49	☽□♅	B
Sa	14 03	☽✱♄	G
	15 24	☽☍♃	B
	16 42	☽△♂	G
	18 02	☽△♆	G
	18 57	☉⚼♄	
	19 22	♄#♇	
	19 58	♀#♆	
	22 13	☽∠♀	b
25	07 57	☽☍♇	B

Day	Time	Aspect	
Su	09 49	☽♋	
	16 28	☽∠♄	b
	17 39	♂☌♆	
	18 16	☽□☉	B
	20 44	☽⚼♆	b
	20 55	☽⚼♂	b
	23 24	☽△☿	G
26 Mo	03 41	☽✱♀	G
	11 19	♀#♂	
	14 36	☽△♅	G
	19 47	☽⊻♄	g
27 Tu	04 21	☉∠♆	
	05 51	☽⚼☿	b
	17 04	☽☊	
	18 50	☽⚼♅	b
28 We	01 57	☽⚼♃	b
	03 01	☽#♃	G
	06 52	☽△☉	G
	18 06	☽□♀	B
	19 06	☿Q♇	
	19 55	☽⚼♇	b
	22 32	♀#♇	
29 Th	02 10	♀∥♄	
	04 55	☽●♄	B
	07 06	☽△♃	G
	07 20	♀±♃	
	09 31	☽∥♀	G
	10 03	☽☍♆	B
	10 07	☽∥♄	B
	10 27	☽#♇	D
	12 57	♀⚼♇	
	13 52	♂∥♆	
	14 39	☽⚼☉	b
	15 45	☽☍♂	B
	19 02	☽#♆	D
	19 18	☽#♂	B
30 Fr	01 24	☽△♇	G
	03 27	☽♍	
	23 19	☽#☿	G
31 Sa	07 55	☽☍☿	B
	08 22	♀✱♅	
	08 47	☽#♅	B
	11 42	☽☍♅	B
	12 03	☽△♀	G
	16 27	☽⊻♄	g
	17 07	☽∥☉	G
	18 58	☽□♃	B
	22 45	♇Stat	
	23 06	☉⊥♀	
	23 22	☉∠♂	
APRIL			
1 Su	13 38	☽□♇	B
	15 43	☽♎	
	18 29	☿☌♅	
	21 45	☽⚼♀	b
	22 42	☽∠♄	b
2 Mo	04 29	☽⚼♆	b
	07 01	♀□♄	
	07 15	☽#☉	G
	12 51	☽∥♅	B
	16 25	☽⚼♂	b
	17 01	☽∥☿	G
	17 15	☽☍☉	B
3 Tu	05 04	☽✱♄	G
	07 50	☽✱♃	G
	08 19	☿▽♄	
	10 00	♀▽♃	
	11 00	☽△♆	G
	21 11	☽∥♂	B
4 We	00 59	☽△♂	G
	02 30	☽✱♇	G
	03 22	☽∥♆	D
	04 36	☽♏	
	07 17	☿□♃	
	07 17	☽⚼♅	b
	12 24	☽∥♇	D
	13 06	☽#♄	B
	14 16	☽∠♃	b
	15 14	☽⚼☿	b
	15 21	☿∥♅	
	18 16	♀□♆	
5 Th	00 22	♂✱♇	
	00 44	☉#☿	
	03 11	☽#♀	G
	08 49	☽∠♇	b
	09 36	☿⊻♆	
	13 01	☉#♅	
	13 43	☽△♅	G
	17 37	☽□♄	B
	20 31	☽⊻♃	g
	21 22	☽∥♃	G
	23 45	☽□♆	B
6 Fr	01 25	♃Stat	
	01 43	☽△☿	G
	02 42	♀±♇	
	02 54	☽☍♀	B
	08 49	♂♓	
	14 52	☽⊻♇	g
	15 29	☉⊻♅	
	16 57	☽♐	
	17 30	☽□♂	B
	20 13	☽⚼☉	b
7 Sa	08 15	☿±♄	
	16 10	☿✱♀	
8 Su	01 33	☽□♅	B
	04 21	☽△☉	G
	04 58	☽△♄	G
	07 52	☽☌♃	G
	11 08	☽✱♆	G
	11 56	☉△♄	
	16 08	♂Q♃	
	21 14	☽□☿	B
9 Mo	01 35	☽☌♇	D
	03 36	☽♑	
	07 57	☽✱♂	G
	09 18	☿⊥♆	
	09 49	☽⚼♄	b
	15 56	☽∠♆	b
10 Tu	00 07	☉△♃	
	03 40	☽⚼♀	b
	07 25	☿□♇	
	10 58	☽✱♅	G
	13 54	☽∠♂	b
	16 42	☽⊻♃	g
	18 04	☽□☉	B
	19 57	☽⊻♆	g
	23 03	♀Q♅	
	23 07	☿♈	
11 We	04 33	♀▽♇	
	09 28	☽⊻♇	g
	09 57	☽△♀	G
	11 23	☽♒	
	13 06	☽✱☿	G
	14 27	☽∠♅	b
	18 50	☽⊻♂	g
	19 33	☉✱♆	
	19 51	☽∠♃	b
	20 19	☽∥♃	G
12 Th	00 34	☽#♀	G
	02 15	♀♊	
	12 06	☽∠♇	b
	17 01	☽⊻♅	g
	19 12	☽∠☿	b
	19 31	☽☍♄	B
	21 45	☿⚼♄	
	22 06	☽✱♃	G
13 Fr	00 00	☽#♄	B
	00 52	☽∥♇	D
	01 18	☽☌♆	D
	01 59	☉⊥♅	
	03 29	☽✱☉	G
	08 41	☽∥♆	D
	13 50	☽✱♇	G
	15 39	☽♓	
	18 59	☽□♀	B
	23 53	☽∥♂	B
14 Sa	00 07	☽⊻☿	g
	01 32	☽●♂	B
	04 49	☽#☉	G
	06 34	☽∠☉	b
	15 39	♀#♃	
	16 50	☽∥♅	B
	19 34	☽☌♅	B
	20 37	☿⊻♂	
	21 46	☿∠♆	
15 Su	00 07	☽□♃	B
	03 16	☽⊻♆	g
	08 47	☽⊻☉	g
	10 02	☽#☿	G
	15 02	☽□♇	B
	16 13	☽∥☿	G
	16 47	☽♈	
	21 50	☽⚼♄	b
16 Mo	00 04	☽✱♀	G
	03 20	☽∠♆	b
	04 47	☽⊻♂	g
	05 23	☉#♂	
	07 08	☽☌☿	G
	08 23	☽#♅	B
	19 40	☽⊻♅	g
	21 34	☽△♄	G
	21 54	☽#♂	B
	23 30	☽∥☉	G
	23 49	☽△♃	G
17 Tu	01 44	☽∠♀	b
	03 03	☽✱♆	G
	05 43	☽∠♂	b
	08 56	♀Q♄	
	11 36	☽☌☉	D
	14 27	☽△♇	G
	14 54	☽#♆	D
	16 11	☽♉	
	19 20	☽∠♅	b
	22 11	☽#♇	D
	23 03	☽∥♄	B
	23 21	☽⚼♃	b
18 We	03 17	☽⊻♀	g
	06 34	☽✱♂	G
	12 42	☽⊻☿	g
	14 05	☽⚼♇	b
	19 06	☽✱♅	G
	20 52	☽□♄	B
19 Th	00 09	☽#♃	G
	02 29	☽□♆	B
	06 33	☽∥♀	G
	07 35	☉△♇	
	14 29	☽⊻☉	g
	15 51	☽♊	
	16 01	☽∠☿	b
	21 23	♄Stat	
20 Fr	07 27	☽☌♀	G
	09 25	☽□♂	B
	11 07	☉♉	
	12 43	♂Q♇	
	16 06	☿⊥♂	
	16 49	☽∠☉	b
	18 10	☿⊻♅	
	20 00	☽□♅	B
	20 16	☽✱☿	G
	21 42	☽✱♄	G
	23 51	☽☍♃	B
21 Sa	03 42	☽△♆	G
	07 09	☿△♄	
	15 52	☽☍♇	B
	17 50	☽♋	
	18 02	☿#♅	
	20 09	☽✱☉	G
	22 39	☿△♃	
	23 18	☽∠♄	b
22 Su	05 33	☽⚼♆	b
	15 18	☽⊻♀	g
	15 44	☽△♂	G
	17 51	☉∠♅	
23 Mo	00 14	☽△♅	G
	01 54	☽⊻♄	g
	04 11	☿✱♆	
	05 30	♀□♂	
	09 10	☽□☿	B
	18 43	☽∥♀	G
	20 42	☽⚼♂	b
	21 11	☽∠♀	b
	22 53	☿⊥♅	
	23 38	☽☊	
24 Tu	03 27	☿#♂	
	03 54	☽⚼♅	b
	06 36	☽□☉	B
	07 37	☽⚼♃	b
	08 01	☉Q♆	
	08 47	☽#♃	G
	19 17	☉⚼♃	
25 We	01 48	☽⚼♇	b
	04 25	☽✱♀	G
	10 14	☽●♄	B
	12 11	☽△♃	G
	15 03	☽∥♄	B
	16 07	☽#♇	D
	17 16	☽☍♆	B
26 Th	01 19	☽#♆	D
	05 00	☽△☿	G
	06 16	☽∥☉	G
	07 02	☽△♇	G
	09 24	☽♍	
	17 06	☿△♇	
	21 21	☽∥☿	G
	21 54	☽△☉	G
27 Fr	03 20	♀□♅	
	07 16	☿♉	
	11 44	☽#♂	B
	16 30	☽#♅	B
	17 04	☽⚼☿	b
	18 12	☽☍♂	B
	20 07	♀✱♄	
	20 18	☽☍♅	B
	21 51	☽⊻♄	g
	22 02	☽□♀	B
	23 31	☽□♃	B
28 Sa	02 52	☿∠♂	
	06 46	☽⚼☉	b
	12 03	☿∠♅	
	12 44	♀☍♃	
	19 14	☽□♇	B
	21 45	☽♎	
29 Su	03 56	☿Q♆	
	04 19	☽∠♄	b
	04 37	♂☌♅	
	05 07	☿⚼♃	
	11 41	☽⚼♆	b
	13 47	☉#♆	
	16 38	☽∥♅	B
	18 40	☽∥♂	B
30 Mo	01 36	☿∠♀	
	04 09	♂▽♄	
	10 52	☽✱♄	G
	12 06	☽✱♃	G
	17 27	☽△♀	G
	18 13	☽△♆	G
	22 21	♂□♃	
MAY			
1 Tu	01 34	♀△♆	
	05 23	☽#☿	G
	08 07	☽✱♇	G
	08 43	☽∥♆	D
	10 41	☽♏	
	10 45	♂∥♅	
	11 37	☽#☉	G
	15 56	☽⚼♅	b
	18 18	☽∠♃	b
	18 21	☽∥♇	D
	19 19	☽#♄	B
	19 48	☽⚼♂	b
2 We	01 09	☿#♆	
	02 59	☽⚼♀	b
	08 00	☽☍☿	B
	10 09	☽☍☉	B
	14 19	☽∠♇	b
	22 12	☽△♅	G
	23 31	☽□♄	B
3 Th	00 15	☽⊻♃	g
	03 10	☽∥♃	G
	03 59	☽△♂	G
	04 05	☉☌☿	
	06 42	☽□♆	B
	07 14	☿±♃	
	10 47	☉±♃	
	11 49	☉∥☿	
	18 52	☿⚼♇	
	20 12	☽⊻♇	g
	22 48	☽♐	
4 Fr	06 04	☽#♀	G
	09 59	☿#♇	
	12 40	☉⚼♇	
	15 06	☿∥♄	
	23 32	♂⊻♆	
5 Sa	09 39	☽□♅	B
	10 52	☽△♄	G
	11 04	☽☌♃	G
	15 53	☿✱♅	
	17 47	☽✱♆	G
	18 58	☽□♂	B
	22 55	☿□♄	
	23 20	☿▽♃	
6 Su	01 51	☉#♇	
	04 50	☽☍♀	B

Day	Time	Aspect	
	06 46	☽☌♇	D
	07 11	♃△♄	
	09 21	☽♑	
	10 22	☽⚼☉	b
	14 56	☉∥♄	
	15 53	☽⚼♄	b
	19 22	☽⚼☿	b
	22 38	☽∠♆	b
7	02 05	♀☍♇	
Mo	14 28	☿□♆	
	17 12	☽△☉	G
	19 12	☽⚹♅	G
	20 00	☽⊻♃	g
	21 58	☿±♇	
	23 37	☽#♀	G
8	02 54	☽⊻♆	g
Tu	05 23	☽△☿	G
	07 16	♂±♄	
	07 28	♀♋	
	07 34	☽⚹♂	G
	15 14	☽⊻♇	g
	17 48	☽♒	
	19 38	☿⊥♀	
	20 25	☉⚹♅	
	23 04	☽∠♅	b
	23 35	☽∠♃	b
9	00 39	☿⚹♂	
We	02 30	☽∥♃	G
	03 10	☉▽♃	
	12 05	☉□♄	
	12 45	☽∠♂	b
	13 25	☽#☿	G
	18 30	☽∠♇	b
10	00 25	☽⚼♀	b
Th	02 14	☽⊻♅	g
	02 28	☽⚹♃	G
	02 36	☽#☉	G
	03 19	☽☍♄	B
	04 27	☽□☉	B
	07 05	☽#♄	B
	07 36	☽∥♇	D
	09 27	☽☌♆	D
	16 04	☽∥♆	D
	16 57	☿▽♇	
	17 03	☽⊻♂	g
	21 02	☽⚹♇	G
	21 47	☽□☿	B
	23 32	☽♓	
11	03 32	♃□♅	
Fr	05 06	☽△♀	G
	08 43	☿Q♅	
	09 17	☿♊	
	13 00	♀∠♄	
12	02 33	☽∥♅	B
Sa	06 03	☽□♃	B
	06 18	☽☌♅	B
	12 02	☽⚹☉	G
	13 01	☽⊻♆	g
	13 49	☽∥♂	B
	19 15	☿#♃	
	22 44	♂⊥♆	
	23 01	☽☌♂	B
	23 53	☽□♇	B
13	02 19	☽♈	
Su	02 56	☉□♆	
	05 01	☽#♂	B
	08 18	☽⚼♄	b
	09 02	☽⚹☿	G
	11 40	☽□♀	B
	13 47	☽∠♆	b
	14 32	☽∠☉	b
	15 15	♂□♇	
	15 54	☉±♇	
	16 36	☽#♅	B
14	07 00	☽△♃	G
Mo	07 41	☽⊻♅	g
	08 42	☽△♄	G
	13 07	☽∠☿	b
	14 02	☽⚹♆	G
	16 12	♀⚼♆	
	16 19	☿Q♄	
	16 26	☽⊻☉	g
15	00 24	☽△♇	G
Tu	00 48	☿⊻♀	
	00 57	☽#♆	D
	02 12	☽⊻♂	g
	02 48	☽♉	
	06 49	☽⚼♃	b
	07 42	☽∠♅	b
	08 39	☽#♇	D
	08 52	☽∥♄	B
	14 06	♂♈	
	15 38	☽⚹♀	G
	16 37	☽⊻☿	g
	19 12	☽∥☉	G
16	00 13	☽⚼♇	b
We	03 19	☽∠♂	b
	07 36	☽⚹♅	G
	08 39	☽□♄	B
	10 14	☽#♃	G
	13 49	☽□♆	B
	17 20	☽∠♀	b
	19 27	☽☌☉	D
	20 33	☽∥☿	G
17	02 34	☽♊	
Th	04 30	☽⚹♂	G
	08 30	☽∥♀	G
	19 19	☽⊻♀	g
	23 31	☽☌☿	G
18	06 23	☽☍♃	B
Fr	07 59	☽□♅	B
	09 08	☽⚹♄	G
	14 20	☽△♆	G
	18 31	☿Q♂	
	23 42	☽⊻☉	g
19	00 03	♄#♇	
Sa	00 57	☽☍♇	B
	03 38	☽♋	
	08 26	☽□♂	B
	10 15	☽∠♄	b
	15 32	☽⚼♆	b
	18 06	☉▽♇	
20	01 30	☽☌♀	G
Su	03 07	☽∠☉	b
	04 34	♀⊥♄	
	05 30	☿☍♃	
	09 11	☽⊻☿	g
	10 56	☽△♅	G
	12 15	☽⊻♄	g
	17 55	☽∥♀	G
	20 39	☽∥☿	G
	20 41	♂⚼♄	
	23 26	☿□♅	
21	07 46	☽⚹☉	G
Mo	07 57	☽♌	
	10 12	☉♊	
	10 48	☿⚹♄	
	11 16	☽⚼♃	b
	13 52	☽⚼♅	b
	15 56	☽∠☿	b
	16 22	☽△♂	G
	16 38	☉Q♅	
	16 44	☽#♃	G
22	00 34	☿∥♀	
Tu	02 43	☽∥☉	G
	08 32	☽⚼♇	b
	12 30	☽⊻♀	g
	14 52	☽△♃	G
	19 26	☽●♄	B
	22 13	☽⚼♂	b
	22 31	☽#♇	D
	22 51	☽∥♄	B
23	00 05	☽⚹☿	G
We	01 02	☽☍♆	B
	01 55	♀±♆	
	07 47	☽#♆	D
	07 47	☿△♆	
	13 09	☽△♇	G
	14 17	♀▽♃	
	16 26	☽♍	
	20 00	☽∠♀	b
	21 03	☽□☉	B
24	21 18	♂∠♆	
Th	23 46	☽#♅	B
25	00 52	☽□♃	B
Fr	01 08	♆Stat	
	04 34	☽⚹♀	G
	04 45	☽☍♅	B
	06 34	☽⊻♄	g
	06 41	♀△♅	
	15 28	☽∥♂	B
	19 38	☽□☿	B
26	00 44	☽□♇	B
Sa	04 16	☽♎	
	04 37	♀⊻♄	
	06 01	☽#♂	B
	13 02	☽∠♄	b
	14 22	☽△☉	G
	18 33	☽⚼♆	b
	21 05	☽∥♅	B
	21 38	☽☍♂	B
27	12 59	☽⚹♃	G
Su	15 13	☿☍♇	
	19 42	☽⚹♄	G
	23 14	☽□♀	B
	23 33	☽⚼☉	b
28	01 02	☽△♆	G
Mo	13 32	☽⚹♇	G
	14 35	☽∥♆	D
	16 17	☽△☿	G
	17 11	☽♏	
	17 58	♀±♃	
	19 06	☽∠♃	b
	19 53	♀▽♆	
	23 25	☽#♄	B
29	00 07	☽⚼♅	b
Tu	00 21	☽∥♇	D
	00 56	☿♋	
	05 22	☉Q♄	
	19 41	☽∠♇	b
30	00 56	☽⊻♃	g
We	01 49	☉∠♀	
	01 51	☽⚼☿	b
	06 14	☽#☉	G
	06 15	☽△♅	G
	07 50	☽∥♃	G
	08 28	☽□♄	B
	13 21	☽□♆	B
	17 11	☽△♀	G
	21 01	☽#♀	G
	22 21	☽⚼♂	b
31	01 26	☽⊻♇	g
Th	05 07	☽♐	
	08 41	☽#☿	G
	20 52	☉#♃	

JUNE

Day	Time	Aspect	
1	01 04	☽☍☉	B
Fr	01 18	☽⚼♀	b
	05 38	☽△♂	G
	11 19	☽☌♃	G
	17 08	☽□♅	B
	19 31	☽△♄	G
	23 54	☽⚹♆	G
2	08 56	☿∠♄	
Sa	11 29	☽☌♇	D
	15 09	☽♑	
3	00 18	☽⚼♄	b
Su	01 27	☽☍☿	B
	04 26	☽∠♆	b
	18 23	♀▽♇	
	18 24	☽□♂	B
	19 47	☽⊻♃	g
4	02 03	☽⚹♅	G
Mo	08 29	☽⊻♆	g
	14 21	☽#☿	G
	14 58	♂△♃	
	19 36	☽⊻♇	g
	21 02	☿⚼♆	
	21 11	☽⚼☉	b
	21 43	☽☍♀	B
	23 15	☽♒	
	23 19	☽∠♃	b
5	03 19	☽#♀	G
Tu	04 45	☽#☉	G
	05 46	☽∠♅	b
	08 20	☽∥♃	G
	16 39	♀⚼♃	
	17 59	♀♌	
	19 42	☉∥♀	
	22 56	☽∠♇	b
	23 13	☉☍♃	
6	02 23	☽⚹♃	G
We	02 40	☽△☉	G
	04 51	☽⚹♂	G
	09 01	☽⊻♅	g
	11 43	☽☍♄	B
	12 15	☽∥♇	D
	13 59	☽#♄	B
	15 09	☽☌♆	D
	17 39	☽⚼☿	b
	20 48	☽∥♆	D
7	00 56	♂#♅	
Th	01 47	☽⚹♇	G
	05 24	☽♓	
	09 11	☽∠♂	b
	21 28	☽△☿	G
8	07 01	☽□♃	B
Fr	07 38	☽#♂	B
	09 01	☽∥♅	B
	11 43	☽□☉	B
	12 21	☽⚼♀	b
	12 52	☽⊻♂	g
	13 55	☽☌♅	B
	14 42	♀#♃	
	19 44	☽⊻♆	g
9	05 52	☽□♇	B
Sa	08 49	♂⊻♅	
	09 26	☽♈	
	11 26	♀⚼♅	
	15 51	☽△♀	G
	18 25	♀±♇	
	18 29	☽⚼♄	b
	20 08	☉□♅	
	21 13	☽∠♆	b
	22 42	☽#♅	B
10	01 51	☽∥♂	B
Su	02 49	☽□☿	B
	09 35	☽△♃	G
	16 42	☽⊻♅	g
	18 09	☽⚹☉	G
	18 24	☽☌♂	B
	19 42	☽△♄	G
	22 14	☽⚹♆	G
11	05 48	☉∥☿	
Mo	07 57	☽△♇	G
	09 06	☽#♆	D
	10 12	☽⚼♃	b
	10 27	☉⚹♂	
	11 29	☽♉	
	14 49	☽∥♄	B
	16 58	☽#♇	D
	17 27	☽∠♅	b
	19 40	☉⚹♄	
	20 34	☽∠☉	b
	21 08	☽□♀	B
	22 43	♂△♄	
12	05 35	☽⚹☿	G
Tu	08 27	☽⚼♇	b
	12 35	☽∥♀	G
	17 45	☽#♃	G
	17 56	☽⚹♅	G
	21 06	☽□♄	B
	22 00	☽∥☿	G
	22 09	☽⊻♂	g
	22 43	☽⊻☉	g
	23 17	☽□♆	B
13	01 12	☽∥☉	G
We	06 24	☽∠☿	b
	07 30	☉△♆	
	12 24	☽♊	
	20 35	♂⚹♆	
	23 51	☽∠♂	b
14	01 17	☽⚹♀	G
Th	07 09	☽⊻☿	g
	10 59	☽☍♃	B
	18 55	☽□♅	B
	22 25	☽⚹♄	G
15	00 18	☽△♆	G
Fr	01 49	☽⚹♂	G
	03 13	☽☌☉	D
	03 36	☽∠♀	b
	09 59	☽☍♇	B
	13 45	☽♋	
	23 37	☽∠♄	b
	23 40	☿Stat	
	23 46	☿#♃	
16	01 23	☽⚼♆	b
Sa	06 30	☽⊻♀	g
	09 21	☽☌☿	G
	21 32	☽△♅	G
17	01 31	☽⊻♄	g
Su	07 39	☽□♂	B
	10 05	☽⊻☉	g
	14 14	♂⊥♅	

Day	Time	Aspect	
	14 39	☽⚼♃	b
	16 57	☽∥☉	G
	17 25	☽☊	
	23 40	☿⊻♀	
	23 59	☽⚼♅	b
18 Mo	02 46	☽⋕♃	G
	06 02	☽∥☿	G
	13 53	☽⊻☿	g
	14 57	☉∠♀	
	15 06	☽●♀	G
	15 06	☽∠☉	b
	16 17	☽⚼♇	b
	17 29	☽△♃	G
	17 55	☽∥♀	G
19 Tu	06 06	☽⋕♇	D
	06 49	☉☍♇	
	08 03	☽●♄	B
	08 16	♀⚼♇	
	09 22	☽☍♆	B
	09 30	♀±♅	
	09 37	☽∥♄	B
	14 57	☽⋕♆	D
	17 19	☽∠☿	b
	17 37	☽△♂	G
	20 14	☽△♇	G
	21 22	☽⚹☉	G
	22 48	♀△♃	
20 We	00 46	☽♍	
	15 03	☽∥♂	B
	21 30	☽⚹☿	G
21 Th	00 20	☽⚼♂	b
	02 00	☽□♃	B
	04 20	☽⊻♀	g
	07 04	☽⋕♅	B
	13 09	☽☍♅	B
	13 36	♂△♇	
	18 06	☉♋	
	18 32	☽⊻♄	g
22 Fr	00 42	♂⚼♃	
	06 50	☽□♇	B
	08 45	☿Q♂	
	11 43	☽♎	
	12 25	☽∠♀	b
	13 15	☽□☉	B
23 Sa	00 52	☽∠♄	b
	01 28	☽⚼♆	b
	02 34	☿⊥♀	
	03 01	☽∥♅	B
	07 22	☽□☿	B
	13 27	☽⚹♃	G
	14 42	♅Stat	
	21 00	☽⚹♀	G
	23 35	☽⋕♂	B
24 Su	07 30	☽⚹♄	G
	07 49	☽△♆	G
	19 23	☽⚹♇	G
	19 35	☽∠♃	b
	21 21	☽∥♆	D
	21 27	♂♉	
25 Mo	00 26	☽♏	
	00 38	☽☍♂	B
	02 06	☽⋕♄	B
	06 50	☽∥♇	D
	07 17	☽△☉	G
	07 54	☽⚼♅	b
	08 34	☽⋕♀	G
	15 54	♄☍♆	
	17 33	☽△☿	G
	22 55	☽⋕☿	G
26 Tu	01 33	☽⊻♃	g
	01 34	☽∠♇	b
	08 22	♀⋕♇	
	12 12	☽∥♃	G
	13 53	☽□♀	B
	14 00	☽△♅	G
	15 43	♀⚻♅	
	16 00	☽⚼☉	b
	20 07	☽□♆	B
	20 23	☽□♄	B
	22 10	☽⚼☿	b
	23 31	☽⋕☉	G
27 We	07 21	☽⊻♇	g
	12 24	☽♐	
28 Th	05 10	☿∠♄	
	12 09	☽☌♃	G
	17 32	☿⚼♆	
	18 40	☉☌☿	
	19 20	☉⚼♆	
	23 12	☽⚼♂	b
29 Fr	00 37	☽□♅	B
	04 18	☽△♀	G
	05 41	☉∠♄	
	06 24	☽⚹♆	G
	07 13	☽△♄	G
	13 00	♀∥♄	
	17 08	☽☌♇	D
	19 34	☿∠♀	
	22 05	☽♑	
	23 43	♂∠♅	
30 Sa	00 37	♂Q♆	
	05 17	☽△♂	G
	08 53	☽☍☿	B
	10 19	☽⚼♀	b
	10 37	☽∠♆	b
	11 41	☽⚼♄	b
	13 49	☽☍☉	B
	15 30	♀☍♆	
	20 23	☽⊻♃	g
JULY			
1 Su	08 45	☽⚹♅	G
	14 15	☽⊻♆	g
	14 38	♀☌♄	
	19 08	☿⚹♂	
	19 13	♀⋕♆	
	23 40	☽∠♃	b
2 Mo	00 32	☽⊻♇	g
	05 24	☽♒	
	06 35	☽⋕☉	G
	12 01	☽∠♅	b
	15 23	☽∥♃	G
	15 28	☽□♂	B
	21 09	♂±♃	
3 Tu	02 29	☽⚹♃	G
	03 29	☽∠♇	b
	06 38	☽⋕☿	G
	14 50	☽⊻♅	g
	15 32	☽⚼☿	b
	16 56	☽∥♇	D
	20 07	☽☌♆	D
	21 52	☽☍♄	B
	22 26	☽⋕♄	B
	23 13	☉⚻♃	
4 We	00 21	☽☍♀	B
	01 02	☽∥♆	D
	04 33	☽⋕♀	G
	05 24	☽⚼☉	b
	06 03	☽⚹♇	G
	09 46	☽⋕♂	B
	10 52	☽♓	
	17 11	☽△☿	G
	23 34	☽⚹♂	G
5 Th	07 01	☽□♃	B
	09 36	☽△☉	G
	13 37	☽∥♅	B
	19 22	☽☌♅	B
6 Fr	00 28	☽⊻♆	g
	03 00	☽∠♂	b
	10 08	☽□♇	B
	11 29	♀∥♂	
	14 57	☽♈	
	19 55	☽□☿	B
7 Sa	02 11	☽∠♆	b
	03 39	☽⋕♅	B
	04 35	☽⚼♄	b
	06 06	☽⊻♂	g
	10 04	☽⚼♀	b
	10 18	☽△♃	G
	16 54	☽□☉	B
	22 40	☽⊻♅	g
8 Su	01 32	☉±♆	
	03 38	☽⚹♆	G
	06 15	☽△♄	G
	06 18	☽∥♀	G
	10 28	☽∥♂	B
	11 33	☽⚼♃	b
	12 34	☽△♀	G
	13 06	☽△♇	G
	15 15	☽⋕♆	D
	16 56	☽∥♄	B
	17 54	☽♉	
	22 09	☽⚹☿	G
	22 55	☽⋕♇	D
	23 57	☽∠♅	b
9 Mo	01 09	♀∠♇	
	09 49	☽∥☿	G
	11 25	☽☌♂	B
	14 16	☽⚼♇	b
	17 23	☉±♃	
	20 54	☉⊥♄	
	22 35	☽⋕♃	G
	23 01	☽⚹☉	G
	23 13	☽∠☿	b
10 Tu	01 04	☽⚹♅	G
	02 15	☿Stat	
	02 47	☽∥☉	G
	05 57	☽□♆	B
	09 00	☽□♄	B
	09 24	♂⚻♃	
	16 54	☽□♀	B
	20 10	☽♊	
11 We	00 22	☽⊻☿	g
	01 54	☽∠☉	b
	05 33	☉△♅	
	14 33	☽☍♃	B
	16 14	☽⊻♂	g
	19 23	♂⚼♇	
12 Th	03 17	☽□♅	B
	04 52	☽⊻☉	g
	08 11	☽△♆	G
	11 45	☽⚹♄	G
	17 39	☽☍♇	B
	18 51	☽∠♂	b
	21 12	☽⚹♀	G
	22 39	☽♋	
13 Fr	03 33	☽☌☿	G
	09 39	☽⚼♆	b
	13 31	☽∠♄	b
	21 53	☽⚹♂	G
	23 36	♂⋕♆	
	23 49	☽∠♀	b
14 Sa	05 10	☉⚻♆	
	06 32	☽△♅	G
	12 04	☽☌☉	D
	15 47	☽⊻♄	g
	16 12	♂∥♄	
	18 23	♀♍	
	19 12	☽⚼♃	b
15 Su	02 43	☽☊	
	03 00	☽⊻♀	g
	08 59	☽⚼♅	b
	09 19	☽⊻☿	g
	12 42	☽∥☉	G
	13 04	☽⋕♃	G
	21 31	☽∥☿	G
	21 53	☽△♃	G
	22 57	☉⋕♃	
16 Mo	00 15	☽⚼♇	b
	06 06	☽□♂	B
	13 42	☽∠☿	b
	14 19	☽⋕♇	D
	17 29	☽☍♆	B
	19 56	☽∥♂	B
	22 23	☽∥♄	B
	22 25	☽⊻☉	g
	22 32	☽●♄	B
	22 33	☽⋕♆	D
17 Tu	00 16	☉⊻♄	
	03 55	☽△♇	G
	09 39	☽♍	
	11 40	☽☌♀	G
	18 51	♄⋕♆	
	19 18	☽⚹☿	G
	21 57	☽∥♀	G
18 We	05 10	☽∠☉	b
	05 44	☽□♃	B
	08 16	☉⊥♀	
	12 10	☉⚼♃	
	14 23	☽⋕♅	B
	18 06	☽△♂	G
	21 06	☽☍♅	B
19 Th	08 43	☽⊻♄	g
	10 03	☿⚼♆	
	12 57	☽⚹☉	G
	13 44	☽□♇	B
	19 53	☽♎	
	22 47	☉⚻♇	
	23 35	☽⊻♀	g
20 Fr	01 29	☽⚼♂	b
	06 14	☉∥☿	
	08 25	☽⚼♆	b
	10 12	☽□☿	B
	10 45	☽∥♅	B
	14 54	☽∠♄	b
	16 40	☽⚹♃	G
	22 13	♂⚹♅	
	23 58	☽⋕♀	G
21 Sa	06 21	☽∠♀	b
	14 34	☽△♆	G
	21 29	☽⚹♄	G
	22 50	☽∠♃	b
22 Su	01 54	☽⚹♇	G
	04 12	☽⋕♄	B
	05 13	☽∥♆	D
	06 29	☽□☉	B
	08 18	☽♏	
	13 16	☽⚹♀	G
	13 38	☽⋕♂	B
	14 06	☽∥♇	D
	15 07	☽⚼♅	b
	23 57	☿∠♄	
23 Mo	01 18	♂⋕♇	
	04 32	☽△☿	G
	05 00	☉☊	
	05 03	☽⊻♃	g
	08 11	☽∠♇	b
	09 46	☿⚻♃	
	09 52	☽⋕☉	G
	17 02	☽⋕☿	G
	17 48	☽∥♃	G
	21 17	☽△♅	G
24 Tu	01 43	☽☍♂	B
	02 58	☽□♆	B
	10 18	♂±♇	
	10 30	☽□♄	B
	13 50	☿⋕♃	
	13 55	☽⚼☿	b
	14 08	☽⊻♇	g
	20 29	☽♐	
	23 10	♂□♆	
	23 51	☽△☉	G
25 We	02 03	☽□♀	B
	16 25	☽☌♃	G
26 Th	02 25	☉±♇	
	06 16	☉⊻♀	
	07 30	☽⚼☉	b
	08 06	☽□♅	B
	13 32	☽⚹♆	G
	15 17	☉⚼♅	
	21 25	☽△♄	G
27 Fr	00 13	☽☌♇	D
	02 36	☿±♆	
	06 21	☽♑	
	11 54	☽△♀	G
	17 28	♀Stat	
	17 44	☽∠♆	b
	18 39	☿±♃	
	21 32	☽⚼♂	b
28 Sa	01 07	☽⊻♃	g
	01 43	☽⚼♄	b
	14 27	☽☍☿	B
	15 31	☽⚼♀	b
	16 01	☽⚹♅	G
	21 10	☽⊻♆	g
	23 09	☿∠♀	
29 Su	02 23	☽△♂	G
	03 25	☿△♅	
	04 22	☽∠♃	b
	07 20	☽⊻♇	g
	13 14	☽♒	
	18 54	☽∠♅	b
	21 50	☽⋕☿	G
	23 44	☽∥♃	G
30 Mo	00 31	☿⊥♄	
	00 48	☽☍☉	B
	05 25	☉Q♂	
	06 58	☽⚹♃	G
	09 53	☽∠♇	b
	14 22	☽⋕☉	G
	17 24	☽⋕♂	B
	20 00	☿⚻♆	
	21 13	☽⊻♅	g
	23 29	☽∥♇	D
31 Tu	02 08	☽☌♆	D
	06 52	☽∥♆	D

Day	Time	Aspect	
	09 35	☽#♄	B
	09 55	☽□♂	B
	10 28	☽☍♄	B
	11 56	☽✱♇	G
	17 40	☽♓	
	22 09	☽☍♀	B
	23 59	♂□♄	

AUGUST

Day	Time	Aspect	
1 We	05 26	☉‖♂	
	08 32	☽⚼☿	b
	10 45	☽□♃	B
	17 08	☽#♀	G
	18 38	☽‖♅	B
2 Th	00 35	☽☌♅	B
	01 35	☿⚼♃	
	03 00	♂⚻♇	
	05 24	☽⊻♆	g
	11 59	☽⚼☉	b
	13 48	☽△☿	G
	15 01	☽□♇	B
	15 12	☉△♃	
	15 16	☿#♃	
	15 37	☽✱♂	G
	16 09	☿⊻♄	
	18 03	☿⊥♀	
	20 43	☽♈	
	22 54	☿⚻♇	
3 Fr	06 42	☽∠♆	b
	09 34	☽#♅	B
	09 53	☿✱♂	
	10 13	☽‖♀	G
	13 30	☽△♃	G
	15 07	☽△☉	G
	15 37	☽⚼♄	b
	18 09	☽∠♂	b
4 Sa	01 12	☽⚼♀	b
	03 08	☽⊻♅	g
	07 55	☽✱♆	G
	08 12	☉⚼♇	
	14 44	☽⚼♃	b
	17 06	☽△♄	G
	17 15	☿♌	
	17 22	☽‖♄	B
	17 31	☽△♇	G
	18 58	☉±♅	
	20 38	☽⊻♂	g
	20 55	☽#♆	D
	23 16	☽♉	
5 Su	00 09	♀#♅	
	00 13	☽□☿	B
	01 56	☽△♀	G
	04 03	☽#♇	D
	04 21	☽∠♅	b
	06 23	☽‖☉	G
	11 00	☿⊻♀	
	14 10	☽‖♂	B
	18 47	☽⚼♇	b
	21 20	☽□☉	B
	22 50	☽‖☿	G
6 Mo	00 29	☿±♇	
	02 58	☽#♃	G
	05 27	☿⚼♅	
	05 37	☽✱♅	G
	10 27	☽□♆	B
	10 35	♄△♇	
	20 16	☽□♄	B
7 Tu	01 50	☽☌♂	B
	02 01	☽♊	

Day	Time	Aspect	
	02 04	♃Stat	
	03 26	☽□♀	B
	04 15	♂Q♅	
	05 33	☉#♇	
	06 01	♂♊	
	11 23	☽✱☿	G
	18 58	☽☍♃	B
	23 36	♀□♂	
8 We	04 07	☽✱☉	G
	08 41	☽□♅	B
	13 37	☽△♆	G
	17 33	☽∠☿	b
	23 34	☽☍♇	B
9 Th	00 11	☽✱♄	G
	01 10	♀♌	
	05 27	☽✱♀	G
	05 36	☽♋	
	05 48	☿‖♂	
	07 57	☽⊻♂	g
	08 00	☽∠☉	b
	15 36	☿△♃	
	15 38	☽⚼♆	b
10 Fr	00 18	☽⊻☿	g
	02 39	☽∠♄	b
	06 51	☽∠♀	b
	09 50	☿⚼♇	
	11 37	☽∠♂	b
	12 21	☽⊻☉	g
	12 57	☽△♅	G
	13 48	☿±♅	
	20 28	☉⚻♅	
11 Sa	01 38	☽⚼♃	b
	05 35	☽⊻♄	g
	08 37	☽⊻♀	g
	10 42	☽♌	
	15 46	☽⚼♅	b
	15 51	☽✱♂	G
	21 16	☽#♃	G
12 Su	04 48	☽△♃	G
	04 49	☿Q♂	
	06 17	☽‖♂	B
	07 34	☽⚼♇	b
	16 13	☽●☿	G
	17 18	☽‖☿	G
	22 04	☽#♇	D
	22 07	☉#♆	
	23 03	☽☌☉	D
13 Mo	00 31	☽☍♆	B
	05 44	☽#♆	D
	06 12	☽‖☉	G
	10 37	☿⚻♅	
	11 23	☽△♇	G
	11 37	☽‖♄	B
	13 15	☽●♄	B
	13 34	☽☌♀	G
	18 03	☽♍	
	18 25	☉☍♆	
	19 16	♀☌♄	
14 Tu	02 24	☽□♂	B
	09 31	☿#♇	
	13 07	☽□♃	B
	20 09	☿☍♆	
	21 12	☽#♅	B
	22 03	☽‖♀	G
15 We	03 56	☽☍♅	B
	12 17	☽⊻☿	g
	13 00	☽⊻☉	g
	13 44	♀△♇	
	19 56	☉☌☿	

Day	Time	Aspect	
	20 42	☽⊻♀	g
	21 02	☽□♇	B
	23 39	☽⊻♄	g
16 Th	04 04	☽♎	
	15 05	☽⚼♆	b
	16 01	☽△♂	G
	19 30	☽#♀	G
	19 48	☽‖♅	B
	21 12	☽∠☉	b
	22 17	☿#♆	
	23 51	☽∠☿	b
17 Fr	00 06	☽✱♃	G
	01 01	☽∠♀	b
	05 27	☿☌♀	
	05 48	☽∠♄	b
	14 26	♀#♅	
	17 23	☿△♇	
	18 00	☉‖♄	
	21 04	☽△♆	G
	23 45	☽⚼♂	b
18 Sa	03 41	☉☌♀	
	05 35	☽#☉	G
	05 42	☽✱♀	G
	05 59	☽✱☉	G
	06 13	☽#♄	B
	06 21	☽∠♃	b
	08 54	☽#☿	G
	08 57	☽✱♇	G
	12 05	☽✱☿	G
	12 21	☽✱♄	G
	13 44	☿☌♄	
	13 48	☽‖♆	D
	16 13	☽♏	
	21 24	☽⚼♅	b
	22 04	☽‖♇	D
19 Su	05 25	☿‖♄	
	12 48	☽⊻♃	g
	13 01	☿♍	
	15 17	☽∠♇	b
	18 14	☉△♇	
	20 50	☽#♂	B
20 Mo	01 42	☽‖♃	G
	03 39	☽△♅	G
	06 28	☉‖☿	
	09 35	☽□♆	B
	15 20	☽□♀	B
	21 30	☽⊻♇	g
	23 54	☽□☉	B
21 Tu	01 34	☽□♄	B
	04 44	☽♐	
	12 20	☽□☿	B
	23 14	☽☍♂	B
	23 28	☉☌♄	
22 We	01 07	☽☌♃	G
	15 07	☽□♅	B
	20 53	☽✱♆	G
	23 08	♀Q♂	
	23 49	☽△♀	G
23 Th	08 23	☽☌♇	D
	12 08	☉♍	
	12 54	☽△♄	G
	15 20	☽♑	
	15 36	☽△☉	G
	16 03	♂☍♃	
24 Fr	01 27	☽∠♆	b
	03 09	☽⚼♀	b
	08 35	☽△☿	G
	10 52	☽⊻♃	g
	17 20	☽⚼♄	b

Day	Time	Aspect	
	21 54	☽⚼☉	b
	23 41	☽✱♅	G
25 Sa	01 03	☿□♃	
	05 09	☽⊻♆	g
	14 26	☽∠♃	b
	15 59	☿□♂	
	16 03	☽⊻♇	g
	16 27	☽⚼♂	b
	16 30	☽⚼☿	b
	21 48	♀☍♆	
	22 35	☽♒	
26 Su	02 39	☽∠♅	b
	08 21	☽‖♃	G
	09 19	☽#♂	B
	17 08	☽✱♃	G
	18 34	☽∠♇	b
	20 11	☽△♂	G
27 Mo	04 49	☽⊻♅	g
	08 09	☽‖♇	D
	08 50	☽☍♀	B
	09 55	☿‖♀	
	10 00	☽☌♆	D
	14 58	☽‖♆	D
	20 22	☽✱♇	G
	23 17	☽#♄	B
28 Tu	01 23	☽☍♄	B
	02 34	☽♓	
	10 35	☽●☉	B
	11 22	☽#☉	G
	14 11	♂#♃	
	19 39	☿☍♅	
	19 55	☽#♀	G
	20 26	☽□♃	B
29 We	01 19	☽□♂	B
	01 21	☽#☿	G
	01 38	☽‖♅	B
	03 42	☿#♅	
	07 15	☽☌♅	B
	08 53	☽☍☿	B
	12 18	☽⊻♆	g
	15 12	☿⊻♀	
	22 22	☽□♇	B
30 Th	04 25	☽♈	
	09 50	☽⚼♀	b
	12 55	☽∠♆	b
	13 14	☿⚻♆	
	14 10	☽‖☿	G
	18 06	☽#♅	B
	22 06	☽△♃	G
31 Fr	01 05	☽‖♀	G
	04 30	☽⚼♄	b
	04 33	☽‖☉	G
	04 44	☽✱♂	G
	08 24	☽⊻♅	g
	09 50	☽△♀	G
	13 26	☽✱♆	G
	18 02	☽⚼☉	b
	19 12	☽‖♄	B
	22 48	☽⚼♃	b
	23 32	☽△♇	G

SEPTEMBER

Day	Time	Aspect	
1 Sa	04 04	☽#♆	D
	05 19	☽△♄	G
	05 35	☽♉	
	06 21	☽∠♂	b
	08 57	☽∠♅	b
	10 36	☽#♇	D
	13 45	☿⊥♀	

Day	Time	Aspect	
	20 28	☽△☉	G
	20 33	☽⚼☿	b
	22 28	☉‖♀	
2 Su	00 15	☽⚼♇	b
	08 11	☽⊻♂	g
	09 42	☽#♃	G
	09 43	☽✱♅	G
	10 19	☽□♀	B
	11 32	☽‖♂	B
	13 49	♄♍	
	14 53	☽□♆	B
3 Mo	00 47	☽△☿	G
	01 56	☿±♆	
	05 04	☿□♇	
	07 30	☽♊	
	07 39	☽□♄	B
	20 09	♂□♅	
	23 36	♀✱♂	
4 Tu	00 04	☉□♃	
	02 23	☽☍♃	B
	02 32	☽□☉	B
	12 22	☽□♅	B
	12 23	☽✱♀	G
	13 06	☽☌♂	B
	15 12	♀⚻♅	
	17 47	☽△♆	G
	23 48	☿Q♃	
5 We	04 39	☽☍♇	B
	11 01	☽□☿	B
	11 08	☽♋	
	11 46	☽✱♄	G
	12 02	☿♎	
	14 16	☽∠♀	b
	18 05	☿⊻♄	
	19 59	☽⚼♆	b
6 Th	11 03	☽✱☉	G
	13 34	☿∠♀	
	14 01	♂Q♄	
	14 41	☽∠♄	b
	16 46	☽⊻♀	g
	17 04	☽△♅	G
	20 20	☽⊻♂	g
7 Fr	10 24	☽⚼♃	b
	14 54	♇Stat	
	16 23	☽∠☉	b
	16 59	☽♌	
	18 11	☽⊻♄	g
	20 16	☽⚼♅	b
	20 58	☉#♅	
	22 20	☽‖♂	B
8 Sa	00 12	☽✱☿	G
	00 56	☽∠♂	b
	02 09	☽#♃	G
	13 53	☽⚼♇	b
	14 16	☽△♃	G
	16 14	♀Stat	
	16 25	☿⚼♆	
	22 27	☽⊻☉	g
	23 47	☽☌♀	G
9 Su	04 05	♂△♆	
	04 21	☽#♇	D
	06 05	☽☍♆	B
	06 10	☽✱♂	G
	07 58	☽∠☿	b
	11 42	☽#♆	D
	16 17	☉⊻♀	
	18 07	☽△♇	G
	18 46	☉☍♅	
	23 42	☿⊥♄	

	23 56	☽∥♄	B
10 Mo	01 10	☽♍	
	02 58	☽●♄	B
	12 24	☽∥♀	G
	16 28	☽⊻☿	g
	17 36	♀∇♅	
	23 46	☽□♃	B
11 Tu	02 53	☽#♅	B
	08 32	☽∥☉	G
	09 18	☽☍♅	B
	09 28	☽⊻♀	g
	10 51	☽#☿	G
	12 44	☽●●	D
	18 31	☽□♂	B
	22 31	☉#☿	
12 We	04 14	☽□♇	B
	11 31	☽♎	
	14 00	☽⊻♄	g
	15 16	☽∠♀	b
	20 41	☽#☉	G
	21 09	☽⚼♆	b
13 Th	00 21	☉∇♆	
	01 27	☽∥☿	G
	05 03	☽∥♅	B
	10 43	☿✶♃	
	11 24	☽✶♃	G
	11 29	☽☌☿	G
	20 13	☽∠♄	b
	21 36	☽#♀	G
	21 38	☽✶♀	G
14 Fr	03 06	☽△♆	G
	05 32	☽⊻☉	g
	07 50	☿∥♅	
	08 13	☽#♄	B
	09 00	☽△♂	G
	16 10	☽✶♇	G
	17 50	☽∠♃	b
	22 20	☽∥♆	D
	23 37	☽♏	
15 Sa	02 06	☿Q♇	
	02 39	☽⚼♅	b
	02 46	☽✶♄	G
	06 14	☽∥♇	D
	14 33	☽∠☉	b
	16 44	☽⚼♂	b
	22 33	☽∠♇	b
16 Su	00 29	☽⊻♃	g
	08 08	☽⊻☿	g
	08 56	☽△♅	G
	11 31	☽□♀	B
	11 38	☽∥♃	G
	14 59	☿∇♅	
	15 41	☽□♆	B
	18 14	☽#♂	B
	20 54	☿∠♄	
	23 40	☽✶☉	G
17 Mo	04 47	☉⊥♀	
	04 56	☽⊻♇	g
	12 21	☽♐	
	16 07	☽□♄	B
	18 21	☽∠☿	b
	20 49	☉□♂	
	21 28	☿✶♀	
18 Tu	13 34	☽☌♃	G
	21 04	☽□♅	B
19 We	00 51	☉±♆	
	01 26	☽△♀	G
	02 00	☿△♆	
	03 44	☽✶♆	G
	03 57	☽✶☿	G
	15 03	☽☍♂	B
	15 59	☉□♇	
	16 44	☽☌♇	D
	16 48	☽□☉	B
	23 52	☽♑	
20 Th	04 04	☽△♄	G
	07 39	☽⚼♀	b
	08 56	☽∠♆	b
	23 26	☿#♀	
21 Fr	00 32	☽⊻♃	g
	01 30	☿±♅	
	06 54	☽✶♅	G
	08 40	♂☍♇	
	08 54	☽⚼♄	b
	13 18	☽⊻♆	g
	19 53	☽□☿	B
	20 03	♀☍♆	
22 Sa	01 39	☽⊻♇	g
	04 42	☽∠♃	b
	06 15	☽△☉	G
	08 18	☽♒	
	09 05	☽#♂	B
	10 30	☽∠♅	b
	15 42	☽∥♃	G
23 Su	04 41	☽∠♇	b
	06 19	☽⚼♂	b
	07 52	☽✶♃	G
	09 51	☉♎	
	11 10	☽⚼☉	b
	13 07	☽⊻♅	g
	14 55	☿#♄	
	17 39	☽∥♇	D
	19 09	☽☌♆	D
	20 52	☽☍♀	B
24 Mo	00 20	☽∥♆	D
	06 23	☽△☿	G
	06 45	☽✶♇	G
	09 14	☽△♂	G
	10 55	☿✶♇	
	12 06	☽∥☿	G
	12 55	☽♓	
	14 07	☽#♄	B
	17 30	☽☍♄	B
	19 17	☉Q♃	
	19 34	☽#♀	G
25 Tu	09 47	☽⚼☿	b
	10 26	☽∥♅	B
	11 24	☽□♃	B
	15 45	☽☌♅	B
	21 29	☽⊻♆	g
26 We	04 19	☽∥☉	G
	08 33	☽□♇	B
	09 00	☉⊻♄	
	09 35	☿∠♃	
	12 05	☽#☉	G
	12 31	☽□♂	B
	14 22	☽♈	
	17 53	☿△♂	
	19 45	☽☍☉	B
	21 44	☽∠♆	b
27 Th	02 10	☽⚼♀	b
	05 18	☽#♅	B
	12 23	☽△♃	G
	16 01	☽⊻♅	g
	17 17	☿♏	
	19 15	☽∥♀	G
	19 17	☽⚼♄	b
	21 39	☽✶♆	G
28 Fr	00 11	☽∥♄	B
	01 25	☉⚼♆	
	03 03	☽△♀	G
	08 34	☽△♇	G
	09 53	☽#☿	G
	12 29	☽⚼♃	b
	13 42	☽#♆	D
	13 59	☽✶♂	G
	14 17	☽♉	
	15 49	☽☍☿	B
	15 50	☽∠♅	b
	15 56	☿⚼♅	
	19 21	☽△♄	G
	19 54	☽#♇	D
	23 55	♂♋	
29 Sa	08 31	☽⚼♇	b
	14 42	☽∠♂	b
	15 46	☽✶♅	G
	20 12	☽#♃	G
	21 32	☽□♆	B
30 Su	00 43	☽⚼☉	b
	02 47	☽∥♂	B
	05 10	☽□♀	B
	14 34	☽♊	
	15 48	☽⊻♂	g
	16 55	☿∥♆	
	20 10	☽□♄	B
OCTOBER			
1 Mo	03 01	☽△☉	G
	06 16	☿✶♄	
	14 16	☽☍♃	B
	16 51	☽□♅	B
	22 13	☽⚼☿	b
	22 58	☽△♆	G
2 Tu	09 31	☽✶♀	G
	10 52	☽☍♇	B
	16 57	☽♋	
	19 55	☽☌♂	B
	23 17	☽✶♄	G
3 We	00 43	☽⚼♆	b
	01 38	☽△☿	G
	06 52	☉⊥♄	
	10 06	☽□☉	B
	13 01	☽∠♀	b
	13 16	♀△♇	
	20 41	☽△♅	G
4 Th	02 03	☽∠♄	b
	17 32	☽⊻♀	g
	20 45	☽∥♂	B
	22 07	☽⚼♃	b
	22 27	☽☊	
	23 49	☽⚼♅	b
5 Fr	03 25	☽⊻♂	g
	04 18	☽#♃	G
	05 39	☽⊻♄	g
	06 26	☿∥♇	
	10 53	☽□☿	B
	19 50	☽⚼♇	b
	21 13	☽✶☉	G
6 Sa	02 24	☽△♃	G
	07 45	☽#☿	G
	08 28	☽∠♂	b
	09 02	☽#♇	D
	10 47	☽☍♆	B
	16 26	☽#♆	D
7 Su	00 22	☽△♇	G
	04 12	☽∠☉	b
	05 28	☽☌♀	G
	07 03	☽♍	
	10 28	☽∥♄	B
	14 13	☽✶♂	G
	15 07	☽●♄	B
	18 38	☽∥♀	G
	22 45	☽✶☿	G
8 Mo	05 14	☉Q♇	
	06 53	♀♍	
	07 17	☽#♅	B
	09 48	☽#☉	G
	11 56	☽⊻☉	g
	13 02	☽□♃	B
	13 30	☽☍♅	B
9 Tu	03 44	♂✶♄	
	04 04	☉✶♃	
	05 13	☽∠☿	b
	06 49	☉∇♅	
	07 27	♂⚼♆	
	11 08	☽□♇	B
	17 58	☽♎	
	18 23	♃□♅	
	20 26	☽⊻♀	g
10 We	00 58	☉∥♅	
	02 41	☽⚼♆	b
	02 47	☽⊻♄	g
	03 21	☽□♂	B
	06 42	☉∠♀	
	11 46	☽⊻☿	g
	13 20	☽∥♅	B
	14 13	☽∥☉	G
11 Th	00 06	☽#♀	G
	01 35	☽✶♃	G
	04 40	☽∠♀	b
	05 01	☽☌☉	D
	08 45	☽△♆	G
	09 09	☽∠♄	b
	10 07	☽#♄	B
	23 23	☽✶♇	G
12 Fr	03 59	☿Stat	
	05 57	☽∥♆	D
	06 13	☽♏	
	07 15	☽⚼♅	b
	08 16	☽∠♃	b
	13 13	☽✶♀	G
	13 57	☽∥♇	D
	15 43	☽✶♄	G
	17 43	☽△♂	G
	18 24	☽∥☿	G
13 Sa	00 31	☽☌☿	G
	01 40	☉△♆	
	05 47	☽∠♇	b
	12 13	☉∠♄	
	13 32	☽△♅	G
	15 05	☽⊻♃	g
	21 23	☽□♆	B
	22 19	☽∥♃	G
	23 12	☽⊻☉	g
14 Su	01 04	☽⚼♂	b
	04 28	♀☌♄	
	06 47	☽#♂	B
	12 13	☽⊻♇	g
	18 47	☉#♀	
	18 58	☽♐	
15 Mo	03 52	☉±♅	
	04 58	☽□♄	B
	06 40	☽□♀	B
	08 18	☽∠☉	b
	11 51	☽⊻☿	g
16 Tu	01 58	☽□♅	B
	04 32	☽☌♃	G
	09 49	☽✶♆	G
	16 38	☽∠☿	b
	17 05	☿∥♇	
	17 05	☽✶☉	G
	17 37	♀✶♂	
17 We	00 32	☽☌♇	D
	03 18	☿✶♀	
	07 03	☽♑	
	08 36	☿△♂	
	15 31	☽∠♆	b
	17 17	☽△♄	G
	20 38	☽✶☿	G
	21 43	☽☍♂	B
	23 07	☽△♀	G
18 Th	12 58	☽✶♅	G
	16 24	☽⊻♃	g
	20 36	☽⊻♆	g
	22 34	☽⚼♄	b
19 Fr	06 14	☽⚼♀	b
	08 33	☽□☉	B
	10 47	☽⊻♇	g
	12 43	☽#♂	B
	13 54	☿✶♄	
	16 52	☽♒	
	17 24	☽∠♅	b
	20 21	☽∥♃	G
	21 12	☽∠♃	b
20 Sa	00 32	☿∥♆	
	01 56	☽□☿	B
	13 39	☉✶♇	
	14 37	☽∠♇	b
	20 55	☽⊻♅	g
21 Su	01 01	☽✶♃	G
	01 57	☽∥♇	D
	04 08	☽☌♆	D
	09 04	☽∥♆	D
	11 45	☽⚼♂	b
	13 18	☽∥☿	G
	17 28	☽✶♇	G
	19 30	☉#♄	
	19 36	☽△☉	G
	23 02	☽♓	
	23 32	☿∠♃	
22 Mo	01 32	♀#♅	
	03 16	☽∥☉	G
	03 23	☽△☿	G
	03 45	☽#♄	B
	08 47	☽☍♄	B
	14 19	☽△♂	G
	19 31	☽∥♅	B
	20 17	☽#♀	G
	20 50	☽☍♀	B
	23 16	☽⚼☉	b
23 Tu	00 59	☽☌♅	B
	02 49	☽⚼☿	b
	05 33	☽□♃	B
	07 46	☽⊻♆	g
	19 15	☉♏	
	20 17	☽□♇	B
	23 31	☉⚼♅	
	23 55	☉☌☿	
24 We	00 15	☿⚼♅	
	01 24	☽♈	
	03 36	☿♎	
	08 18	☽∠♆	b
	14 58	☿∠♀	
	15 01	☽∥♀	G
	16 38	☽□♂	B

Day	h	m	Aspect	
	17	26	☽#♅	B
	21	36	☉‖☿	
25	01	43	☽⊻♅	g
Th	06	44	☽△♃	G
	07	46	☽‖♄	B
	08	13	☽✱♆	G
	09	08	♀☍♅	
	10	35	☽#☿	G
	10	51	☽⚼♄	b
	12	51	☽#☉	G
	20	16	☽△♇	G
	21	46	☽☍☿	B
26	01	02	☽#♆	D
Fr	01	07	☽♉	
	01	19	☽∠♅	b
	02	26	☽⚼♀	b
	04	52	☽☍☉	B
	06	36	☽⚼♃	b
	07	25	☽#♇	D
	10	32	☽△♄	G
	13	27	☿#♄	
	16	41	☽✱♂	G
	17	51	☿✱♇	
	19	47	☽⚼♇	b
27	00	45	☽✱♅	G
Sa	03	31	☽△♀	G
	07	15	☽□♆	B
	09	39	☽#♃	G
	13	32	☉∠♃	
	16	15	☽‖♂	B
	16	35	☽∠♂	b
28	00	11	☽♊	
Su	10	01	☽□♄	B
	16	17	☽⚼☿	b
	16	47	☽⊻♂	g
29	00	17	☽□♅	B
Mo	01	53	☿⊥♀	
	06	40	☽□♀	B
	06	48	☽☍♃	B
	07	05	☽△♆	G
	09	08	♀□♃	
	09	14	☽⚼☉	b
	12	47	♀⊽♆	
	15	33	☽△☿	G
	19	50	☽☍♇	B
30	00	49	☽♋	
Tu	03	42	☉✱♄	
	03	58	♃✱♆	
	07	57	☽⚼♆	b
	11	31	☽✱♄	G
	12	04	☽△☉	G
	19	11	☽☌♂	B
31	02	21	☽△♅	G
We	13	19	☽✱♀	G
	13	35	☽∠♄	b
	17	13	☽□☿	B
	20	06	♆Stat	
	22	36	☽‖♂	B

NOVEMBER

Day	h	m	Aspect	
1	04	48	☽⚼♅	b
Th	04	48	☽☊	
	06	14	☽#♃	G
	13	21	☽⚼♃	b
	16	40	☽⊻♄	g
	18	30	☽∠♀	b
	21	18	☽□☉	B
	22	59	☿Stat	
2	01	22	☽⊻♂	g
Fr	02	54	☽⚼♇	b
	13	19	☽#♇	D
	13	32	♀Q♂	
	14	27	☿⊻♀	
	16	16	☽☍♆	B
	17	35	☽△♃	G
	21	07	☽#♆	D
	23	16	☽#☉	G
3	00	14	☽✱☿	G
Sa	00	59	☽⊻♀	g
	05	58	☽∠♂	b
	07	13	☽△♇	G
	12	45	☽♍	
	19	14	☽‖♄	B
4	01	46	☽☌♄	B
Su	05	52	☽∠☿	b
	07	58	☽#☿	G
	09	17	♀±♆	
	10	38	☉‖♆	
	11	17	☽#♅	B
	11	19	☉△♂	
	11	24	☽✱♂	G
	11	24	☽✱☉	G
	17	51	☽☍♅	B
	23	44	☉∠♇	
5	04	44	☽□♃	B
Mo	05	47	☽‖♀	G
	12	46	☽⊻☿	g
	17	04	☽☌♀	G
	18	10	☽□♇	B
	19	48	☽∠☉	b
	23	47	☽♎	
	23	58	☽#♀	G
6	06	01	♀□♇	
Tu	08	19	☽⚼♆	b
	13	40	☽⊻♄	g
	20	02	☽‖♅	B
	23	51	☽□♂	B
7	01	09	☽‖☿	G
We	04	43	☽⊻☉	g
	12	15	☽#♄	B
	14	34	☽△♆	G
	16	49	☉△♅	
	18	00	☽✱♃	G
	18	36	☉⊥♃	
	20	07	☽∠♄	b
8	05	24	☽☌☿	G
Th	06	46	☽✱♇	G
	11	26	☽⊻♀	g
	12	04	☽⚼♅	b
	12	10	☽‖♆	D
	12	18	☽♏	
	18	50	☽‖☉	G
	20	48	☽‖♇	D
	21	05	♀♎	
	22	27	☿✱♇	
9	00	55	☽∠♃	b
Fr	02	41	☽✱♄	G
	13	03	☽△♂	G
	13	13	☽∠♇	b
	18	24	☽△♅	G
	20	49	☽∠♀	b
	23	03	☽☌☉	D
10	02	43	☉‖♇	
Sa	03	19	☽□♆	B
	07	48	☽⊻♃	g
	08	16	☽‖♃	G
	18	29	☽#♂	B
	19	33	☽⚼♂	b

Day	h	m	Aspect	
	19	37	☽⊻♇	g
11	00	07	☽⊻☿	g
Su	00	59	☽♐	
	05	39	☿⚼♅	
	06	08	☽✱♀	G
	08	41	☿♏	
	15	37	☽□♄	B
12	01	42	☉□♆	
Mo	02	04	☉Q♄	
	06	48	☽□♅	B
	09	43	☽∠☿	b
	15	42	☽✱♆	G
	16	58	☽⊻☉	g
	20	26	♀⚼♆	
	21	09	☽☌♃	G
13	01	57	☿#♄	
Tu	07	53	☽☌♇	D
	13	00	☽♑	
	19	12	☽✱☿	G
	21	30	☽∠♆	b
	23	58	☽□♀	B
14	01	26	☽∠☉	b
We	03	41	☽△♄	G
	05	16	☉⊥♇	
	13	32	☽☍♂	B
	18	09	☽✱♅	G
15	02	54	☽⊻♆	g
Th	07	12	☉⊻♃	
	08	24	♂Stat	
	09	06	☽⚼♄	b
	09	11	☽⊻♃	g
	09	19	☽✱☉	G
	11	44	☽#♂	B
	18	42	☽⊻♇	g
	19	28	♀⊻♄	
	22	28	☽‖♃	G
	23	07	☽∠♅	b
	23	30	☽♒	
16	12	42	☽□☿	B
Fr	14	19	☽∠♃	b
	15	32	☽△♀	G
	22	47	☽‖☉	G
	23	11	☽∠♇	b
	23	22	☿✱♄	
17	03	24	☽⊻♅	g
Sa	04	57	☿∠♃	
	07	41	☽‖♇	D
	11	48	☽☌♆	D
	15	47	☽‖♆	D
	18	39	☽✱♃	G
	21	56	☽⚼♀	b
	22	33	☽□☉	B
18	02	29	☽‖☿	G
Su	02	33	☽⚼♂	b
	02	51	☽✱♇	G
	07	14	☽♓	
	13	57	☽#♄	B
	21	00	☽☍♄	B
19	02	21	☽△☿	G
Mo	03	06	☽‖♅	B
	05	09	☽△♂	G
	06	51	♀Q♃	
	09	25	☽☌♅	B
	16	44	☽‖♀	G
	17	18	☽⊻♆	g
20	00	29	☽□♃	B
Tu	00	33	☉⚼♂	
	02	18	♀□♂	
	02	52	☿△♂	

Day	h	m	Aspect	
	04	34	☿⊻♀	
	07	19	☽⚼☿	b
	07	20	☽△☉	G
	07	26	☽□♇	B
	08	27	☿∠♇	
	08	49	☉⊻♇	
	11	24	☽♈	
	16	16	☽#♀	G
	18	41	☽∠♆	b
	19	13	☉∠♀	
21	03	55	☽#♅	B
We	07	37	☽□♂	B
	10	05	☽⚼☉	b
	10	12	☽☍♀	B
	11	31	♀⊥♄	
	11	50	☽⊻♅	g
	15	55	☽‖♄	B
	17	57	☿△♅	
	19	17	☽✱♆	G
22	00	55	☽⚼♄	b
Th	02	43	☽△♃	G
	07	23	♀⊽♅	
	08	40	☽△♇	G
	11	33	☿‖♆	
	11	48	☽#♆	D
	11	50	☽#☿	G
	11	57	☽∠♅	b
	12	18	☽♉	
	16	50	☉♐	
	18	58	☽#♇	D
23	00	51	☽△♄	G
Fr	02	53	☽⚼♃	b
	03	49	♀Q♇	
	07	16	☽✱♂	G
	08	26	☽⚼♇	b
	09	10	☽#☉	G
	11	38	☽✱♅	G
	16	19	☽☍☿	B
	18	53	☽□♆	B
	23	25	☽#♃	G
24	02	46	☿⊥♃	
Sa	06	36	☽∠♂	b
	10	16	♅Stat	
	11	02	☽‖♂	B
	11	29	☽♊	
	14	30	☽☍☉	B
	15	16	☽⚼♀	b
	17	49	☿□♆	
25	00	04	☽□♄	B
Su	03	11	☿Q♄	
	05	58	☽⊻♂	g
	10	44	☽□♅	B
	16	51	☽△♀	G
	18	08	☽△♆	G
	19	45	☿‖♇	
26	02	51	☽☍♃	B
Mo	07	17	☿⊥♇	
	07	38	☽☍♇	B
	09	55	♀△♆	
	11	07	☽♋	
	18	20	☽⚼♆	b
27	00	05	☽⚼☿	b
Tu	00	21	☽✱♄	G
	05	53	☽☌♂	B
	11	26	☽△♅	G
	14	09	♀±♅	
	20	35	☽⚼☉	b
	20	57	☽‖♂	B
	22	12	☽□♀	B

Day	h	m	Aspect	
	23	06	☉±♂	
28	01	34	☽∠♄	b
We	04	22	☽△☿	G
	11	00	☽#♃	G
	13	01	☽⚼♅	b
	13	23	☽☊	
	14	11	☿⊻♃	
	20	57	♀‖♅	
	21	26	☽#☉	G
29	00	37	☽△☉	G
Th	00	52	☿⚼♂	
	03	47	☽⊻♄	g
	08	04	☽⚼♃	b
	08	54	☽⊻♂	g
	10	28	☽#☿	G
	12	19	☽⚼♇	b
	16	47	♀∠♄	
	19	09	☽#♇	D
30	00	12	☽☍♆	B
Fr	02	34	☉Q♆	
	03	39	☽#♆	D
	05	24	☿⊻♇	
	08	26	☽✱♀	G
	11	54	☽∠♂	b
	11	57	☽△♃	G
	15	58	☽△♇	G
	17	25	☽□☿	B
	19	44	☽♍	
	20	23	☉□♄	

DECEMBER

Day	h	m	Aspect	
1	03	04	☽‖♄	B
Sa	11	27	☽☌♄	B
	12	13	☽#♀	G
	12	21	☿♐	
	12	44	☽□☉	B
	15	40	☽∠♀	b
	15	52	☽✱♂	G
	16	41	☽#♅	B
2	00	04	☽☍♅	B
Su	08	14	♀✱♃	
	20	27	☉⊽♂	
	22	51	☽□♃	B
3	00	06	☽⊻♀	g
Mo	02	12	☽□♇	B
	06	01	☽♎	
	12	16	☽✱☿	G
	15	06	☽⚼♆	b
	22	34	♀✱♇	
	22	42	☽⊻♄	g
4	01	07	☿±♂	
Tu	01	28	☽‖♅	B
	01	58	☽□♂	B
	05	24	☽✱☉	G
	11	26	☽‖♀	G
	15	46	☽#♄	B
	16	58	☿⊥♀	
	21	23	☽△♆	G
	23	03	☽∠☿	b
5	05	04	☽∠♄	b
We	09	53	♀⚼♅	
	12	22	☽✱♃	G
	13	29	♀♏	
	14	36	☽∠☉	b
	14	48	☽✱♇	G
	17	13	☽‖♆	D
	18	10	☽⚼♅	b
	18	31	☽♏	
	19	04	☽☌♀	G

6	02 59	☽∥♇	D
Th	08 47	☿Q♆	
	10 07	☽⚺☿	g
	11 34	☽⚹♄	G
	13 19	☽△♂	G
	19 23	☽∠♃	b
	20 53	♀⋕♄	
	21 16	☿□♄	
	21 19	☽∠♇	b
	23 52	☽⚺☉	g
7	00 36	☽△♅	G
Fr	06 59	☿▽♂	
	08 34	☉□♅	
	08 57	☽∥☿	G
	10 16	☽□♆	B
	11 57	☽∥☉	G
	16 21	☽∥♃	G
	18 54	☽⚼♂	b
8	02 16	☽⚺♃	g
Sa	03 41	☽⚺♇	g
	07 11	☽♐	
	14 19	☽⚺♀	g
	15 48	☽⋕♂	B
9	00 09	☽□♄	B
Su	03 59	♂⚹♄	
	06 18	☉∥☿	
	07 40	☽☌☿	G
	12 55	☽□♅	B
	17 40	☽☌☉	D
	22 28	☽⚹♆	G
	23 27	☽∠♀	b
10	15 09	☽☌♃	G
Mo	15 36	☽☌♇	D
	17 40	☿∥♃	
	18 51	☽♑	
11	00 25	☿□♅	
Tu	04 04	☽∠♆	b
	08 08	☽⚹♀	G
	09 58	☽☍♂	B
	11 30	☽△♄	G
	19 36	♃☌♇	
	23 16	♀△♂	
	23 57	☽⚹♅	G

12	00 23	☽⋕♂	B
We	03 20	☽⚺☿	g
	03 48	☉⚹♆	
	09 18	☽⚺♆	g
	09 46	☽⚺☉	g
	16 36	☽⚼♄	b
	19 33	♀⚹♄	
	20 55	☽∥☿	G
13	00 54	☽∥♃	G
Th	01 45	☽∥☉	G
	02 03	☽⚺♇	g
	02 31	☽⚺♃	g
	04 53	☽∠♅	b
	05 01	☽♒	
	12 16	☽∠☿	b
	17 01	☽∠☉	b
	23 52	☽□♀	B
14	03 02	☿⚹♆	
Fr	06 35	☽∠♇	b
	07 29	☽∠♃	b
	09 19	☽⚺♅	g
	11 45	☽∥♇	D
	18 22	☽☌♆	D
	20 28	☽⚹☿	G
	21 04	☽∥♆	D
	21 30	☽⚼♂	b
	23 36	☽⚹☉	G
15	03 27	☉∥♃	
Sa	06 25	☽∥♀	G
	10 33	☽⚹♇	G
	11 51	☽⚹♃	G
	13 15	☽♓	
	19 57	☽⋕♄	B
16	00 18	☽△♂	G
Su	04 50	☽☍♄	B
	08 56	☽∥♅	B
	12 43	☽△♀	G
	16 24	☽☌♅	B
17	01 02	☽⚺♆	g
Mo	01 58	♀∠♇	
	10 03	☽□☿	B
	10 18	☽□☉	B
	15 27	☉☌☿	

	16 27	☽□♇	B
	17 47	☽⚼♀	b
	18 27	☽□♃	B
	18 52	☽♈	
18	03 07	♀∠♃	
Tu	03 18	☽∠♆	b
	03 56	☽□♂	B
	06 43	♀△♅	
	10 46	☽⋕♅	B
	20 11	♃♑	
	20 38	☽⚺♅	g
	23 03	☽∥♄	B
19	01 10	♂⚼♆	
We	04 50	☽⚹♆	G
	10 58	☽⚼♄	b
	14 10	♄ Stat	
	17 23	☽△☉	G
	17 51	☽⋕♀	G
	18 50	☿☌♇	
	19 28	☽△♇	G
	19 33	☽△☿	G
	19 42	☽⋕♆	D
	21 38	☽♉	
	21 43	☽∠♅	b
	22 02	☽△♃	G
20	04 11	☽⋕♇	D
Th	04 56	☽⚹♂	G
	11 41	☽△♄	G
	14 43	☿♑	
	19 46	☽⚼☉	b
	20 04	☽⚼♇	b
	21 54	☿☌♃	
	22 14	☽⚹♅	G
	22 54	☽⚼♃	b
	23 00	☽⚼☿	b
21	00 17	☉☌♇	
Fr	00 58	♀∥♆	
	03 41	☽☍♀	B
	04 39	☽∠♂	b
	06 06	☽□♆	B
	10 15	☽⋕♃	G
	11 20	☽⋕☉	G
	12 59	♀⚼♂	

	22 14	☽♊	
	22 21	☽⋕☿	G
22	04 06	☽⚺♂	g
Sa	06 08	☉♑	
	10 22	♀□♆	
	11 55	☽□♄	B
	12 02	☽∥♂	B
	13 43	☿Q♅	
	18 29	☿☍♂	
	21 56	♀Q♄	
	22 24	☽□♅	B
23	05 56	☉☌♃	
Su	06 13	☽△♆	G
	18 25	☿∠♆	
	20 26	☽☍♇	B
	22 18	☽♋	
24	00 13	☽☍♃	B
Mo	01 16	☽☍☉	B
	02 59	☽•♂	B
	06 27	☽⚼♆	b
	07 53	☽☍☿	B
	10 16	☽⚼♀	b
	12 11	☽⚹♄	G
	16 12	☽∥♂	B
	19 47	☉☍♂	
	20 16	♀⊥♇	
	23 03	☽△♅	G
25	07 07	☽⋕☿	G
Tu	09 04	☉Q♅	
	12 57	☽∠♄	b
	13 17	☽△♀	G
	18 57	☽⋕☉	G
	19 49	☽⋕♃	G
	23 10	☿△♄	
	23 52	☽♌	
26	00 12	☽⚼♅	b
We	03 26	☽⚺♂	g
	14 29	☽⚺♄	g
	19 52	♂☍♃	
	23 58	☽⚼♇	b
27	03 34	☽⋕♇	D
Th	03 52	☽⋕♀	G
	04 26	♀±♂	

	04 47	☽∠♂	b
	05 12	☽⚼♃	b
	06 40	☉∠♆	
	09 07	♀∥♇	
	09 50	♀⊥♃	
	10 53	☽☍♆	B
	11 13	☽⚼☉	b
	13 01	☽⋕♆	D
	16 35	☿∠♀	
	22 33	☽□♀	B
	22 45	☽⚼☿	b
28	02 54	☽△♇	G
Fr	04 44	☽♍	
	07 03	☽⚹♂	G
	08 44	☽△♃	G
	10 50	☽∥♄	B
	16 51	☽△☉	G
	20 26	☽☌♄	B
29	00 57	☽⋕♅	B
Sa	06 31	☽△☿	G
	07 27	☉∥♃	
	09 15	☽☍♅	B
	11 22	☿⊥♆	
	23 27	♀⚺♇	
30	04 10	☿⚹♅	
Su	11 50	☽□♇	B
	13 08	☽⚹♀	G
	13 23	☉△♄	
	13 37	☽♎	
	14 23	☽□♂	B
	18 02	♀♐	
	19 00	☽□♃	B
	23 09	♀▽♂	
	23 54	☽⚼♆	b
31	06 16	☽⚺♄	g
Mo	06 49	☽∥♅	B
	07 51	☽□☉	B
	16 00	♂♊	
	22 10	☽∠♀	b
	22 17	☽⋕♄	B

Note: The Distances Apart are in Declination

JANUARY

Day	h	m	Aspect	°	'
1	01	21	☽☍♃	5	34
1	20	04	☽☍♂	4	43
2	10	06	☽☍♇	11	51
3	09	32	☽☍☿	3	02
3	13	57	☽☍☉	4	34
4	23	08	☽☍♀	2	14
6	07	38	☽☍♆	2	11
6	18	57	☽●♄	0	47
7	06	05	☉☌☿	1	52
8	05	37	☽☍♅	0	12
13	10	02	♂☌♇	7	18
15	15	10	☽☌♃	5	43
16	21	28	☽☌♇	11	54
17	02	06	☽☌♂	4	30
19	02	48	♀☌♆	1	17
19	04	01	☽☌☉	3	45
19	18	56	☽●☿	1	11
20	14	02	☽☌♆	2	06
20	17	18	☽●♀	0	40
20	21	33	☽☍♄	0	46
22	05	29	☽☌♅	0	19
22	15	38	♀☍♄	0	18
26	13	20	☿☌♆	1	18
28	16	46	☽☍♃	5	49
28	18	07	☿☍♄	0	03
29	18	40	☽☍♇	11	57
30	16	45	☽☍♂	4	06

FEBRUARY

Day	h	m	Aspect	°	'
2	05	45	☽☍☉	2	45
2	17	47	☽☍♆	2	02
2	23	34	☽●♄	0	47
3	18	26	☽☍☿	0	55
4	08	09	☽☍♀	0	45
4	16	18	☽☍♅	0	25
7	18	57	♀☌♅	0	37
8	15	52	☉☌♆	0	13
10	18	42	☉☍♄	1	14
12	09	16	☽☌♃	5	55
13	08	45	☽☌♇	12	02
15	02	21	☽☌♂	3	26
17	01	47	☽☌♆	2	00
17	03	57	☽☍♄	0	52
17	16	14	☽☌☉	1	29
18	08	43	☽☌☿	3	40
18	16	58	☽☌♅	0	29
19	15	43	☽☌♀	2	00
23	04	45	☉☌☿	3	28
25	05	11	☽☍♃	5	58
26	01	21	☽☍♇	12	04
28	12	01	♄☍♆	1	02
28	15	11	☽☍♂	2	41

MARCH

Day	h	m	Aspect	°	'
2	02	12	☽●♄	0	57
2	02	32	☽☍♆	1	58
2	15	53	☽☍☿	4	19
3	23	17	☽●☉	0	16
4	02	28	☽☍♅	0	33
5	15	39	☉☌♅	0	41
6	18	48	☽☍♀	2	55
11	23	21	☽☌♃	5	59
12	18	27	☽☌♇	12	06
16	02	25	☽☌♂	1	40
16	11	36	☽☍♄	1	01
16	14	18	☽☌♆	1	56
17	03	56	☽●☿	1	10
18	06	26	☽☌♅	0	37
19	02	43	☽●●	1	00
21	12	11	☽☌♀	3	27
22	19	34	♂☍♄	0	10
24	15	24	☽☍♃	5	58
25	07	57	☽☍♇	12	06
25	17	39	♂☌♆	0	54
29	04	55	☽●♄	1	03
29	10	03	☽☍♆	1	53
29	15	45	☽☍♂	0	43
31	07	55	☽☍☿	1	50
31	11	42	☽☍♅	0	41

APRIL

Day	h	m	Aspect	°	'
1	18	29	☿☌♅	1	24
2	17	15	☽☍☉	2	09
6	02	54	☽☍♀	3	33
8	07	52	☽☌♃	5	54
9	01	35	☽☌♇	12	04
12	19	31	☽☍♄	1	02
13	01	18	☽☌♆	1	47
14	01	32	☽●♂	0	26
14	19	34	☽☌♅	0	47
16	07	08	☽☌☿	4	00
17	11	36	☽☌☉	3	12
20	07	27	☽☌♀	3	14
20	23	51	☽☍♃	5	51
21	15	52	☽☍♇	12	02
25	10	14	☽●♄	0	58
25	17	16	☽☍♆	1	41
27	18	12	☽☍♂	1	26
27	20	18	☽☍♅	0	53
28	12	44	♀☍♃	2	56
29	04	37	♂☌♅	0	38

MAY

Day	h	m	Aspect	°	'
2	08	00	☽☍☿	4	18
2	10	09	☽☍☉	4	03
3	04	05	☉☌☿	0	10
5	11	04	☽☌♃	5	46
6	04	50	☽☍♀	2	27
6	06	46	☽☌♇	11	57
7	02	05	♀☍♇	9	33
10	03	19	☽☍♄	0	50
10	09	27	☽☌♆	1	33
12	06	18	☽☌♅	1	03
12	23	01	☽☌♂	2	31
16	19	27	☽☌☉	4	39
17	23	31	☽☌☿	2	59
18	06	23	☽☍♃	5	43
19	00	57	☽☍♇	11	54
20	01	30	☽☌♀	1	38
20	05	30	☿☍♃	2	54
22	19	26	☽●♄	0	42
23	01	02	☽☍♆	1	26
25	04	45	☽☍♅	1	10
26	21	38	☽☍♂	3	26
27	15	13	☿☍♇	9	16

JUNE

Day	h	m	Aspect	°	'
1	01	04	☽☍☉	4	56
1	11	19	☽☌♃	5	39
2	11	29	☽☌♇	11	50
3	01	27	☽☍☿	2	57
4	21	43	☽☍♀	0	49
5	23	13	☉☍♃	0	42
6	11	43	☽☍♄	0	30
6	15	09	☽☌♆	1	18
8	13	55	☽☌♅	1	20
10	18	24	☽☌♂	4	20
14	10	59	☽☍♃	5	39
15	03	13	☽☌☉	4	52
15	09	59	☽☍♇	11	49
16	09	21	☽☌☿	5	33
18	15	06	☽●♀	0	31
19	06	49	☉☍♇	7	02
19	08	03	☽●♄	0	20
19	09	22	☽☍♆	1	13
21	13	09	☽☍♅	1	27
25	00	38	☽☍♂	5	02
25	15	54	♄☍♆	0	56
28	12	09	☽☌♃	5	38
28	18	40	☉☌☿	4	18
29	17	08	☽☌♇	11	48
30	08	53	☽☍☿	9	01
30	13	49	☽☍☉	4	24
30	15	30	♀☍♆	0	24

JULY

Day	h	m	Aspect	°	'
1	14	38	♀☌♄	0	38
3	20	07	☽☌♆	1	09
3	21	52	☽☍♄	0	08
4	00	21	☽☍♀	0	56
5	19	22	☽☌♅	1	34
9	11	25	☽☌♂	5	37
11	14	33	☽☍♃	5	39
12	17	39	☽☍♇	11	49
13	03	33	☽☌☿	8	39
14	12	04	☽☌☉	3	39
16	17	29	☽☍♆	1	07
16	22	32	☽●♄	0	02
17	11	40	☽☌♀	2	17
18	21	06	☽☍♅	1	37
24	01	43	☽☍♂	6	00
25	16	25	☽☌♃	5	40
27	00	13	☽☌♇	11	49
28	14	27	☽☍☿	4	30
30	00	48	☽☍☉	2	35
31	02	08	☽☌♆	1	07
31	10	28	☽☍♄	0	13
31	22	09	☽☍♀	4	58

AUGUST

Day	h	m	Aspect	°	'
2	00	35	☽☌♅	1	39
7	01	50	☽☌♂	6	10
7	18	58	☽☍♃	5	41
8	23	34	☽☍♇	11	49
12	16	13	☽●☿	0	12
12	23	03	☽☌☉	1	29
13	00	31	☽☍♆	1	09
13	13	15	☽●♄	0	22
13	13	34	☽☌♀	7	47
13	18	25	☉☍♆	0	16
13	19	16	♀☌♄	8	12
14	20	09	☿☍♆	1	23
15	03	56	☽☍♅	1	39
15	19	56	☉☌☿	1	40
17	05	27	☿☌♀	9	06
18	03	41	☉☌♀	7	32
18	13	44	☿☌♄	0	26
21	23	14	☽☍♂	6	07
21	23	28	☉☌♄	1	12
22	01	07	☽☌♃	5	40
23	08	23	☽☌♇	11	47
23	16	03	♂☍♃	0	25
25	21	48	♀☍♆	8	06
27	08	50	☽☍♀	9	19
27	10	00	☽☌♆	1	11
28	01	23	☽☍♄	0	32
28	10	35	☽●☉	0	12
28	19	39	☿☍♅	0	16
29	07	15	☽☌♅	1	36
29	08	53	☽☍☿	1	54

SEPTEMBER

Day	h	m	Aspect	°	'
4	02	23	☽☍♃	5	38
4	13	06	☽☌♂	5	51
5	04	39	☽☍♇	11	43
8	23	47	☽☌♀	8	22
9	06	05	☽☍♆	1	13
9	18	46	☉☍♅	0	45
10	02	58	☽●♄	0	41
11	09	18	☽☍♅	1	33
11	12	44	☽●●	0	57
13	11	29	☽☌☿	2	03
18	13	34	☽☌♃	5	34
19	15	03	☽☍♂	5	20
19	16	44	☽☌♇	11	36
21	08	40	♂☍♇	6	20
21	20	03	♀☍♆	4	53
23	19	09	☽☌♆	1	13
23	20	52	☽☍♀	5	42
24	17	30	☽☍♄	0	53
25	15	45	☽☌♅	1	31
26	19	45	☽☍☉	2	08
28	15	49	☽☍☿	1	25

OCTOBER

Day	h	m	Aspect	°	'
1	14	16	☽☍♃	5	28
2	10	52	☽☍♇	11	29
2	19	55	☽☌♂	4	44
6	10	47	☽☍♆	1	12
7	05	28	☽☌♀	2	57
7	15	07	☽●♄	1	04
8	13	30	☽☍♅	1	29
11	05	01	☽☌☉	3	07
13	00	31	☽☌☿	1	09
14	04	28	♀☌♄	2	42
16	04	32	☽☌♃	5	19
17	00	32	☽☌♇	11	18
17	21	43	☽☍♂	3	55
21	04	08	☽☌♆	1	07
22	08	47	☽☍♄	1	18
22	20	50	☽☍♀	0	09
23	00	59	☽☌♅	1	31
23	23	55	☉☌☿	1	00
25	09	08	♀☍♅	0	55
25	21	46	☽☍☿	3	22
26	04	52	☽☍☉	4	00
29	06	48	☽☍♃	5	11
29	19	50	☽☍♇	11	10
30	19	11	☽☌♂	3	11

NOVEMBER

Day	h	m	Aspect	°	'
2	16	16	☽☍♆	1	02

DISTANCES APART OF ALL ☌s AND ☍s IN 2007

Note: The Distances Apart are in Declination

4	01 46	☽☌♄	1 30	24	14 30	☽☍☉	4 54	10	15 36	☽☌♇	10 45	23	20 26	☽☍♇	10 43
4	17 51	☽☍♅	1 33	26	02 51	☽☍♃	4 50	11	09 58	☽☍♂	1 07	24	00 13	☽☍♃	4 30
5	17 04	☽☌♀	2 31	26	07 38	☽☍♇	10 52	11	19 36	♃☌♇	6 07	24	01 16	☽☍☉	4 17
8	05 24	☽☌☿	5 47	27	05 53	☽☌♂	1 40	14	18 22	☽☌♆	0 35	24	02 59	☽●♂	0 54
9	23 03	☽☌☉	4 35	30	00 12	☽☍♆	0 45	16	04 50	☽☍♄	2 12	24	07 53	☽☍☿	2 14
12	21 09	☽☌♃	4 59	DECEMBER				16	16 24	☽☌♅	1 55	24	19 47	☉☍♂	3 21
13	07 53	☽☌♇	10 59					17	15 27	☉☌☿	1 21	26	19 52	♂☍♃	3 35
14	13 32	☽☍♂	2 18	1	11 27	☽☌♄	1 58	19	18 50	☿☌♇	7 50	27	10 53	☽☍♆	0 29
17	11 48	☽☌♆	0 52	2	00 04	☽☍♅	1 46	20	21 54	☿☌♃	1 48	28	20 26	☽☌♄	2 20
18	21 00	☽☍♄	1 47	5	19 04	☽☌♀	6 07	21	00 17	☉☌♇	6 18	29	09 15	☽☍♅	2 01
19	09 25	☽☌♅	1 40	9	07 40	☽☌☿	4 19	21	03 41	☽☍♀	6 56				
21	10 12	☽☍♀	4 43	9	17 40	☽☌☉	4 46	22	18 29	☿☍♂	1 33				
23	16 19	☽☍☿	5 50	10	15 09	☽☌♃	4 39	23	05 56	☉☌♃	0 11				

PHENOMENA IN 2007

d h	JANUARY
2 12	☽ Max. Dec.28°N24′
3 19	⊕ in perihelion
9 14	☽ Zero Dec.
10 16	☽ in Apogee
16 22	☽ Max. Dec.28°S27′
22 12	☽ in Perigee
23 07	☽ Zero Dec.
29 18	☽ Max. Dec.28°N30′
	FEBRUARY
5 05	☿ ☊
5 21	☽ Zero Dec.
7 13	☽ in Apogee
7 18	☿ Gt.Elong. 18 ° E.
9 21	☿ in perihelion
13 08	☽ Max. Dec.28°S34′
19 09	☽ in Perigee
19 15	☽ Zero Dec.
26 00	☽ Max. Dec.28°N36′
	MARCH
3 23	☽ Total eclipse
5 05	☽ Zero Dec.
7 03	☽ in Apogee
12 16	☽ Max. Dec.28°S36′
15 12	☿ ☋
16 13	♀ ☊
19 02	☽ Zero Dec.
19 03	● Partial eclipse
19 19	☽ in Perigee
21 00	☉ enters ♈,Equinox
22 02	☿ Gt.Elong. 28 ° W.
25 06	☽ Max. Dec.28°N35′
25 20	☿ in aphelion
	APRIL
1 11	☽ Zero Dec.
3 08	☽ in Apogee
8 23	☽ Max. Dec.28°S31′
15 13	☽ Zero Dec.
17 06	☽ in Perigee
19 05	♀ in perihelion
21 14	☽ Max. Dec.28°N27′
28 17	☽ Zero Dec.
30 11	☽ in Apogee

d h	MAY
4 04	☿ ☊
6 04	☽ Max. Dec.28°S21′
8 20	☿ in perihelion
12 22	☽ Zero Dec.
15 15	☽ in Perigee
18 23	☽ Max. Dec.28°N17′
25 22	☽ Zero Dec.
27 22	☽ in Apogee
	JUNE
2 09	☽ Max. Dec.28°S13′
2 10	☿ Gt.Elong. 23 ° E.
4 12	♂ in perihelion
9 02	♀ Gt.Elong. 45 ° E.
9 04	☽ Zero Dec.
11 11	☿ ☋
12 17	☽ in Perigee
15 08	☽ Max. Dec.28°N13′
21 18	☉ enters ♋,Solstice
21 20	☿ in aphelion
22 05	☽ Zero Dec.
24 14	☽ in Apogee
29 16	☽ Max. Dec.28°S13′
	JULY
6 03	♀ ☋
6 09	☽ Zero Dec.
7 01	⊕ in aphelion
9 22	☽ in Perigee
12 17	☽ Max. Dec.28°N15′
19 12	☽ Zero Dec.
20 15	☿ Gt.Elong. 20 ° W.
22 09	☽ in Apogee
26 23	☽ Max. Dec.28°S18′
31 03	☿ ☊
	AUGUST
2 14	☽ Zero Dec.
4 00	☽ in Perigee
4 19	☿ in perihelion
8 23	☽ Max. Dec.28°N20′
9 18	♀ in aphelion
15 20	☽ Zero Dec.
19 04	☽ in Apogee
23 08	☽ Max. Dec.28°S22′
28 11	☽ Total eclipse
29 22	☽ Zero Dec.
31 00	☽ in Perigee

d h	SEPTEMBER
5 04	☽ Max. Dec.28°N23′
7 10	☿ ☋
11 13	● Partial eclipse
12 04	☽ Zero Dec.
15 21	☽ in Apogee
17 19	☿ in aphelion
19 16	☽ Max. Dec.28°S21′
23 10	☉ enters ♎,Equinox
26 08	☽ Zero Dec.
28 02	☽ in Perigee
29 16	☿ Gt.Elong. 26 ° E.
	OCTOBER
2 10	☽ Max. Dec.28°N18′
3 11	♂ ☊
9 10	☽ Zero Dec.
13 10	☽ in Apogee
16 23	☽ Max. Dec.28°S12′
23 19	☽ Zero Dec.
26 12	☽ in Perigee
27 03	☿ ☊
27 06	♀ ☊
29 18	☽ Max. Dec.28°N07′
31 19	☿ in perihelion
	NOVEMBER
5 15	☽ Zero Dec.
8 20	☿ Gt.Elong. 19 ° W.
9 13	☽ in Apogee
13 05	☽ Max. Dec.28°S00′
20 04	☽ Zero Dec.
24 00	☽ in Perigee
26 04	☽ Max. Dec.27°N57′
30 05	♀ in perihelion
	DECEMBER
2 21	☽ Zero Dec.
4 10	☿ ☋
6 17	☽ in Apogee
10 10	☽ Max. Dec.27°S54′
14 18	☿ in aphelion
17 10	☽ Zero Dec.
22 06	☉ enters ♑,Solstice
22 10	☽ in Perigee
23 14	☽ Max. Dec.27°N55′
30 04	☽ Zero Dec.

LOCAL MEAN TIME OF SUNRISE FOR LATITUDES
60° North to 50° South
FOR ALL SUNDAYS IN 2007 (ALL TIMES ARE A.M.)

Date	NORTHERN LATITUDES									SOUTHERN LATITUDES				
	LONDON	60°	55°	50°	40°	30°	20°	10°	0°	10°	20°	30°	40°	50°
	H M	H M	H M	H M	H M	H M	H M	H M	H M	H M	H M	H M	H M	H M
2006 Dec. 31	8 6	9 3	8 25	7 59	7 22	6 55	6 35	6 16	5 59	5 42	5 23	5 1	4 34	3 54
2007 Jan. 7	8 4	8 58	8 23	7 57	7 22	6 57	6 37	6 19	6 3	5 46	5 28	5 7	4 40	4 2
,, 14	8 0	8 50	8 17	7 54	7 21	6 57	6 38	6 21	6 5	5 49	5 32	5 13	4 47	4 12
,, 21	7 54	8 38	8 9	7 48	7 17	6 55	6 38	6 22	6 8	5 53	5 37	5 19	4 55	4 22
,, 28	7 45	8 24	7 59	7 40	7 12	6 53	6 37	6 23	6 9	5 56	5 42	5 25	5 4	4 34
Feb. 4	7 34	8 8	7 46	7 30	7 6	6 49	6 35	6 22	6 10	5 59	5 46	5 31	5 12	4 46
,, 11	7 22	7 50	7 32	7 18	6 58	6 44	6 32	6 21	6 11	6 1	5 50	5 37	5 21	4 59
,, 18	7 9	7 31	7 17	7 6	6 50	6 38	6 28	6 19	6 11	6 2	5 53	5 42	5 29	5 11
,, 25	6 55	7 12	7 1	6 53	6 40	6 31	6 23	6 16	6 10	6 3	5 56	5 48	5 38	5 23
Mar. 4	6 40	6 51	6 44	6 38	6 30	6 23	6 18	6 13	6 9	6 4	5 59	5 53	5 46	5 35
,, 11	6 24	6 30	6 26	6 23	6 19	6 15	6 12	6 10	6 7	6 4	6 1	5 58	5 53	5 47
,, 18	6 9	6 9	6 9	6 8	6 8	6 7	6 6	6 6	6 5	6 4	6 3	6 2	6 0	5 58
,, 25	5 53	5 48	5 51	5 53	5 56	5 59	6 0	6 2	6 3	6 4	6 5	6 6	6 8	6 9
Apr. 1	5 37	5 27	5 33	5 38	5 45	5 50	5 54	5 58	6 1	6 4	6 7	6 11	6 15	6 20
,, 8	5 21	5 6	5 15	5 23	5 34	5 42	5 48	5 54	5 59	6 4	6 9	6 15	6 22	6 31
,, 15	5 5	4 45	4 58	5 8	5 23	5 34	5 43	5 50	5 57	6 4	6 11	6 19	6 29	6 42
,, 22	4 51	4 24	4 41	4 54	5 13	5 26	5 37	5 47	5 55	6 4	6 13	6 23	6 36	6 52
,, 29	4 37	4 4	4 25	4 41	5 3	5 20	5 32	5 44	5 54	6 4	6 15	6 28	6 43	7 3
May 6	4 24	3 46	4 10	4 29	4 55	5 13	5 28	5 41	5 53	6 5	6 18	6 32	6 50	7 13
,, 13	4 12	3 28	3 57	4 18	4 47	5 8	5 25	5 40	5 53	6 6	6 20	6 36	6 56	7 23
,, 20	4 2	3 12	3 45	4 8	4 41	5 4	5 22	5 38	5 53	6 8	6 23	6 41	7 3	7 33
,, 27	3 54	2 58	3 35	4 1	4 36	5 1	5 21	5 38	5 54	6 9	6 26	6 45	7 8	7 41
June 3	3 47	2 47	3 27	3 55	4 33	4 59	5 20	5 38	5 55	6 11	6 29	6 49	7 14	7 49
,, 10	3 44	2 39	3 22	3 51	4 31	4 58	5 20	5 39	5 56	6 13	6 31	6 52	7 18	7 54
,, 17	3 42	2 36	3 20	3 50	4 31	4 59	5 21	5 40	5 57	6 15	6 33	6 54	7 21	7 58
,, 24	3 43	2 37	3 21	3 51	4 32	5 0	5 22	5 41	5 59	6 16	6 35	6 56	7 23	8 0
July 1	3 47	2 42	3 25	3 55	4 35	5 2	5 24	5 43	6 0	6 17	6 36	6 57	7 23	8 0
,, 8	3 53	2 51	3 32	4 0	4 39	5 5	5 26	5 45	6 1	6 18	6 36	6 56	7 22	7 57
,, 15	4 0	3 3	3 41	4 7	4 43	5 9	5 29	5 46	6 2	6 18	6 35	6 55	7 19	7 52
,, 22	4 9	3 17	3 51	4 15	4 49	5 13	5 32	5 48	6 3	6 18	6 34	6 52	7 14	7 45
,, 29	4 19	3 33	4 3	4 25	4 55	5 17	5 34	5 49	6 3	6 17	6 31	6 48	7 8	7 37
Aug. 5	4 29	3 49	4 15	4 34	5 2	5 21	5 37	5 50	6 3	6 15	6 28	6 43	7 1	7 26
,, 12	4 40	4 6	4 28	4 45	5 8	5 25	5 39	5 51	6 2	6 13	6 24	6 37	6 53	7 14
,, 19	4 51	4 23	4 41	4 55	5 15	5 30	5 41	5 51	6 0	6 10	6 19	6 30	6 44	7 2
,, 26	5 2	4 40	4 54	5 5	5 22	5 34	5 43	5 51	5 59	6 6	6 14	6 23	6 34	6 48
Sept. 2	5 14	4 56	5 7	5 16	5 28	5 37	5 45	5 51	5 57	6 2	6 8	6 15	6 23	6 33
,, 9	5 25	5 13	5 21	5 26	5 35	5 41	5 46	5 50	5 54	5 58	6 2	6 6	6 12	6 18
,, 16	5 36	5 29	5 34	5 37	5 42	5 45	5 48	5 50	5 52	5 54	5 56	5 58	6 0	6 3
,, 23	5 47	5 46	5 47	5 47	5 48	5 49	5 49	5 49	5 49	5 49	5 49	5 49	5 49	5 48
,, 30	5 58	6 2	6 0	5 58	5 55	5 53	5 51	5 49	5 47	5 45	5 43	5 40	5 37	5 32
Oct. 7	6 10	6 19	6 13	6 9	6 2	5 57	5 52	5 49	5 45	5 41	5 37	5 32	5 26	5 17
,, 14	6 22	6 36	6 27	6 20	6 9	6 1	5 54	5 49	5 43	5 37	5 31	5 24	5 15	5 2
,, 21	6 34	6 53	6 41	6 31	6 17	6 6	5 57	5 49	5 42	5 34	5 26	5 16	5 4	4 48
,, 28	6 46	7 11	6 55	6 42	6 24	6 11	6 0	5 50	5 41	5 31	5 21	5 9	4 55	4 35
Nov. 4	6 58	7 29	7 9	6 54	6 32	6 16	6 3	5 51	5 40	5 29	5 17	5 3	4 46	4 22
,, 11	7 10	7 47	7 24	7 6	6 40	6 22	6 6	5 53	5 41	5 28	5 14	4 59	4 39	4 11
,, 18	7 23	8 5	7 38	7 17	6 48	6 27	6 10	5 56	5 42	5 28	5 12	4 55	4 33	4 1
,, 25	7 34	8 22	7 50	7 28	6 56	6 33	6 15	5 59	5 43	5 28	5 12	4 52	4 28	3 54
Dec. 2	7 44	8 37	8 2	7 38	7 3	6 39	6 19	6 2	5 46	5 29	5 12	4 51	4 26	3 48
,, 9	7 53	8 49	8 12	7 46	7 10	6 44	6 24	6 6	5 49	5 32	5 13	4 52	4 25	3 46
,, 16	8 0	8 58	8 20	7 53	7 15	6 49	6 28	6 9	5 52	5 34	5 16	5 54	4 26	3 45
,, 23	8 4	9 3	8 24	7 57	7 19	6 53	6 31	6 13	5 55	5 38	5 19	4 57	4 29	3 48
,, 30	8 6	9 3	8 25	7 59	7 22	6 55	6 34	6 16	5 59	5 41	5 23	5 1	4 33	3 53
2008 Jan. 6	8 5	9 0	8 24	7 58	7 22	6 57	6 37	6 19	6 2	5 45	5 27	5 6	4 39	4 1

Example:—To find the time of Sunrise in Jamaica (Latitude 18°N.) on Wednesday June 13th. 2007. On June 10th. L.M.T. = 5h. 20m. + $\frac{2}{10}$ × 19m. = 5h. 24m., on June 17th. L.M.T. = 5h. 21m. + $\frac{2}{10}$ × 19m. = 5h. 25m., therefore L.M.T. on June 13th. = 5h. 24m. + $\frac{3}{7}$ × 1m. = 5h. 24m. A.M.

LOCAL MEAN TIME OF SUNSET FOR LATITUDES
60° North to 50° South
FOR ALL SUNDAYS IN 2007 (ALL TIMES ARE P.M.)

Date	NORTHERN LATITUDES									SOUTHERN LATITUDES				
	LONDON	60°	55°	50°	40°	30°	20°	10°	0°	10°	20°	30°	40°	50°
2006	H M	H M	H M	H M	H M	H M	H M	H M	H M	H M	H M	H M	H M	H M
Dec. 31	4 0	3 3	3 41	4 7	4 44	5 10	5 31	5 50	6 7	6 24	6 43	7 4	7 32	8 12
2007														
Jan. 7	4 8	3 14	3 50	4 15	4 50	5 15	5 35	5 53	6 10	6 26	6 45	7 5	7 32	8 10
,, 14	4 18	3 28	4 1	4 24	4 57	5 21	5 40	5 57	6 13	6 28	6 46	7 5	7 30	8 6
,, 21	4 29	3 44	4 13	4 35	5 5	5 27	5 45	6 0	6 15	6 30	6 45	7 4	7 27	8 0
,, 28	4 41	4 2	4 27	4 46	5 13	5 33	5 49	6 3	6 16	6 30	6 44	7 1	7 22	7 52
Feb. 4	4 54	4 20	4 42	4 58	5 22	5 39	5 53	6 6	6 17	6 29	6 42	6 57	7 15	7 41
,, 11	5 6	4 39	4 56	5 10	5 30	5 45	5 57	6 8	6 18	6 28	6 39	6 52	7 8	7 30
,, 18	5 19	4 57	5 11	5 22	5 38	5 50	6 0	6 9	6 17	6 26	6 35	6 46	6 59	7 17
,, 25	5 32	5 15	5 26	5 34	5 47	5 56	6 3	6 10	6 17	6 23	6 30	6 39	6 49	7 3
Mar. 4	5 44	5 33	5 40	5 46	5 54	6 1	6 6	6 11	6 15	6 20	6 25	6 31	6 39	6 49
,, 11	5 56	5 50	5 54	5 57	6 2	6 5	6 8	6 11	6 14	6 16	6 20	6 23	6 28	6 34
,, 18	6 8	6 8	6 8	6 8	6 9	6 10	6 10	6 11	6 12	6 13	6 14	6 15	6 16	6 19
,, 25	6 20	6 25	6 22	6 20	6 16	6 14	6 12	6 11	6 10	6 9	6 7	6 6	6 5	6 3
Apr. 1	6 32	6 42	6 35	6 31	6 23	6 18	6 14	6 11	6 8	6 4	6 1	5 58	5 54	5 48
,, 8	6 44	6 59	6 49	6 42	6 31	6 23	6 16	6 11	6 6	6 1	5 55	5 50	5 43	5 33
,, 15	6 55	7 16	7 3	6 52	6 38	6 27	6 18	6 11	6 4	5 57	5 50	5 42	5 32	5 19
,, 22	7 7	7 33	7 16	7 3	6 45	6 31	6 20	6 11	6 2	5 54	5 45	5 34	5 22	5 5
,, 29	7 19	7 51	7 30	7 14	6 52	6 36	6 23	6 11	6 1	5 51	5 40	5 28	5 13	4 52
May 6	7 30	8 8	7 43	7 25	6 59	6 40	6 25	6 12	6 0	5 48	5 36	5 22	5 4	4 40
,, 13	7 41	8 25	7 56	7 35	7 6	6 45	6 28	6 13	6 0	5 47	5 33	5 17	4 57	4 30
,, 20	7 51	8 41	8 9	7 45	7 12	6 49	6 31	6 15	6 0	5 46	5 30	5 12	4 51	4 20
,, 27	8 1	8 56	8 20	7 54	7 18	6 53	6 34	6 17	6 1	5 45	5 29	5 10	4 46	4 13
June 3	8 9	9 9	8 29	8 1	7 24	6 57	6 36	6 18	6 2	5 45	5 28	5 8	4 43	4 8
,, 10	8 15	9 19	8 37	8 7	7 28	7 0	6 39	6 20	6 3	5 46	5 28	5 7	4 41	4 4
,, 17	8 19	9 26	8 41	8 11	7 31	7 3	6 41	6 22	6 4	5 47	5 29	5 7	4 41	4 3
,, 24	8 21	9 28	8 43	8 13	7 33	7 5	6 43	6 24	6 6	5 49	5 30	5 9	4 42	4 5
July 1	8 21	9 26	8 42	8 13	7 33	7 5	6 44	6 25	6 7	5 50	5 32	5 11	4 45	4 8
,, 8	8 18	9 19	8 38	8 10	7 32	7 5	6 44	6 26	6 9	5 52	5 34	5 14	4 49	4 13
,, 15	8 12	9 9	8 31	8 5	7 29	7 3	6 43	6 26	6 10	5 54	5 37	5 17	4 53	4 20
,, 22	8 4	8 56	8 22	7 58	7 24	7 0	6 41	6 25	6 10	5 55	5 39	5 21	4 59	4 28
,, 29	7 54	8 40	8 10	7 49	7 18	6 56	6 39	6 24	6 10	5 56	5 42	5 25	5 5	4 37
Aug. 5	7 43	8 23	7 57	7 38	7 11	6 51	6 36	6 22	6 10	5 57	5 44	5 29	5 11	4 46
,, 12	7 30	8 4	7 42	7 26	7 2	6 45	6 31	6 20	6 9	5 58	5 46	5 33	5 18	4 56
,, 19	7 16	7 45	7 26	7 13	6 53	6 38	6 27	6 17	6 7	5 58	5 48	5 37	5 24	5 6
,, 26	7 2	7 24	7 10	6 59	6 42	6 31	6 21	6 13	6 5	5 58	5 50	5 41	5 31	5 16
Sept. 2	6 46	7 4	6 53	6 44	6 32	6 23	6 15	6 9	6 3	5 58	5 52	5 45	5 37	5 27
,, 9	6 31	6 42	6 35	6 29	6 20	6 14	6 9	6 5	6 1	5 57	5 53	5 49	5 44	5 37
,, 16	6 14	6 21	6 17	6 14	6 9	6 5	6 3	6 1	5 59	5 57	5 55	5 53	5 50	5 47
,, 23	5 58	6 0	5 59	5 58	5 57	5 57	5 56	5 56	5 56	5 56	5 56	5 56	5 57	5 58
,, 30	5 42	5 39	5 41	5 43	5 46	5 48	5 50	5 52	5 54	5 56	5 58	6 0	6 4	6 8
Oct. 7	5 26	5 17	5 23	5 28	5 34	5 40	5 44	5 48	5 51	5 55	6 0	6 4	6 11	6 19
,, 14	5 11	4 57	5 6	5 13	5 24	5 32	5 38	5 44	5 50	5 55	6 2	6 9	6 18	6 30
,, 21	4 56	4 37	4 49	4 59	5 13	5 24	5 33	5 41	5 48	5 56	6 4	6 14	6 25	6 42
,, 28	4 42	4 17	4 33	4 46	5 4	5 17	5 28	5 38	5 47	5 57	6 7	6 19	6 33	6 54
Nov. 4	4 29	3 58	4 18	4 33	4 55	5 12	5 25	5 36	5 47	5 58	6 10	6 24	6 41	7 5
,, 11	4 18	3 40	4 4	4 22	4 48	5 6	5 22	5 35	5 48	6 0	6 14	6 30	6 50	7 17
,, 18	4 8	3 25	3 52	4 13	4 42	5 3	5 20	5 35	5 49	6 3	6 18	6 36	6 58	7 29
,, 25	4 0	3 12	3 43	4 6	4 38	5 1	5 19	5 35	5 51	6 6	6 22	6 42	7 6	7 40
Dec. 2	3 55	3 2	3 36	4 1	4 35	5 0	5 20	5 37	5 53	6 9	6 27	6 47	7 13	7 50
,, 9	3 52	2 55	3 32	3 58	4 35	5 0	5 21	5 39	5 56	6 13	6 31	6 53	7 20	7 59
,, 16	3 51	2 53	3 32	3 59	4 36	5 2	5 24	5 42	5 59	6 17	6 36	6 58	7 26	8 6
,, 23	3 54	2 55	3 34	4 1	4 39	5 6	5 27	5 45	6 3	6 20	6 39	7 1	7 29	8 10
,, 30	3 59	3 2	3 40	4 7	4 44	5 10	5 31	5 49	6 6	6 23	6 42	7 4	7 32	8 12
2008														
Jan. 6	4 7	3 12	3 48	4 14	4 49	5 15	5 35	5 53	6 9	6 26	6 44	7 6	7 32	8 11

Example:—To find the time of Sunset in Canberra (Latitude 35.3°S.) on Friday July 27th. 2007. On July 22nd. L.M.T. = 5h. 21m. − $\frac{5 \cdot 3}{10}$ × 22m. = 5h. 9m., on July 29th. L.M.T. = 5h. 25m. − $\frac{5 \cdot 3}{10}$ × 20m. = 5h. 14m., therefore L.M.T. on July 27th. = 5h. 9m. + $\frac{5}{7}$ × 5m. = 5h. 13m. P.M.

TABLES OF HOUSES FOR LONDON, Latitude 51º 32' *N.*

Sidereal Time.	10 ♈	11 ♉	12 ♊	Ascen ♋	2 ♌	3 ♍
H. M. S.	º	º	º	º '	º	º
0 0 0	0	9	22	26 36	12	3
0 3 40	1	10	23	27 17	13	3
0 7 20	2	11	24	27 56	14	4
0 11 0	3	12	25	28 42	15	5
0 14 41	4	13	25	29 17	15	6
0 18 21	5	14	26	29 55	16	7
0 22 2	6	15	27	0♌34	17	8
0 25 42	7	16	28	1 14	18	8
0 29 23	8	17	29	1 55	18	9
0 33 4	9	18	♋	2 33	19	10
0 36 45	10	19	1	3 14	20	11
0 40 26	11	20	1	3 54	20	12
0 44 8	12	21	2	4 33	21	13
0 47 50	13	22	3	5 12	22	14
0 51 32	14	23	4	5 52	23	15
0 55 14	15	24	5	6 30	23	15
0 58 57	16	25	6	7 9	24	16
1 2 40	17	26	6	7 50	25	17
1 6 23	18	27	7	8 30	26	18
1 10 7	19	28	8	9 9	26	19
1 13 51	20	29	9	9 48	27	19
1 17 35	21	♊	10	10 28	28	20
1 21 20	22	1	10	11 8	28	21
1 25 6	23	2	11	11 48	29	22
1 28 52	24	3	12	12 28	♍	23
1 32 38	25	4	13	13 8	1	24
1 36 25	26	5	14	13 48	1	25
1 40 12	27	6	14	14 28	2	25
1 44 0	28	7	15	15 8	3	26
1 47 48	29	8	16	15 48	4	27
1 51 37	30	9	17	16 28	4	28

Sidereal Time.	10 ♉	11 ♊	12 ♋	Ascen ♌	2 ♍	3 ♍
H. M. S.	º	º	º	º '	º	º
1 51 37	0	9	17	16 28	4	28
1 55 27	1	10	18	17 8	5	29
1 59 17	2	11	19	17 48	6	♎
2 3 8	3	12	19	18 28	7	1
2 6 59	4	13	20	19 9	8	2
2 10 51	5	14	21	19 49	9	2
2 14 44	6	15	22	20 29	9	3
2 18 37	7	16	22	21 10	10	4
2 22 31	8	17	23	21 51	11	5
2 26 25	9	18	24	22 32	11	6
2 30 20	10	19	25	23 14	12	7
2 34 16	11	20	25	23 55	13	8
2 38 13	12	21	26	24 36	14	9
2 42 10	13	22	27	25 17	15	10
2 46 8	14	23	28	25 58	15	11
2 50 7	15	24	29	26 40	16	12
2 54 7	16	25	29	27 22	17	12
2 58 7	17	26	♌	28 4	18	13
3 2 8	18	27	1	28 46	18	14
3 6 9	19	27	2	29 28	19	15
3 10 12	20	28	3	0♍12	20	16
3 14 15	21	29	3	0 54	21	17
3 18 19	22	♋	4	1 36	22	18
3 22 23	23	1	5	2 20	22	19
3 26 29	24	2	6	3 2	23	20
3 30 35	25	3	7	3 45	24	21
3 34 41	26	4	7	4 28	25	22
3 38 49	27	5	8	5 11	26	23
3 42 57	28	6	9	5 54	27	24
3 47 6	29	7	10	6 38	27	25
3 51 15	30	8	11	7 21	28	25

Sidereal Time.	10 ♊	11 ♋	12 ♌	Ascen ♍	2 ♍	3 ♎
H. M. S.	º	º	º	º '	º	º
3 51 15	0	8	11	7 21	28	25
3 55 25	1	9	12	8 5	29	26
3 59 36	2	10	12	8 49	♎	27
4 3 48	3	10	13	9 33	1	28
4 8 0	4	11	14	10 17	2	29
4 12 13	5	12	15	11 2	2	♏
4 16 26	6	13	16	11 46	3	1
4 20 40	7	14	17	12 30	4	2
4 24 55	8	15	17	13 15	5	3
4 29 10	9	16	18	14 0	6	4
4 33 26	10	17	19	14 45	7	5
4 37 42	11	18	20	15 30	8	6
4 41 59	12	19	21	16 15	8	7
4 46 16	13	20	21	17 0	9	8
4 50 34	14	21	22	17 45	10	9
4 54 52	15	22	23	18 30	11	10
4 59 10	16	23	24	19 16	12	11
5 3 29	17	24	25	20 3	13	12
5 7 49	18	25	26	20 49	14	13
5 12 9	19	25	27	21 35	14	14
5 16 29	20	26	28	22 20	15	14
5 20 49	21	27	28	23 6	16	15
5 25 9	22	28	29	23 51	17	16
5 29 30	23	29	♍	24 37	18	17
5 33 51	24	♌	1	25 23	19	18
5 38 12	25	1	2	26 9	20	19
5 42 34	26	2	3	26 55	21	20
5 46 55	27	3	4	27 41	21	21
5 51 17	28	4	4	28 27	22	22
5 55 38	29	5	5	29 13	23	23
6 0 0	30	6	6	30 0	24	24

Sidereal Time.	10 ♋	11 ♌	12 ♍	Ascen ♎	2 ♎	3 ♏
H. M. S.	º	º	º	º '	º	º
6 0 0	0	6	6	0 0	24	24
6 4 22	1	7	7	0 47	25	25
6 8 43	2	8	8	1 33	26	26
6 13 5	3	9	9	2 19	27	27
6 17 26	4	10	10	3 5	27	28
6 21 48	5	11	10	3 51	28	29
6 26 9	6	12	11	4 37	29	♐
6 30 30	7	13	12	5 23	♏	1
6 34 51	8	14	13	6 9	1	2
6 39 11	9	15	14	6 55	2	3
6 43 31	10	16	15	7 40	2	4
6 47 51	11	16	16	8 26	3	4
6 52 11	12	17	16	9 12	4	5
6 56 31	13	18	17	9 58	5	6
7 0 50	14	19	18	10 43	6	7
7 5 8	15	20	19	11 28	7	8
7 9 26	16	21	20	12 14	8	9
7 13 44	17	22	21	12 59	8	10
7 18 1	18	23	22	13 45	9	11
7 22 18	19	24	23	14 30	10	12
7 26 34	20	25	24	15 15	11	13
7 30 50	21	26	25	16 0	12	14
7 35 5	22	27	25	16 45	13	15
7 39 20	23	28	26	17 30	13	16
7 43 34	24	29	27	18 15	14	17
7 47 47	25	♍	28	18 59	15	18
7 52 0	26	1	29	19 43	16	19
7 56 12	27	2	29	20 27	17	20
8 0 24	28	3	♎	21 11	18	20
8 4 35	29	4	1	21 56	18	21
8 8 45	30	5	2	22 40	19	22

Sidereal Time.	10 ♌	11 ♍	12 ♎	Ascen ♎	2 ♏	3 ♐
H. M. S.	º	º	º	º '	º	º
8 8 45	0	5	2	22 40	19	22
8 12 54	1	5	3	23 24	20	23
8 17 3	2	6	3	24 7	21	24
8 21 11	3	7	4	24 50	22	25
8 25 19	4	8	5	25 34	23	26
8 29 26	5	9	6	26 18	23	27
8 33 31	6	10	7	27 1	24	28
8 37 37	7	11	8	27 44	25	29
8 41 41	8	12	8	28 26	26	♑
8 45 45	9	13	9	29 8	27	1
8 49 48	10	14	10	29 50	27	2
8 53 51	11	15	11	0♏32	28	3
8 57 52	12	16	12	1 15	29	4
9 1 53	13	17	12	1 58	♐	4
9 5 53	14	18	13	2 39	1	5
9 9 53	15	18	14	3 21	1	6
9 13 52	16	19	15	4 3	2	7
9 17 50	17	20	16	4 44	3	8
9 21 47	18	21	16	5 26	3	9
9 25 44	19	22	17	6 7	4	10
9 29 40	20	23	18	6 48	5	11
9 33 35	21	24	18	7 29	5	12
9 37 29	22	25	19	8 9	6	13
9 41 23	23	26	20	8 50	7	14
9 45 16	24	27	21	9 31	8	15
9 49 9	25	28	22	10 11	9	16
9 53 1	26	28	23	10 51	9	17
9 56 52	27	29	23	11 32	10	18
10 0 43	28	♎	24	12 12	11	19
10 4 33	29	1	25	12 53	12	20
10 8 23	30	2	26	13 33	13	20

Sidereal Time.	10 ♍	11 ♎	12 ♎	Ascen ♏	2 ♐	3 ♑
H. M. S.	º	º	º	º '	º	º
10 8 23	0	2	26	13 33	13	20
10 12 12	1	3	26	14 13	14	21
10 16 0	2	4	27	14 53	15	22
10 19 48	3	5	28	15 33	15	23
10 23 35	4	5	29	16 13	16	24
10 27 22	5	6	29	16 52	17	25
10 31 8	6	7	♏	17 32	18	26
10 34 54	7	8	1	18 12	19	27
10 38 40	8	9	2	18 52	20	28
10 42 25	9	10	2	19 31	20	29
10 46 9	10	11	3	20 11	21	♒
10 49 53	11	11	4	20 50	22	1
10 53 37	12	12	4	21 30	23	2
10 57 20	13	13	5	22 9	24	3
11 1 3	14	14	6	22 49	24	4
11 4 46	15	15	7	23 28	25	5
11 8 28	16	16	7	24 8	26	6
11 12 10	17	17	8	24 47	27	8
11 15 52	18	17	9	25 27	28	9
11 19 34	19	18	10	26 6	29	10
11 23 15	20	19	10	26 45	♑	11
11 26 56	21	20	11	27 25	0	12
11 30 37	22	21	12	28 5	1	13
11 34 18	23	22	13	28 44	2	14
11 37 58	24	23	13	29 24	3	15
11 41 39	25	23	14	0♐3	4	16
11 45 19	26	24	15	0 43	5	17
11 49 0	27	25	15	1 23	6	18
11 52 40	28	26	16	2 3	6	19
11 56 20	29	27	17	2 43	7	20
12 0 0	30	27	17	3 23	8	21

TABLES OF HOUSES FOR LONDON, Latitude 51º 32' N.

Sidereal Time.	10 ♎	11 ♎	12 ♏	Ascen ♐	2 ♑	3 ♒
H. M. S.	°	°	°	° '	°	°
12 0 0	0	27	17	3 23	8	21
12 3 40	1	28	18	4 4	9	23
12 7 20	2	29	19	4 45	10	24
12 11 0	3	♏	20	5 26	11	25
12 14 41	4	1	20	6 7	12	26
12 18 21	5	1	21	6 48	13	27
12 22 2	6	2	22	7 29	14	28
12 25 42	7	3	23	8 10	15	29
12 29 23	8	4	23	8 51	16	♓
12 33 4	9	5	24	9 33	17	2
12 36 45	10	6	25	10 15	18	3
12 40 26	11	6	25	10 57	19	4
12 44 8	12	7	26	11 40	20	5
12 47 50	13	8	27	12 22	21	6
12 51 32	14	9	28	13 4	22	7
12 55 14	15	10	28	13 47	23	9
12 58 57	16	11	29	14 30	24	10
13 2 40	17	11	♐	15 14	25	11
13 6 23	18	12	1	15 59	26	12
13 10 7	19	13	1	16 44	27	13
13 13 51	20	14	2	17 29	28	15
13 17 35	21	15	3	18 14	29	16
13 21 20	22	16	4	19 0	♒	17
13 25 6	23	16	4	19 45	1	18
13 28 52	24	17	5	20 31	2	20
13 32 38	25	18	6	21 18	4	21
13 36 25	26	19	7	22 6	5	22
13 40 12	27	20	7	22 54	6	23
13 44 0	28	21	8	23 42	7	25
13 47 48	29	21	9	24 31	8	26
13 51 37	30	22	10	25 20	10	27

Sidereal Time.	10 ♏	11 ♏	12 ♐	Ascen ♐	2 ♒	3 ♓
H. M. S.	°	°	°	° '	°	°
13 51 37	0	22	10	25 20	10	27
13 55 27	1	23	11	26 10	11	28
13 59 17	2	24	11	27 2	12	♈
14 3 8	3	25	12	27 53	14	1
14 6 59	4	26	13	28 45	15	2
14 10 51	5	26	14	29 36	16	4
14 14 44	6	27	15	0♑29	18	5
14 18 37	7	28	15	1 23	19	6
14 22 31	8	29	16	2 18	20	8
14 26 25	9	♐	17	3 14	22	9
14 30 20	10	1	18	4 11	23	10
14 34 16	11	2	19	5 9	25	11
14 38 13	12	2	20	6 7	26	13
14 42 10	13	3	20	7 6	28	14
14 46 8	14	4	21	8 6	29	15
14 50 7	15	5	22	9 8	♓	17
14 54 7	16	6	23	10 11	2	18
14 58 7	17	7	24	11 15	4	19
15 2 8	18	8	25	12 20	6	21
15 6 9	19	9	26	13 27	8	22
15 10 12	20	9	27	14 35	9	23
15 14 15	21	10	27	15 43	11	24
15 18 19	22	11	28	16 52	13	26
15 22 23	23	12	29	18 3	14	27
15 26 29	24	13	♑	19 16	16	28
15 30 35	25	14	1	20 32	17	29
15 34 41	26	15	2	21 48	19	♉
15 38 49	27	16	3	23 8	21	2
15 42 57	28	17	4	24 29	22	3
15 47 6	29	18	5	25 51	24	5
15 51 15	30	18	6	27 15	26	6

Sidereal Time.	10 ♐	11 ♐	12 ♑	Ascen ♑	2 ♓	3 ♉
H. M. S.	°	°	°	° '	°	°
15 51 15	0	18	6	27 15	26	6
15 55 25	1	19	7	28 42	28	7
15 59 36	2	20	8	0♒11	♈	9
16 3 48	3	21	9	1 42	2	10
16 8 0	4	22	10	3 16	3	11
16 12 13	5	23	11	4 53	5	12
16 16 26	6	24	12	6 32	7	14
16 20 40	7	25	13	8 13	9	15
16 24 55	8	26	14	9 57	11	16
16 29 10	9	27	16	11 44	12	17
16 33 26	10	28	17	13 34	14	18
16 37 42	11	29	18	15 26	16	20
16 41 59	12	♑	19	17 20	18	21
16 46 16	13	1	20	19 18	20	22
16 50 34	14	2	21	21 22	21	23
16 54 52	15	3	22	23 29	23	25
16 59 10	16	4	24	25 36	25	26
17 3 29	17	5	25	27 46	27	27
17 7 49	18	6	26	0♓ 0	28	28
17 12 9	19	7	27	2 19	♉	29
17 16 29	20	8	29	4 40	2	♊
17 20 49	21	9	♒	7 2	3	1
17 25 9	22	10	1	9 26	5	2
17 29 30	23	11	3	11 54	7	3
17 33 51	24	12	4	14 24	8	5
17 38 12	25	13	5	17 0	10	6
17 42 34	26	14	7	19 33	11	7
17 46 55	27	15	8	22 6	13	8
17 51 17	28	16	10	24 40	14	9
17 55 38	29	17	11	27 20	16	10
18 0 0	30	18	13	30 0	17	11

Sidereal Time.	10 ♑	11 ♑	12 ♒	Ascen ♈	2 ♉	3 ♊
H. M. S.	°	°	°	° '	°	°
18 0 0	0	18	13	0 0	17	11
18 4 22	1	20	14	2 39	19	13
18 8 43	2	21	16	5 19	20	14
18 13 5	3	22	17	7 55	22	15
18 17 26	4	23	19	10 29	23	16
18 21 48	5	24	20	13 2	25	17
18 26 9	6	25	22	15 36	26	18
18 30 30	7	26	23	18 6	28	19
18 34 51	8	27	25	20 34	29	20
18 39 11	9	29	27	22 59	♊	21
18 43 31	10	♒	28	25 22	1	22
18 47 51	11	1	♓	27 42	2	23
18 52 11	12	2	2	29 58	4	24
18 56 31	13	3	3	2♉13	5	25
19 0 50	14	4	5	4 24	6	26
19 5 8	15	6	7	6 30	8	27
19 9 26	16	7	9	8 36	9	28
19 13 44	17	8	10	10 40	10	29
19 18 1	18	9	12	12 39	11	♋
19 22 18	19	10	14	14 35	12	1
19 26 34	20	12	16	16 28	13	2
19 30 50	21	13	18	18 17	14	3
19 35 5	22	14	19	20 3	16	4
19 39 20	23	15	21	21 48	17	5
19 43 34	24	16	23	23 29	18	6
19 47 47	25	18	25	25 9	19	7
19 52 0	26	19	27	26 45	20	8
19 56 12	27	20	28	28 18	21	9
20 0 24	28	21	♈	29 49	22	10
20 4 35	29	23	2	1♊19	23	11
20 8 45	30	24	4	2 45	24	12

Sidereal Time.	10 ♒	11 ♒	12 ♈	Ascen ♊	2 ♊	3 ♋
H. M. S.	°	°	°	° '	°	°
20 8 45	0	24	4	2 45	24	12
20 12 54	1	25	6	4 9	25	12
20 17 3	2	27	7	5 32	26	13
20 21 11	3	28	9	6 53	27	14
20 25 19	4	29	11	8 12	28	15
20 29 26	5	♓	13	9 27	29	16
20 33 31	6	2	14	10 43	♋	17
20 37 37	7	3	16	11 58	1	18
20 41 41	8	4	18	13 9	2	19
20 45 45	9	6	19	14 18	3	20
20 49 48	10	7	21	15 25	3	21
20 53 51	11	8	23	16 32	4	21
20 57 52	12	9	24	17 39	5	22
21 1 53	13	11	26	18 44	6	23
21 5 53	14	12	28	19 48	7	24
21 9 53	15	13	29	20 51	8	25
21 13 52	16	15	♉	21 53	9	26
21 17 50	17	16	2	22 53	10	27
21 21 47	18	17	4	23 52	10	28
21 25 44	19	19	5	24 51	11	28
21 29 40	20	20	7	25 48	12	29
21 33 35	21	22	8	26 44	13	♌
21 37 29	22	23	10	27 40	14	1
21 41 23	23	24	11	28 34	15	2
21 45 16	24	25	13	29 29	15	3
21 49 9	25	26	14	0♋22	16	4
21 53 1	26	28	15	1 15	17	4
21 56 52	27	29	16	2 7	18	5
22 0 43	28	♈	18	2 57	19	6
22 4 33	29	2	19	3 48	19	7
22 8 23	30	3	20	4 38	20	8

Sidereal Time.	10 ♓	11 ♈	12 ♉	Ascen ♋	2 ♋	3 ♌
H. M. S.	°	°	°	° '	°	°
22 8 23	0	3	20	4 38	20	8
22 12 12	1	4	21	5 28	21	8
22 16 0	2	6	23	6 17	22	9
22 19 48	3	7	24	7 5	23	10
22 23 35	4	8	25	7 53	23	11
22 27 22	5	9	26	8 42	24	12
22 31 8	6	10	28	9 29	25	13
22 34 54	7	12	29	10 16	26	14
22 38 40	8	13	♊	11 2	26	14
22 42 25	9	14	1	11 47	27	15
22 46 9	10	15	2	12 31	28	16
22 49 53	11	17	3	13 16	29	17
22 53 37	12	18	4	14 1	29	18
22 57 20	13	19	5	14 45	♌	19
23 1 3	14	20	6	15 28	1	19
23 4 46	15	21	7	16 11	2	20
23 8 28	16	23	8	16 54	2	21
23 12 10	17	24	9	17 37	3	22
23 15 52	18	25	10	18 20	4	23
23 19 34	19	26	11	19 3	5	24
23 23 15	20	27	12	19 45	5	24
23 26 56	21	29	13	20 26	6	25
23 30 37	22	♉	14	21 8	7	26
23 34 18	23	1	15	21 50	7	27
23 37 58	24	2	16	22 31	8	28
23 41 39	25	3	17	23 12	9	28
23 45 19	26	4	18	23 53	9	29
23 49 0	27	5	19	24 32	10	♍
23 52 40	28	6	20	25 15	11	1
23 56 20	29	8	21	25 56	12	2
24 0 0	30	9	22	26 36	13	3

TABLES OF HOUSES FOR LIVERPOOL, Latitude 53º 25' *N.*

Sidereal Time.	10 ♈	11 ♉	12 ♊	Ascen ♋	2 ♌	3 ♍	Sidereal Time.	10 ♉	11 ♊	12 ♋	Ascen ♌	2 ♍	3 ♍	Sidereal Time.	10 ♊	11 ♋	12 ♌	Ascen ♍	2 ♍	3 ♎
H. M. S.	º	º	º	º '	º	º	H. M. S.	º	º	º	º '	º	º	H. M. S.	º	º	º	º '	º	º
0 0 0	0	9	24	28 12	14	3	1 51 37	0	10	18	17 32	5	28	3 51 15	0	9	12	7 55	28	25
0 3 40	1	10	25	28 51	14	4	1 55 27	1	11	19	18 11	6	29	3 55 25	1	10	13	8 37	29	26
0 7 20	2	12	25	29 30	15	4	1 59 17	2	12	20	18 51	6	♎	3 59 36	2	11	13	9 20	♎	27
0 11 0	3	13	26	0♌ 9	16	5	2 3 8	3	13	21	19 30	7	1	4 3 48	3	12	14	10 3	1	28
0 14 41	4	14	27	0 48	17	6	2 6 59	4	14	22	20 9	8	2	4 8 0	4	12	15	10 46	2	29
0 18 21	5	15	28	1 27	17	7	2 10 51	5	15	22	20 49	9	2	4 12 13	5	13	16	11 30	2	♏
0 22 2	6	16	29	2 6	18	8	2 14 44	6	16	23	21 28	9	3	4 16 26	6	14	17	12 13	3	1
0 25 42	7	17	♋	2 44	19	9	2 18 37	7	17	24	22 8	10	4	4 20 40	7	15	18	12 56	4	2
0 29 23	8	18	1	3 22	19	10	2 22 31	8	18	25	22 48	11	5	4 24 55	8	16	18	13 40	5	3
0 33 4	9	19	1	4 1	20	10	2 26 25	9	19	25	23 28	12	6	4 29 10	9	17	19	14 24	6	4
0 36 45	10	20	2	4 39	21	11	2 30 20	10	20	26	24 8	12	7	4 33 26	10	18	20	15 8	7	5
0 40 26	11	21	3	5 18	22	12	2 34 16	11	21	27	24 48	13	8	4 37 42	11	19	21	15 52	7	6
0 44 8	12	22	4	5 56	22	13	2 38 13	12	22	28	25 28	14	9	4 41 59	12	20	21	16 36	8	6
0 47 50	13	23	5	6 34	23	14	2 42 10	13	23	29	26 8	15	10	4 46 16	13	21	22	17 20	9	7
0 51 32	14	24	6	7 13	24	14	2 46 8	14	24	29	26 49	15	10	4 50 34	14	22	23	18 4	10	8
0 55 14	15	25	6	7 51	24	15	2 50 7	15	25	♌	27 29	16	11	4 54 52	15	23	24	18 48	11	9
0 58 57	16	26	7	8 30	25	16	2 54 7	16	26	1	28 10	17	12	4 59 10	16	24	25	19 32	12	10
1 2 40	17	27	8	9 8	26	17	2 58 7	17	27	2	28 51	18	13	5 3 29	17	24	26	20 17	12	11
1 6 23	18	28	9	9 47	26	18	3 2 8	18	28	2	29 32	19	14	5 7 49	18	25	26	21 1	13	12
1 10 7	19	29	10	10 25	27	19	3 6 9	19	29	3	0♍13	19	15	5 12 9	19	26	27	21 46	14	13
1 13 51	20	♊	11	11 4	28	19	3 10 12	20	29	4	0 54	20	16	5 16 29	20	27	28	22 31	15	14
1 17 35	21	1	11	11 43	28	20	3 14 15	21	♋	5	1 36	21	17	5 20 49	21	28	29	23 16	16	15
1 21 20	22	2	12	12 21	29	21	3 18 19	22	1	5	2 17	22	18	5 25 9	22	29	♍	24 0	17	16
1 25 6	23	3	13	13 0	♍	22	3 22 23	23	2	6	2 59	23	19	5 29 30	23	♌	1	24 45	18	17
1 28 52	24	4	14	13 39	1	23	3 26 29	24	3	7	3 41	23	20	5 33 51	24	1	1	25 30	18	18
1 32 38	25	5	15	14 17	1	24	3 30 35	25	4	8	4 23	24	21	5 38 12	25	2	2	26 15	19	19
1 36 25	26	6	15	14 56	2	25	3 34 41	26	5	9	5 5	25	22	5 42 34	26	3	3	27 0	20	20
1 40 12	27	7	16	15 35	3	25	3 38 49	27	6	10	5 47	26	22	5 46 55	27	4	4	27 45	21	21
1 44 0	28	8	17	16 14	3	26	3 42 57	28	7	10	6 29	27	23	5 51 17	28	5	5	28 30	22	21
1 47 48	29	9	18	16 53	4	27	3 47 6	29	8	11	7 12	27	24	5 55 38	29	6	6	29 15	23	22
1 51 37	30	10	18	17 32	5	28	3 51 15	30	9	12	7 55	28	25	6 0 0	30	7	7	30 0	23	23

Sidereal Time.	10 ♋	11 ♌	12 ♍	Ascen ♎	2 ♎	3 ♏	Sidereal Time.	10 ♌	11 ♍	12 ♎	Ascen ♎	2 ♏	3 ♐	Sidereal Time.	10 ♍	11 ♎	12 ♎	Ascen ♏	2 ♐	3 ♑
H. M. S.	º	º	º	º '	º	º	H. M. S.	º	º	º	º '	º	º	H. M. S.	º	º	º	º '	º	º
6 0 0	0	7	7	0 0	23	23	8 8 45	0	5	2	22 5	18	21	10 8 23	0	2	25	12 28	11	19
6 4 22	1	8	7	0 45	24	24	8 12 54	1	6	2	22 48	19	22	10 12 12	1	3	26	13 6	12	20
6 8 43	2	9	8	1 30	25	25	8 17 3	2	7	3	23 30	20	23	10 16 0	2	4	27	13 45	13	21
6 13 5	3	9	9	2 15	26	26	8 21 11	3	8	4	24 13	20	24	10 19 48	3	4	27	14 25	14	22
6 17 26	4	10	10	3 0	27	27	8 25 19	4	8	5	24 55	21	25	10 23 35	4	5	28	15 4	15	23
6 21 48	5	11	11	3 45	28	28	8 29 26	5	9	6	25 37	22	26	10 27 22	5	6	29	15 42	15	24
6 26 9	6	12	12	4 30	29	29	8 33 31	6	10	7	26 19	23	27	10 31 8	6	7	29	16 21	16	25
6 30 30	7	13	12	5 15	29	♐	8 37 37	7	11	7	27 1	24	28	10 34 54	7	8	♏	17 0	17	26
6 34 51	8	14	13	6 0	♏	1	8 41 41	8	12	8	27 43	25	29	10 38 40	8	9	1	17 39	18	27
6 39 11	9	15	14	6 44	1	2	8 45 45	9	13	9	28 24	25	♑	10 42 25	9	10	2	18 17	18	28
6 43 31	10	16	15	7 29	2	3	8 49 48	10	14	10	29 6	26	1	10 46 9	10	10	2	18 55	19	29
6 47 51	11	17	16	8 14	3	4	8 53 51	11	15	11	29 47	27	1	10 49 53	11	11	3	19 34	20	♒
6 52 11	12	18	17	8 59	4	5	8 57 52	12	16	11	0♏28	28	2	10 53 37	12	12	4	20 13	21	1
6 56 31	13	19	18	9 43	4	6	9 1 53	13	17	12	1 9	28	3	10 57 20	13	13	4	20 52	22	2
7 0 50	14	20	18	10 27	5	6	9 5 53	14	18	13	1 50	29	4	11 1 3	14	14	5	21 30	22	3
7 5 8	15	21	19	11 11	6	7	9 9 53	15	19	14	2 31	♐	5	11 4 46	15	15	6	22 8	23	5
7 9 26	16	22	20	11 56	7	8	9 13 52	16	19	15	3 11	1	6	11 8 28	16	16	7	22 46	24	6
7 13 44	17	23	21	12 40	8	9	9 17 50	17	20	15	3 52	1	7	11 12 10	17	16	7	23 25	25	7
7 18 1	18	24	22	13 24	8	10	9 21 47	18	21	16	4 32	2	8	11 15 52	18	17	8	24 4	26	8
7 22 18	19	24	23	14 8	9	11	9 25 44	19	22	17	5 12	3	9	11 19 34	19	18	9	24 42	26	9
7 26 34	20	25	23	14 52	10	12	9 29 40	20	23	18	5 52	4	10	11 23 15	20	19	9	25 21	27	10
7 30 50	21	26	24	15 36	11	13	9 33 35	21	24	18	6 32	5	11	11 26 56	21	20	10	25 59	28	11
7 35 5	22	27	25	16 20	12	14	9 37 29	22	25	19	7 12	5	12	11 30 37	22	20	11	26 38	29	12
7 39 20	23	28	26	17 4	13	15	9 41 23	23	26	20	7 52	6	13	11 34 18	23	21	12	27 16	♑	13
7 43 34	24	29	27	17 47	13	16	9 45 16	24	27	21	8 32	7	14	11 37 58	24	22	12	27 54	1	14
7 47 47	25	♍	28	18 30	14	17	9 49 9	25	27	21	9 12	8	15	11 41 39	25	23	13	28 33	1	15
7 52 0	26	1	28	19 13	15	18	9 53 1	26	28	22	9 51	8	16	11 45 19	26	24	14	29 11	2	16
7 56 12	27	2	29	19 57	16	18	9 56 52	27	29	23	10 30	9	17	11 49 0	27	25	14	29 50	3	17
8 0 24	28	3	♎	20 40	17	19	10 0 43	28	♎	24	11 9	10	17	11 52 40	28	26	15	0♐30	4	18
8 4 35	29	4	1	21 23	17	20	10 4 33	29	1	24	11 49	11	18	11 56 20	29	26	16	1 9	5	20
8 8 45	30	5	2	22 5	18	21	10 8 23	30	2	25	12 28	11	19	12 0 0	30	27	16	1 48	6	21

TABLES OF HOUSES FOR LIVERPOOL, Latitude 53º 25' *N.*

Sidereal Time.	10 ♎	11 ♎	12 ♏	Ascen ♐	2 ♑	3 ♒
H. M. S.	º	º	º	º '	º	º
12 0 0	0	27	16	1 48	6	21
12 3 40	1	28	17	2 27	7	22
12 7 20	2	29	18	3 6	8	23
12 11 0	3	♏	18	3 46	9	24
12 14 41	4	0	19	4 25	10	25
12 18 21	5	1	20	5 6	10	26
12 22 2	6	2	21	5 46	11	28
12 25 42	7	3	21	6 26	12	29
12 29 23	8	4	22	7 6	13	♓
12 33 4	9	4	23	7 46	14	1
12 36 45	10	5	24	8 27	15	2
12 40 26	11	6	24	9 8	16	3
12 44 8	12	7	25	9 49	17	5
12 47 50	13	8	26	10 30	18	6
12 51 32	14	9	26	11 12	19	7
12 55 14	15	9	27	11 54	20	8
12 58 57	16	10	28	12 36	21	10
13 2 40	17	11	28	13 19	22	11
13 6 23	18	12	29	14 2	23	12
13 10 7	19	13	♐	14 45	25	13
13 13 51	20	13	1	15 28	26	15
13 17 35	21	14	1	16 12	27	16
13 21 20	22	15	2	16 56	28	17
13 25 6	23	16	3	17 41	29	18
13 28 52	24	17	4	18 26	♒	19
13 32 38	25	17	4	19 11	1	21
13 36 25	26	18	5	19 57	3	22
13 40 12	27	19	6	20 44	4	23
13 44 0	28	20	7	21 31	5	24
13 47 48	29	21	7	22 18	7	26
13 51 37	30	21	8	23 6	8	27

Sidereal Time.	10 ♏	11 ♏	12 ♐	Ascen ♐	2 ♒	3 ♓
H. M. S.	º	º	º	º '	º	º
13 51 37	0	21	8	23 6	8	27
13 55 27	1	22	9	23 55	9	28
13 59 17	2	23	10	24 43	10	♈
14 3 8	3	24	10	25 33	12	1
14 6 59	4	25	11	26 23	13	2
14 10 51	5	26	12	27 14	15	4
14 14 44	6	26	13	28 6	16	5
14 18 37	7	27	13	28 59	18	6
14 22 31	8	28	14	29 52	19	8
14 26 25	9	29	15	0♑46	20	9
14 30 20	10	♐	16	1 41	22	10
14 34 16	11	1	17	2 36	23	11
14 38 13	12	2	18	3 33	25	13
14 42 10	13	2	18	4 30	26	14
14 46 8	14	3	19	5 29	28	16
14 50 7	15	4	20	6 29	♓	17
14 54 7	16	5	21	7 30	1	18
14 58 7	17	6	22	8 32	3	20
15 2 8	18	7	23	9 35	5	21
15 6 9	19	8	24	10 39	6	22
15 10 12	20	8	24	11 45	8	23
15 14 15	21	9	25	12 52	10	25
15 18 19	22	10	26	14 1	11	26
15 22 23	23	11	27	15 11	13	27
15 26 29	24	12	28	16 23	15	29
15 30 35	25	13	29	17 37	17	♉
15 34 41	26	14	♑	18 53	19	1
15 38 49	27	15	1	20 10	21	3
15 42 57	28	16	2	21 29	22	4
15 47 6	29	16	3	22 51	24	5
15 51 15	30	17	4	24 15	26	7

Sidereal Time.	10 ♐	11 ♐	12 ♑	Ascen ♑	2 ♓	3 ♉
H. M. S.	º	º	º	º '	º	º
15 51 15	0	17	4	24 15	26	7
15 55 25	1	18	5	25 41	28	8
15 59 36	2	19	6	27 10	♈	9
16 3 48	3	20	7	28 41	2	10
16 8 0	4	21	8	0♒14	4	12
16 12 13	5	22	9	1 50	5	13
16 16 26	6	23	10	3 30	7	14
16 20 40	7	24	11	5 13	9	15
16 24 55	8	25	12	6 58	11	17
16 29 10	9	26	13	8 46	13	18
16 33 26	10	27	14	10 38	15	19
16 37 42	11	28	15	12 32	17	20
16 41 59	12	29	16	14 31	19	22
16 46 16	13	♑	18	16 33	20	23
16 50 34	14	1	19	18 40	22	24
16 54 52	15	2	20	20 50	24	25
16 59 10	16	3	21	23 4	26	26
17 3 29	17	4	22	25 21	28	28
17 7 49	18	5	24	27 42	29	29
17 12 9	19	6	25	0♓ 8	♉	♊
17 16 29	20	7	26	2 37	3	1
17 20 49	21	8	28	5 10	5	3
17 25 9	22	9	29	7 46	6	4
17 29 30	23	10	♒	10 24	8	5
17 33 51	24	11	2	13 7	10	6
17 38 12	25	12	3	15 52	11	7
17 42 34	26	13	4	18 38	13	8
17 46 55	27	14	6	21 27	15	9
17 51 17	28	15	7	24 17	16	10
17 55 38	29	16	9	27 8	18	12
18 0 0	30	17	11	30 0	19	13

Sidereal Time.	10 ♑	11 ♑	12 ♒	Ascen ♈	2 ♉	3 ♊
H. M. S.	º	º	º	º '	º	º
18 0 0	0	17	11	0 0	19	13
18 4 22	1	18	12	2 52	21	14
18 8 43	2	20	14	5 43	23	15
18 13 5	3	21	15	8 33	24	16
18 17 26	4	22	17	11 22	25	17
18 21 48	5	23	19	14 8	27	18
18 26 9	6	24	20	16 53	28	19
18 30 30	7	25	22	19 36	♊	20
18 34 51	8	26	24	22 14	1	21
18 39 11	9	27	25	24 50	2	22
18 43 31	10	29	27	27 23	4	23
18 47 51	11	♒	28	29 52	5	24
18 52 11	12	1	♓	2♉18	6	25
18 56 31	13	2	2	4 39	8	26
19 0 50	14	4	4	6 56	9	27
19 5 8	15	5	6	9 10	10	28
19 9 26	16	6	8	11 20	11	29
19 13 44	17	7	10	13 27	12	♋
19 18 1	18	8	11	15 29	14	1
19 22 18	19	9	13	17 28	15	2
19 26 34	20	11	15	19 22	16	3
19 30 50	21	12	17	21 14	17	4
19 35 5	22	13	19	23 2	18	5
19 39 20	23	15	21	24 47	19	6
19 43 34	24	16	23	26 30	20	7
19 47 47	25	17	25	28 10	21	8
19 52 0	26	18	26	29 46	22	9
19 56 12	27	20	28	1♊19	23	10
20 0 24	28	21	♈	2 50	24	11
20 4 35	29	22	2	4 19	25	12
20 8 45	30	23	4	5 45	26	13

Sidereal Time.	10 ♒	11 ♒	12 ♈	Ascen ♊	2 ♊	3 ♋
H. M. S.	º	º	º	º '	º	º
20 8 45	0	23	4	5 45	26	13
20 12 54	1	25	6	7 9	27	14
20 17 3	2	26	8	8 31	28	14
20 21 11	3	27	9	9 50	29	15
20 25 19	4	29	11	11 7	♋	16
20 29 26	5	♓	13	12 23	1	17
20 33 31	6	1	15	13 37	2	18
20 37 37	7	3	17	14 49	3	19
20 41 41	8	4	19	15 59	4	20
20 45 45	9	5	20	17 8	5	21
20 49 48	10	7	22	18 15	6	22
20 53 51	11	8	24	19 21	7	22
20 57 52	12	10	25	20 25	7	23
21 1 53	13	11	27	21 28	8	24
21 5 53	14	12	29	22 30	9	25
21 9 53	15	13	♉	23 31	10	26
21 13 52	16	14	2	24 31	11	27
21 17 50	17	16	4	25 30	12	28
21 21 47	18	17	5	26 27	12	28
21 25 44	19	18	7	27 24	13	29
21 29 40	20	20	8	28 19	14	♌
21 33 35	21	21	10	29 14	15	1
21 37 29	22	22	11	0♋ 8	16	2
21 41 23	23	24	12	1 1	17	3
21 45 16	24	25	14	1 54	17	4
21 49 9	25	26	15	2 46	18	4
21 53 1	26	28	17	3 37	19	5
21 56 52	27	29	18	4 27	20	6
22 0 43	28	♈	20	5 17	20	7
22 4 33	29	2	21	6 5	21	8
22 8 23	30	3	22	6 54	22	8

Sidereal Time.	10 ♓	11 ♈	12 ♉	Ascen ♋	2 ♋	3 ♌
H. M. S.	º	º	º	º '	º	º
22 8 23	0	3	22	6 54	22	8
22 12 12	1	4	23	7 42	23	9
22 16 0	2	5	25	8 29	23	10
22 19 48	3	7	26	9 16	24	11
22 23 35	4	8	27	10 3	25	12
22 27 22	5	9	29	10 49	26	13
22 31 8	6	11	♊	11 34	26	13
22 34 54	7	12	1	12 19	27	14
22 38 40	8	13	2	13 3	28	15
22 42 25	9	14	3	13 48	29	16
22 46 9	10	16	4	14 32	29	17
22 49 53	11	17	5	15 15	♌	17
22 53 37	12	18	7	15 58	1	18
22 57 20	13	19	8	16 41	2	19
23 1 3	14	20	9	17 24	2	20
23 4 46	15	22	10	18 6	3	21
23 8 28	16	23	11	18 48	4	21
23 12 10	17	24	12	19 30	4	22
23 15 52	18	25	13	20 11	5	23
23 19 34	19	27	14	20 52	6	24
23 23 15	20	28	15	21 33	6	25
23 26 56	21	29	16	22 14	7	26
23 30 37	22	♉	17	22 54	8	26
23 34 18	23	1	18	23 34	9	27
23 37 58	24	2	19	24 14	9	28
23 41 39	25	4	20	24 54	10	29
23 45 19	26	5	21	25 35	11	♍
23 49 0	27	6	22	26 14	11	0
23 52 40	28	7	22	26 54	12	1
23 56 20	29	8	23	27 33	13	2
24 0 0	30	9	24	28 12	14	3

TABLES OF HOUSES FOR NEW YORK, *Latitude* 40º 43' N.

Sidereal Time. H. M. S.	10 ♈ º	11 ♉ º	12 ♊ º	Ascen ♋ º '	2 ♌ º	3 ♍ º
0 0 0	0	6	15	18 53	8	1
0 3 40	1	7	16	19 38	9	2
0 7 20	2	8	17	20 23	10	3
0 11 0	3	9	18	21 12	11	4
0 14 41	4	11	19	21 55	12	5
0 18 21	5	12	20	22 40	12	5
0 22 2	6	13	21	23 24	13	6
0 25 42	7	14	22	24 8	14	7
0 29 23	8	15	23	24 54	15	8
0 33 4	9	16	23	25 37	15	9
0 36 45	10	17	24	26 22	16	10
0 40 26	11	18	25	27 5	17	11
0 44 8	12	19	26	27 50	18	12
0 47 50	13	20	27	28 33	19	13
0 51 32	14	21	28	29 18	19	13
0 55 14	15	22	28	0♌ 3	20	14
0 58 57	16	23	29	0 46	21	15
1 2 40	17	24	♋	1 31	22	16
1 6 23	18	25	1	2 14	22	17
1 10 7	19	26	2	2 58	23	18
1 13 51	20	27	3	3 43	24	19
1 17 35	21	28	3	4 27	25	20
1 21 20	22	29	4	5 12	25	21
1 25 6	23	♊	5	5 56	26	22
1 28 52	24	1	6	6 40	27	22
1 32 38	25	2	7	7 25	28	23
1 36 25	26	2	8	8 9	29	24
1 40 12	27	3	9	8 53	♍	25
1 44 0	28	4	10	9 38	1	26
1 47 48	29	5	10	10 24	1	27
1 51 37	30	6	11	11 8	2	28

Sidereal Time. H. M. S.	10 ♉ º	11 ♊ º	12 ♋ º	Ascen ♌ º '	2 ♍ º	3 ♍ º
1 51 37	0	6	11	11 8	2	28
1 55 27	1	7	12	11 53	3	29
1 59 17	2	8	13	12 38	4	♎
2 3 8	3	9	14	13 22	5	1
2 6 59	4	10	15	14 8	5	2
2 10 51	5	11	15	14 53	6	3
2 14 44	6	12	16	15 39	7	4
2 18 37	7	13	17	16 24	8	4
2 22 31	8	14	18	17 10	9	5
2 26 25	9	15	19	17 56	10	6
2 30 20	10	16	20	18 41	10	7
2 34 16	11	17	20	19 27	11	8
2 38 13	12	18	21	20 14	12	9
2 42 10	13	19	22	21 0	13	10
2 46 8	14	19	23	21 47	14	11
2 50 7	15	20	24	22 33	15	12
2 54 7	16	21	25	23 20	16	13
2 58 7	17	22	25	24 7	17	14
3 2 8	18	23	26	24 54	17	15
3 6 9	19	24	27	25 42	18	16
3 10 12	20	25	28	26 29	19	17
3 14 15	21	26	29	27 17	20	18
3 18 19	22	27	♌	28 4	21	19
3 22 23	23	28	1	28 52	22	20
3 26 29	24	29	1	29 40	23	21
3 30 35	25	♋	2	0♍29	24	22
3 34 41	26	1	3	1 17	24	23
3 38 49	27	2	4	2 6	25	24
3 42 57	28	3	5	2 55	26	25
3 47 6	29	4	6	3 43	27	26
3 51 15	30	5	7	4 32	28	27

Sidereal Time. H. M. S.	10 ♊ º	11 ♋ º	12 ♌ º	Ascen ♍ º '	2 ♍ º	3 ♎ º
3 51 15	0	5	7	4 32	28	27
3 55 25	1	6	8	5 22	29	28
3 59 36	2	6	8	6 10	♎	29
4 3 48	3	7	9	7 0	1	♏
4 8 0	4	8	10	7 49	2	1
4 12 13	5	9	11	8 40	3	2
4 16 26	6	10	12	9 30	4	3
4 20 40	7	11	13	10 19	4	4
4 24 55	8	12	14	11 10	5	5
4 29 10	9	13	15	12 0	6	6
4 33 26	10	14	16	12 51	7	7
4 37 42	11	15	16	13 41	8	8
4 41 59	12	16	17	14 32	9	9
4 46 16	13	17	18	15 23	10	10
4 50 34	14	18	19	16 14	11	11
4 54 52	15	19	20	17 5	12	12
4 59 10	16	20	21	17 56	13	13
5 3 29	17	21	22	18 47	14	14
5 7 49	18	22	23	19 39	15	15
5 12 9	19	23	24	20 30	16	16
5 16 29	20	24	25	21 22	17	17
5 20 49	21	25	25	22 13	18	18
5 25 9	22	26	26	23 5	18	19
5 29 30	23	27	27	23 57	19	20
5 33 51	24	28	28	24 49	20	21
5 38 12	25	29	29	25 40	21	22
5 42 34	26	♌	♍	26 32	22	22
5 46 55	27	1	1	27 25	23	23
5 51 17	28	2	2	28 16	24	24
5 55 38	29	3	3	29 8	25	25
6 0 0	30	4	4	30 0	26	26

Sidereal Time. H. M. S.	10 ♋ º	11 ♌ º	12 ♍ º	Ascen ♎ º '	2 ♎ º	3 ♏ º
6 0 0	0	4	4	0 0	26	26
6 4 22	1	5	5	0 52	27	27
6 8 43	2	6	6	1 44	28	28
6 13 5	3	6	7	2 35	29	29
6 17 26	4	7	8	3 28	♏	♐
6 21 48	5	8	9	4 20	1	1
6 26 9	6	9	10	5 11	2	2
6 30 30	7	10	11	6 3	3	3
6 34 51	8	11	12	6 55	3	4
6 39 11	9	12	13	7 47	4	5
6 43 31	10	13	14	8 38	5	6
6 47 51	11	14	15	9 30	6	7
6 52 11	12	15	15	10 21	7	8
6 56 31	13	16	16	11 13	8	9
7 0 50	14	17	17	12 4	9	10
7 5 8	15	18	18	12 55	10	11
7 9 26	16	19	19	13 46	11	12
7 13 44	17	20	20	14 37	12	13
7 18 1	18	21	21	15 28	13	14
7 22 18	19	22	22	16 19	14	15
7 26 34	20	23	23	17 9	14	16
7 30 50	21	24	23	18 0	15	17
7 35 5	22	25	24	18 50	16	18
7 39 20	23	26	25	19 41	17	19
7 43 34	24	27	26	20 30	18	20
[illegible] 47	25	28	27	21 20	19	21
[illegible]	26	29	28	22 11	20	22
[illegible]	[illegible]	♍	29	23 0	21	23
[illegible]	[illegible]	[illegible]	♎	23 50	21	24
[illegible]	[illegible]	[illegible]	1	24 38	22	24
[illegible]	[illegible]	[illegible]	[illegible]	[illegible] 28	23	25

Sidereal Time. H. M. S.	10 ♌ º	11 ♍ º	12 ♎ º	Ascen ♎ º '	2 ♏ º	3 ♐ º
8 8 45	0	3	2	25 28	23	25
8 12 54	1	4	3	26 17	24	26
8 17 3	2	5	4	27 5	25	27
8 21 11	3	6	5	27 54	26	28
8 25 19	4	7	6	28 43	27	29
8 29 26	5	8	7	29 31	28	♑
8 33 31	6	9	7	0♏20	28	1
8 37 37	7	10	8	1 8	29	2
8 41 41	8	11	9	1 56	♐	3
8 45 45	9	12	10	2 43	1	4
8 49 48	10	13	11	3 31	2	5
8 53 51	11	14	12	4 18	3	6
8 57 52	12	15	12	5 6	4	7
9 1 53	13	16	13	5 53	5	8
9 5 53	14	17	14	6 40	5	9
9 9 53	15	18	15	7 27	6	10
9 13 52	16	19	16	8 13	7	10
9 17 50	17	20	17	9 0	8	11
9 21 47	18	21	18	9 46	9	12
9 25 44	19	22	19	10 33	10	13
9 29 40	20	23	19	11 19	10	14
9 33 35	21	24	20	12 4	11	15
9 37 29	22	24	21	12 50	12	16
9 41 23	23	25	22	13 36	13	17
9 45 16	24	26	23	14 21	14	18
9 49 9	25	27	24	15 7	15	19
9 53 1	26	28	24	15 52	15	20
9 56 52	27	29	25	16 38	16	21
10 0 43	28	♎	26	17 22	17	22
10 4 33	29	1	27	18 7	18	23
10 8 23	30	2	28	18 52	19	24

Sidereal Time. H. M. S.	10 ♍ º	11 ♎ º	12 ♎ º	Ascen ♏ º '	2 ♐ º	3 ♑ º
10 8 23	0	2	28	18 52	19	24
10 12 12	1	3	29	19 36	20	25
10 16 0	2	4	29	20 22	20	26
10 19 48	3	5	♏	21 7	21	27
10 23 35	4	6	1	21 51	22	28
10 27 22	5	7	1	22 35	23	28
10 31 8	6	7	2	23 20	24	29
10 34 54	7	8	3	24 4	25	♒
10 38 40	8	9	4	24 48	25	1
10 42 25	9	10	5	25 33	26	2
10 46 9	10	11	6	26 17	27	3
10 49 53	11	12	7	27 2	28	4
10 53 37	12	13	7	27 46	29	5
10 57 20	13	14	8	28 29	♑	6
11 1 3	14	15	9	29 14	1	7
11 4 46	15	16	10	29 57	1	8
11 8 28	16	17	11	0♐42	2	9
11 12 10	17	17	11	1 27	3	10
11 15 52	18	18	12	2 10	4	11
11 19 34	19	19	13	2 55	5	12
11 23 15	20	20	14	3 38	6	13
11 26 56	21	21	14	4 23	7	14
11 30 37	22	22	15	5 6	7	15
11 34 18	23	23	16	5 52	8	16
11 37 58	24	23	17	6 36	9	17
11 41 39	25	24	18	7 20	10	18
11 45 19	26	25	18	8 5	11	19
11 49 0	27	26	19	8 48	12	20
11 52 40	28	27	20	9 37	13	22
11 56 20	29	28	21	10 22	14	23
12 0 0	30	29	21	11 7	15	24

TABLES OF HOUSES FOR NEW YORK, Latitude 40º 43' *N.*

Sidereal Time.	10 ♎	11 ♎	12 ♏	Ascen ♐	2 ♑	3 ♒	Sidereal Time.	10 ♏	11 ♏	12 ♐	Ascen ♑	2 ♒	3 ♓	Sidereal Time.	10 ♐	11 ♐	12 ♑	Ascen ♒	2 ♓	3 ♉
H. M. S.	º	º	º	º '	º	º	H. M. S.	º	º	º	º '	º	º	H. M. S.	º	º	º	º '	º	º
12 0 0	0	29	21	11 7	15	24	13 51 37	0	25	15	5 35	16	27	15 51 15	0	21	13	9 8	27	4
12 3 40	1	♏	22	11 52	16	25	13 55 27	1	25	16	6 30	17	29	15 55 25	1	22	14	10 31	28	5
12 7 20	2	1	23	12 37	17	26	13 59 17	2	26	17	7 27	18	♈	15 59 36	2	23	15	11 56	♈	6
12 11 0	3	1	24	13 19	17	27	14 3 8	3	27	18	8 23	20	1	16 3 48	3	24	16	13 23	1	7
12 14 41	4	2	25	14 7	18	28	14 6 59	4	28	18	9 20	21	2	16 8 0	4	25	17	14 50	3	9
12 18 21	5	3	25	14 52	19	29	14 10 51	5	29	19	10 18	22	3	16 12 13	5	26	18	16 9	4	10
12 22 2	6	4	26	15 38	20	♓	14 14 44	6	♐	20	11 16	23	5	16 16 26	6	27	19	17 50	6	11
12 25 42	7	5	27	16 23	21	1	14 18 37	7	1	21	12 15	24	6	16 20 40	7	28	20	19 22	7	12
12 29 23	8	6	28	17 11	22	2	14 22 31	8	2	22	13 15	26	7	16 24 55	8	29	21	20 56	9	13
12 33 4	9	6	28	17 58	23	3	14 26 25	9	2	23	14 16	27	8	16 29 10	9	♑	22	22 30	11	15
12 36 45	10	7	29	18 45	24	4	14 30 20	10	3	24	15 17	28	9	16 33 26	10	1	23	24 7	12	16
12 40 26	11	8	♐	19 32	25	5	14 34 16	11	4	24	16 19	♓	11	16 37 42	11	2	24	25 44	14	17
12 44 8	12	9	1	20 20	26	7	14 38 13	12	5	25	17 23	1	12	16 41 59	12	3	26	27 23	15	18
12 47 50	13	10	2	21 8	27	8	14 42 10	13	6	26	18 27	2	13	16 46 16	13	4	27	29 4	17	19
12 51 32	14	11	2	21 57	28	9	14 46 8	14	7	27	19 32	4	14	16 50 34	14	5	28	0♓45	18	20
12 55 14	15	12	3	22 43	29	10	14 50 7	15	8	28	20 37	5	16	16 54 52	15	6	29	2 27	20	22
12 58 57	16	13	4	23 33	♒	11	14 54 7	16	9	29	21 44	6	17	16 59 10	16	7	♒	4 11	21	23
13 2 40	17	13	5	24 22	1	12	14 58 7	17	10	♑	22 51	8	18	17 3 29	17	8	2	5 56	23	24
13 6 23	18	14	6	25 11	2	13	15 2 8	18	10	1	23 59	9	19	17 7 49	18	9	3	7 43	24	25
13 10 7	19	15	7	26 1	3	15	15 6 9	19	11	2	25 9	11	20	17 12 9	19	10	4	9 30	26	26
13 13 51	20	16	7	26 51	5	16	15 10 12	20	12	3	26 19	12	22	17 16 29	20	11	5	11 18	27	27
13 17 35	21	17	8	27 40	6	17	15 14 15	21	13	4	27 31	14	23	17 20 49	21	12	7	13 8	29	28
13 21 20	22	18	9	28 32	7	18	15 18 19	22	14	5	28 43	15	24	17 25 9	22	13	8	14 57	♉	♊
13 25 6	23	19	10	29 23	8	19	15 22 23	23	15	6	29 57	16	25	17 29 30	23	14	9	16 48	2	1
13 28 52	24	19	10	0♑14	9	20	15 26 29	24	16	6	1♒14	18	26	17 33 51	24	15	10	18 41	3	2
13 32 38	25	20	11	1 7	10	21	15 30 35	25	17	7	2 28	19	28	17 38 12	25	16	12	20 33	5	3
13 36 25	26	21	12	2 0	11	23	15 34 41	26	18	8	3 46	21	29	17 42 34	26	17	13	22 25	6	4
13 40 12	27	22	13	2 52	12	24	15 38 49	27	19	9	5 5	22	♉	17 46 55	27	19	14	24 19	7	5
13 44 0	28	23	13	3 46	13	25	15 42 57	28	20	10	6 25	24	1	17 51 17	28	20	16	26 12	9	6
13 47 48	29	24	14	4 41	15	26	15 47 6	29	21	11	7 46	25	3	17 55 38	29	21	17	28 7	10	7
13 51 37	30	25	15	5 35	16	27	15 51 15	30	21	13	9 8	27	4	18 0 0	30	22	18	30 0	12	9

Sidereal Time.	10 ♑	11 ♑	12 ♒	Ascen ♈	2 ♉	3 ♊	Sidereal Time.	10 ♒	11 ♒	12 ♈	Ascen ♉	2 ♊	3 ♋	Sidereal Time.	10 ♓	11 ♈	12 ♉	Ascen ♊	2 ♋	3 ♌
H. M. S.	º	º	º	º '	º	º	H. M. S.	º	º	º	º '	º	º	H. M. S.	º	º	º	º '	º	º
18 0 0	0	22	18	0 0	12	9	20 8 45	0	26	3	20 52	17	9	22 8 23	0	3	14	24 25	15	5
18 4 22	1	23	20	1 53	13	10	20 12 54	1	27	5	22 14	18	9	22 12 12	1	4	15	25 19	16	6
18 8 43	2	24	21	3 48	14	11	20 17 3	2	29	6	23 35	19	10	22 16 0	2	5	17	26 14	17	7
18 13 5	3	25	23	5 41	16	12	20 21 11	3	♓	8	24 55	20	11	22 19 48	3	6	18	27 8	17	8
18 17 26	4	26	24	7 35	17	13	20 25 19	4	1	9	26 14	21	12	22 23 35	4	7	19	28 0	18	9
18 21 48	5	27	25	9 27	18	14	20 29 26	5	2	11	27 32	22	13	22 27 22	5	8	20	28 53	19	10
18 26 9	6	28	27	11 19	20	15	20 33 31	6	3	12	28 46	23	14	22 31 8	6	10	21	29 46	20	11
18 30 30	7	29	28	13 12	21	16	20 37 37	7	5	14	0♊3	24	15	22 34 54	7	11	22	0♋37	21	11
18 34 51	8	♒	♓	15 3	22	17	20 41 41	8	6	15	1 17	25	16	22 38 40	8	12	23	1 28	21	12
18 39 11	9	2	1	16 52	23	18	20 45 45	9	7	16	2 29	26	17	22 42 25	9	13	24	2 20	22	13
18 43 31	10	3	3	18 42	25	19	20 49 48	10	8	18	3 41	27	18	22 46 9	10	14	25	3 9	23	14
18 47 51	11	4	4	20 30	26	20	20 53 51	11	10	19	4 51	28	19	22 49 53	11	15	27	3 59	24	15
18 52 11	12	5	5	22 17	27	21	20 57 52	12	11	21	6 1	29	20	22 53 37	12	17	28	4 49	24	16
18 56 31	13	6	7	24 4	29	22	21 1 53	13	12	22	7 9	♋	20	22 57 20	13	18	29	5 38	25	17
19 0 50	14	7	9	25 49	♊	23	21 5 53	14	13	24	8 16	1	21	23 1 3	14	19	♊	6 27	26	17
19 5 8	15	9	10	27 33	1	24	21 9 53	15	14	25	9 23	2	22	23 4 46	15	20	1	7 17	27	18
19 9 26	16	10	12	29 15	2	25	21 13 52	16	16	26	10 30	3	23	23 8 28	16	21	2	8 3	28	19
19 13 44	17	11	13	0♉56	3	26	21 17 50	17	17	28	11 33	4	24	23 12 10	17	22	3	8 52	28	20
19 18 1	18	12	15	2 37	4	27	21 21 47	18	18	29	12 37	5	25	23 15 52	18	23	4	9 40	29	21
19 22 18	19	13	16	4 16	6	28	21 25 44	19	19	♉	13 41	6	26	23 19 34	19	24	5	10 28	♌	22
19 26 34	20	14	18	5 53	7	29	21 29 40	20	21	2	14 43	6	27	23 23 15	20	26	6	11 15	1	23
19 30 50	21	16	19	7 30	8	♋	21 33 35	21	22	3	15 44	7	28	23 26 56	21	27	7	12 2	2	23
19 35 5	22	17	21	9 4	9	1	21 37 29	22	23	4	16 45	8	28	23 30 37	22	28	8	12 49	2	24
19 39 20	23	18	22	10 38	10	2	21 41 23	23	24	6	17 45	9	29	23 34 18	23	29	9	13 37	3	25
19 43 34	24	19	24	12 10	11	3	21 45 16	24	25	7	18 44	10	♌	23 37 58	24	♉	10	14 22	4	26
19 47 47	25	20	25	13 41	12	4	21 49 9	25	27	8	19 42	11	1	23 41 39	25	1	11	15 8	5	27
19 52 0	26	21	27	15 10	13	5	21 53 1	26	28	9	20 40	12	2	23 45 19	26	2	12	15 53	5	28
19 56 12	27	23	29	16 37	14	6	21 56 52	27	29	11	21 37	12	3	23 49 0	27	3	12	16 41	6	29
20 0 24	28	24	♈	18 4	15	7	22 0 43	28	♈	12	22 33	13	4	23 52 40	28	4	13	17 23	7	29
20 4 35	29	25	2	19 29	16	8	22 4 33	29	1	13	23 30	14	5	23 56 20	29	5	14	18 8	8	♍
20 8 45	30	26	3	20 52	17	9	22 8 23	30	3	14	24 25	15	5	24 0 0	30	6	15	18 53	9	1

PROPORTIONAL LOGARITHMS FOR FINDING THE PLANETS' PLACES

DEGREES OR HOURS

Min	0	1	2	3	4	5	6	7	8	9	10	11	12	13	14	15	Min
0	3.1584	1.3802	1.0792	9031	7781	6812	6021	5351	4771	4260	3802	3388	3010	2663	2341	2041	0
1	3.1584	1.3730	1.0756	9007	7763	6798	6009	5341	4762	4252	3795	3382	3004	2657	2336	2036	1
2	2.8573	1.3660	1.0720	8983	7745	6784	5997	5330	4753	4244	3788	3375	2998	2652	2330	2032	2
3	2.6812	1.3590	1.0685	8959	7728	6769	5985	5320	4744	4236	3780	3368	2992	2646	2325	2027	3
4	2.5563	1.3522	1.0649	8935	7710	6755	5973	5310	4735	4228	3773	3362	2986	2640	2320	2022	4
5	2.4594	1.3454	1.0614	8912	7692	6741	5961	5300	4726	4220	3766	3355	2980	2635	2315	2017	5
6	2.3802	1.3388	1.0580	8888	7674	6726	5949	5289	4717	4212	3759	3349	2974	2629	2310	2012	6
7	2.3133	1.3323	1.0546	8865	7657	6712	5937	5279	4708	4204	3752	3342	2968	2624	2305	2008	7
8	2.2553	1.3258	1.0511	8842	7639	6698	5925	5269	4699	4196	3745	3336	2962	2618	2300	2003	8
9	2.2041	1.3195	1.0478	8819	7622	6684	5913	5259	4690	4188	3737	3329	2956	2613	2295	1998	9
10	2.1584	1.3133	1.0444	8796	7604	6670	5902	5249	4682	4180	3730	3323	2950	2607	2289	1993	10
11	2.1170	1.3071	1.0411	8773	7587	6656	5890	5239	4673	4172	3723	3316	2944	2602	2284	1988	11
12	2.0792	1.3010	1.0378	8751	7570	6642	5878	5229	4664	4164	3716	3310	2938	2596	2279	1984	12
13	2.0444	1.2950	1.0345	8728	7552	6628	5866	5219	4655	4156	3709	3303	2933	2591	2274	1979	13
14	2.0122	1.2891	1.0313	8706	7535	6614	5855	5209	4646	4148	3702	3297	2927	2585	2269	1974	14
15	1.9823	1.2833	1.0280	8683	7518	6600	5843	5199	4638	4141	3695	3291	2921	2580	2264	1969	15
16	1.9542	1.2775	1.0248	8661	7501	6587	5832	5189	4629	4133	3688	3284	2915	2574	2259	1965	16
17	1.9279	1.2719	1.0216	8639	7484	6573	5820	5179	4620	4125	3681	3278	2909	2569	2254	1960	17
18	1.9031	1.2663	1.0185	8617	7467	6559	5809	5169	4611	4117	3674	3271	2903	2564	2249	1955	18
19	1.8796	1.2607	1.0153	8595	7451	6546	5797	5159	4603	4109	3667	3265	2897	2558	2244	1950	19
20	1.8573	1.2553	1.0122	8573	7434	6532	5786	5149	4594	4102	3660	3258	2891	2553	2239	1946	20
21	1.8361	1.2499	1.0091	8552	7417	6519	5774	5139	4585	4094	3653	3252	2885	2547	2234	1941	21
22	1.8159	1.2445	1.0061	8530	7401	6505	5763	5129	4577	4086	3646	3246	2880	2542	2229	1936	22
23	1.7966	1.2393	1.0030	8509	7384	6492	5752	5120	4568	4079	3639	3239	2874	2536	2223	1932	23
24	1.7781	1.2341	1.0000	8487	7368	6478	5740	5110	4559	4071	3632	3233	2868	2531	2218	1927	24
25	1.7604	1.2289	0.9970	8466	7351	6465	5729	5100	4551	4063	3625	3227	2862	2526	2213	1922	25
26	1.7434	1.2239	0.9940	8445	7335	6451	5718	5090	4542	4055	3618	3220	2856	2520	2208	1917	26
27	1.7270	1.2188	0.9910	8424	7318	6438	5706	5081	4534	4048	3611	3214	2850	2515	2203	1913	27
28	1.7112	1.2139	0.9881	8403	7302	6425	5695	5071	4525	4040	3604	3208	2845	2509	2198	1908	28
29	1.6960	1.2090	0.9852	8382	7286	6412	5684	5061	4516	4032	3597	3201	2839	2504	2193	1903	29
30	1.6812	1.2041	0.9823	8361	7270	6398	5673	5051	4508	4025	3590	3195	2833	2499	2188	1899	30
31	1.6670	1.1993	0.9794	8341	7254	6385	5662	5042	4499	4017	3583	3189	2827	2493	2183	1894	31
32	1.6532	1.1946	0.9765	8320	7238	6372	5651	5032	4491	4010	3576	3183	2821	2488	2178	1889	32
33	1.6398	1.1899	0.9737	8300	7222	6359	5640	5023	4482	4002	3570	3176	2816	2483	2173	1885	33
34	1.6269	1.1852	0.9708	8279	7206	6346	5629	5013	4474	3994	3563	3170	2810	2477	2168	1880	34
35	1.6143	1.1806	0.9680	8259	7190	6333	5618	5003	4466	3987	3556	3164	2804	2472	2164	1875	35
36	1.6021	1.1761	0.9652	8239	7174	6320	5607	4994	4457	3979	3549	3157	2798	2467	2159	1871	36
37	1.5902	1.1716	0.9625	8219	7159	6307	5596	4984	4449	3972	3542	3151	2793	2461	2154	1866	37
38	1.5786	1.1671	0.9597	8199	7143	6294	5585	4975	4440	3964	3535	3145	2787	2456	2149	1862	38
39	1.5673	1.1627	0.9570	8179	7128	6282	5574	4965	4432	3957	3529	3139	2781	2451	2144	1857	39
40	1.5563	1.1584	0.9542	8159	7112	6269	5563	4956	4424	3949	3522	3133	2775	2445	2139	1852	40
41	1.5456	1.1540	0.9515	8140	7097	6256	5552	4947	4415	3942	3515	3126	2770	2440	2134	1848	41
42	1.5351	1.1498	0.9488	8120	7081	6243	5541	4937	4407	3934	3508	3120	2764	2435	2129	1843	42
43	1.5249	1.1455	0.9462	8101	7066	6231	5531	4928	4399	3927	3501	3114	2758	2430	2124	1838	43
44	1.5149	1.1413	0.9435	8081	7050	6218	5520	4918	4390	3919	3495	3108	2753	2424	2119	1834	44
45	1.5051	1.1372	0.9409	8062	7035	6205	5509	4909	4382	3912	3488	3102	2747	2419	2114	1829	45
46	1.4956	1.1331	0.9383	8043	7020	6193	5498	4900	4374	3905	3481	3096	2741	2414	2109	1825	46
47	1.4863	1.1290	0.9356	8023	7005	6180	5488	4890	4365	3897	3475	3089	2736	2409	2104	1820	47
48	1.4771	1.1249	0.9330	8004	6990	6168	5477	4881	4357	3890	3468	3083	2730	2403	2099	1816	48
49	1.4682	1.1209	0.9305	7985	6975	6155	5466	4872	4349	3882	3461	3077	2724	2398	2095	1811	49
50	1.4594	1.1170	0.9279	7966	6960	6143	5456	4863	4341	3875	3454	3071	2719	2393	2090	1806	50
51	1.4508	1.1130	0.9254	7947	6945	6131	5445	4853	4333	3868	3448	3065	2713	2388	2085	1802	51
52	1.4424	1.1091	0.9228	7929	6930	6118	5435	4844	4324	3860	3441	3059	2707	2382	2080	1797	52
53	1.4341	1.1053	0.9203	7910	6915	6106	5424	4835	4316	3853	3434	3053	2702	2377	2075	1793	53
54	1.4260	1.1015	0.9178	7891	6900	6094	5414	4826	4308	3846	3428	3047	2696	2372	2070	1788	54
55	1.4180	1.0977	0.9153	7873	6885	6081	5403	4817	4300	3838	3421	3041	2691	2367	2065	1784	55
56	1.4102	1.0939	0.9128	7854	6871	6069	5393	4808	4292	3831	3415	3034	2685	2362	2061	1779	56
57	1.4025	1.0902	0.9104	7836	6856	6057	5382	4798	4284	3824	3408	3028	2679	2356	2056	1774	57
58	1.3949	1.0865	0.9079	7818	6841	6045	5372	4789	4276	3817	3401	3022	2674	2351	2051	1770	58
59	1.3875	1.0828	0.9055	7800	6827	6033	5361	4780	4268	3809	3395	3016	2668	2346	2046	1765	59
	0	**1**	**2**	**3**	**4**	**5**	**6**	**7**	**8**	**9**	**10**	**11**	**12**	**13**	**14**	**15**	

RULE: – Add proportional log. of planet's ...ly motion to log. of time from noon, ... sum will be the log. of the motion ...dd this to planet's place at ...he p.m., but subtract if ... will be planet's true ... subtract for p.m.,

What is the Long. of ☽ August 2, 2007 at 2.15 p.m.?

☽'s daily motion – 14° 12′

Prop. Log. of 14° 12′ .... .2279

Prop. Log. of 2h. 15m. 1.0280

☽'s motion in 2h. 15m. = 1° 20′ or Log. 1.2559

☽'s Long. = 24° ♓ 51′ + 1° 20′ = 26° ♓ 11′

The Daily Motions of the Sun, Moon, Mercury, Venus and Mars will be found on pages 26 to 28.